Certified <allaire> ColdFusion Developer Study Guide

Ben Forta
with Emily Kim, Geoff Bowers, Matthew Boles, Matt Reider

201 West 103rd Street,
Indianapolis, Indiana 46290

Certified ColdFusion Developer Study Guide

International Standard Book Number: 0-7897-2565-7

Library of Congress Catalog Card Number: 00-111735

Printed in the United States of America

First Printing: March 2001

03 02 01 4 3 2

Trademarks

All terms mentioned in this book that are known to be trademarks or service marks have been appropriately capitalized. Que cannot attest to the accuracy of this information. Use of a term in this book should not be regarded as affecting the validity of any trademark or service mark.

ColdFusion is a registered trademark of Allaire Corporation.

Warning and Disclaimer

Every effort has been made to make this book as complete and as accurate as possible, but no warranty or fitness is implied. The information provided is on an "as is" basis. The author(s) and the publisher shall have neither liability nor responsibility to any person or entity with respect to any loss or damages arising from the information contained in this book.

Executive Editor
Rosemarie Graham

Acquisitions Editor
Angela Kozlowski

Development Editor
Mark Kozlowski

Managing Editor
Charlotte Clapp

Project Editor
Leah Kirkpatrick

Copy Editors
Chuck Hutchinson
Michael Henry

Indexer
Eric Schroeder

Proofreader
Daniel Ponder

Technical Editor
Jason Wright

Team Coordinator
Pamalee Nelson

Interior Designer
Ann Jones

Cover Designer
Maureen McCarty

Page Layout
Ayanna Lacey
Heather Hiatt Miller
Stacey Richwine-DeRome

Overview

Contents

Part VII Databases 281

Part IX Appendix 343

A Answers 345

Index 355

About the Author

Ben Forta is Allaire Corporation's Product Evangelist for the ColdFusion product line. He has more than 15 years of experience in the computer industry in product development, support, training, and product marketing. Ben is the author of the best-selling *ColdFusion Web Application Construction Kit* (now in its third edition), and its sequel *Advanced ColdFusion 4 Development* (both published by Que), as well as titles on ColdFusion Express, Allaire Spectra, Allaire HomeSite, SQL, WAP, and JavaServer Pages (the complete list of his books can be found at `http://www.forta.com/books/`). Ben coauthored the official Allaire ColdFusion training courses, helped create the content for the Certified Developer exam, writes regular columns on ColdFusion and Internet development, and now spends a considerable amount of time lecturing and speaking on ColdFusion and Internet application development worldwide. Born in London, England, and educated in London, New York, and Los Angeles, Ben now lives in Oak Park, Michigan, with his wife, Marcy, and their six children. Ben welcomes your email at `ben@forta.com`, and invites you to visit his Web site at `http://www.forta.com/`.

Matthew Boles started training for Allaire in 1997, making him one of the first Allaire instructors. He is currently a Senior Instructor. In addition to training, Matthew also has some responsibility for curriculum development and instructor readiness. Matthew is also a certified Microsoft and Novell instructor.

Geoffrey Bowers was educated in Scotland and studied biochemistry at Oxford before returning home to Australia as an options derivatives dealer. Leaving the City, Geoff founded Daemon Internet Consultants in 1995 (`http://www.daemon.com.au/`) and has been building Web applications ever since. Based in Sydney, Geoff is the Allaire Master Instructor for Australasia and divides his time between teaching, consulting, and playing the ancient game of Real Tennis. He can be reached at `modius@daemon.com.au`.

Emily Kim is Director of Business Development and co-founder of Trilemetry, Inc., a Web design and programming company. She has coauthored a college-level workbook about the Internet and was contributing author to a popular ColdFusion book, and occasionally writes for ColdFusion magazines. She is also a Certified Allaire Instructor and teaches both ColdFusion and Spectra courses for Allaire. You can reach Emily at `emily@trilemetry.com`.

Matthew Reider has been working for commercial software vendors since 1992, beginning with the database driver team at Q+E in Raleigh, North Carolina. Initially, Allaire hired Matt to manage West Coast partner and customer relationships. After joining the education team as a Master Instructor in 1999, he coauthored the Advanced ColdFusion, Advanced Spectra Development, and Fast-track to JRun curriculum. Before joining Allaire, Matt enjoyed a position at Sybase as a product specialist for the Watcom SQL database family. Matt loves to backpack in California's Sierra Nevada mountains.

Dedication

To Poppet, Flambeau, Harry, and James for being all the things I love the most. To Mum, Dad, and Dan for loving me and not dropping me on the floor too often as a baby.
—Geoffrey Bowers

To my parents, whom I feel so lucky to have, and Irene, who breaks the mother-in-law stereotype.
—Matthew Boles

To Mom, Dad, Jacob, Sooz and Alison. —Matthew Reider

To Mommy, Daddy, Elicia, Irene, Elizabeth, Yoon, Thomas, Gwen, Kevin, Aimee, Michael...and the little niece or nephew who will born about the time of publication!
—Emily Kim

Acknowledgments

First of all, I'd like to thank my coauthors, Emily Kim, Geoff Bowers, Matt Boles, and Matt Reider for their outstanding contributions (and for agreeing to such aggressive deadlines).

Thanks to Carolyn Lightner and Steve Curtin (fellow Allaireites) for their support of this project. Thanks also to Sue Hove and Robert Crooks (also fellow Allaireites) for their honest advice and criticism (fortunately very little of the latter).

Thanks once again to everyone at Sams and Que for their hard work and dedication to this project, and for granting me the freedom to shape this book as I saw fit. A very special thank you to my Acquisitions Editor, Angela Kozlowski, without whom I'd not even considered taking on this project.

And finally, a special thank you to the most dedicated, selfless, and hard-working person I know—my wife, Marcy. It is she who makes all I do possible.
—Ben Forta

Thanks to the following people: all my colleagues in Allaire Educational Services, but especially Carolyn Lightner, Sue Hove, and Robert Crooks, who have supported me from my first day at Allaire; Sam Calvin, Bill Whittaker, Ron Lekrone, and Ron Pope from the Department of Defense Dependents Schools in Germany, who helped me develop my interest in, and my skills for, training adults; Alberto Chalas, who gave me technical free rein in his fledgling Internet company, which allowed me to discover ColdFusion; and Sandra, my wife, who has encouraged me in all my career decisions.
—Matthew Boles

Thanks to Team Daemon for keeping the world super green and lumber enabled. Special thanks to Julie, my wife, for all her love and the maniacal things she does to keep me going.
—Geoffrey Bowers

Very few people have the patience to live with an unwilling workaholic! Thank you, Michael, for always being so supportive. Thank you to Annette Kunovic for being the best business partner a girl could ask for. Thank you to Jeremy Taylor, Tammie O'Brien, Tammy Smith, and Lisa Kissler for working so hard. And thank you, Denise Rolen, for being such an important organizational part of our team! Also, I'd like to thank each and every one of my students for keeping me on my toes and making teaching so fun and fulfilling! I hope you'll find this book useful!

—Emily Kim

Tell Us What You Think!

As the reader of this book, *you* are our most important critic and commentator. We value your opinion and want to know what we're doing right, what we could do better, what areas you'd like to see us publish in, and any other words of wisdom you're willing to pass our way.

As an Acquisitions Editor for Que, I welcome your comments. You can fax, email, or write me directly to let me know what you did or didn't like about this book—as well as what we can do to make our books stronger.

Please note that I cannot help you with technical problems related to the topic of this book, and that due to the high volume of mail I receive, I might not be able to reply to every message.

When you write, please be sure to include this book's title and author as well as your name and phone or fax number. I will carefully review your comments and share them with the author and editors who worked on the book.

Fax: 317-581-4770
Email: `allairefeedback@quepublishing.com`
Mail: Angela Kozlowski
Que
201 West 103rd Street
Indianapolis, IN 46290 USA

Introduction

What Is the *Certified ColdFusion Developer* Exam?

The popularity of Allaire's products continues to grow, and along with it, so has the demand for experienced developers. Once upon a time (Internet time, that is, and actually not that long ago in conventional time), claiming to be a ColdFusion developer was easy; the product was simple enough that, with a minimal investment of time and energy, developers could realistically consider themselves experts.

This is not the case anymore. The product line has grown both in actual products and in their complexity, and the levels of expertise and experience among developers are diverse. Claiming to be an expert is not that easy, and recognizing legitimate expertise is even harder.

The Allaire Certified Professional Program

This is where certification comes into play. Formal, official certification by Allaire helps to mark a threshold that explicitly separates developers by their knowledge and experience, making it possible to identify who is who.

The *Certified ColdFusion Developer* certification is the first in a series of certification tracks from Allaire—this one concentrating on developers using Allaire's flagship product, ColdFusion. Other exams and certification programs being developed concentrate on other products and areas of expertise.

Reasons to Get Certified

There's really only one important reason for ColdFusion developers to become certified (aside from the goodies you'll receive): Being able to call yourself an *Allaire Certified ColdFusion Developer* means that you can command the respect and recognition that goes along with being one of the best at what you do.

Just as has happened with other products and technologies in this space, certification is likely to become a prerequisite for employers—an additional barometer by which to measure the potential of candidates and applicants.

Whether being certified helps you find a new (or better) job, helps persuade your boss that the pay raise you want is justified, helps you find new clients, or gets you listed on Allaire's Web site so that you can attract new work or prospects—whatever the reason—it will help you stick out from the crowd.

About the Exam

Becoming a *Certified ColdFusion Developer* involves being examined on your knowledge of ColdFusion and related technologies. As far as exams go, this one is not easy—nor should it be. In fact, more than a third of all examinees fail their first test. This is not a bad thing; on the contrary, this is a good thing because it means that you really have to know your stuff to pass. You do not merely receive a paper certificate; the exam and subsequent certification have real value and real significance. "Very challenging but fair" is how many examinees describe the exam itself.

The Exam Itself

The exam itself is a set of multiple-choice questions you answer electronically. A computer application issues the test, and you'll know whether you passed immediately upon test completion.

You are presented with questions and possible answers. Some questions have a single correct answer; others have two or more (you'll be told how many answers to provide). If a question stumps you, you can skip it and then come back to it later.

After you have answered all your questions, you can review them to check your answers. And after you are done (or the time is up; yes, the test has a 60-minute time limit), you'll get your results. You need at least 60% correct to pass. If you do not pass, you need to wait at least 30 days before you can try again. You may take the test no more than three times in a single year (starting from the date of your first test).

What You'll Be Tested On

Being a ColdFusion expert requires that you know more than just ColdFusion. As such, the exam includes questions on related technologies. The subjects you'll be tested on are as follows:

- ColdFusion functionality
- ColdFusion Markup Language (CFML) usage and syntax
- Internet and IP fundamentals
- Basic Hypertext Markup Language (HTML) and related client technologies
- Database fundamentals and concepts
- Structured Query Language (SQL)

Every question counts, and you cannot assume that one particular topic is more or less significant than others. You need to know it all, and you need to know it all well.

Preparing for the Exam

Obviously, the most important preparation for the exam is the use of ColdFusion itself. If you do not use ColdFusion regularly, or have not done so for an extended period, then you probably will not pass the exam.

Having said that, we can tell you that many experienced ColdFusion developers still find the exam challenging. Usually, they say so because they don't use some features and technologies, or because they have learned the product but have never paid attention to changing language and feature details (and thus are not using the product as effectively as they could be).

And this is where this book fits in. This book is not a cheat-sheet. It will not teach you ColdFusion from scratch, nor will it give you a list of things to remember to pass the test. What it will do is help you systematically review every major (and not so major) feature and technology in the product—everything that you need to know to pass the test.

Where to Take the Exam

To offer the exams locally in as many locations as possible, Allaire has partnered with a company called Virtual University Enterprises (VUE). VUE offers exams and certification programs for a wide range of companies and products, and it has more than 2,000 regional testing facilities in more than 100 countries.

You can take the *ColdFusion Certified Developer* exam in any VUE testing center. For a current list of locations, visit the following Web site:

`http://www.vue.com/allaire/`

How Much It Costs

The fee to take the exam in North America is $150 (U.S.). Pricing in other countries varies. The fee must be paid at the time you register for the exam. If you need to cancel, you must do so at least 24 hours before the exam, or the fee will not be refunded.

As a special gift to readers of this book, and to encourage you to study appropriately for the test, Allaire has sponsored a coupon that you can use for a discount off the exam fee. Refer to the coupon for details and usage information.

How to Use This Book

This book is designed to be used in two ways:

- To prepare for your exam, you should start at the beginning of the book and systematically work your way through it. The book flow, layout, and form-factor have all been especially designed to make reviewing content as pleasant an experience as possible. The content has been designed to be highly readable and digestible in small, bite-sized chunks so that it will feel more like reading than studying.
- After you have reviewed all content, reread the topics that you feel you need extra help brushing up on. Topics are all covered in highly focused and very manageable chapters so that you can easily drill-down to the exact content you need. And extensive cross-referencing allows you to read up on related topics as needed.

And even after the exam, you'll find that the style and design of this book makes it an invaluable desktop reference tool as well.

Contents

The book is divided into eight parts, each containing a set of highly focused chapters. Each chapter concludes with a summary and sample questions (the answers to which are in Appendix A).

Part I: The Basics

This part covers the basics of Internet development in general and ColdFusion in particular, and includes chapters on the following topics:

- Web Technology and Terminology
- Working with Variables and Expressions
- Conditional Processing
- Looping
- Redirects and Reuse
- The Application Framework
- Using Databases

Part II: Variables and Expressions

This part covers the use of different variable types, scopes, and expressions, and includes chapters on the following topics:

- `URL` Variables
- `FORM` Variables
- `APPLICATION` and `SERVER` Variables
- Session State Management
- Locking

Part III: Data Types

This part covers the data types supported by ColdFusion, and includes chapters on the following topics:

- Lists
- Arrays
- Structures

Part IV: Advanced ColdFusion

This part covers a wide range of advanced development technologies and features, and includes chapters on the following topics:

- Scripting
- Dynamic Functions
- Stored Procedures
- Transactions
- Debugging
- Error Handling

Part V: Extending ColdFusion

This part covers ColdFusion's extensibility features, and includes chapters on the following topics:

- Custom Tags
- Advanced Custom Tags
- COM, CORBA, CFX, and Java
- WDDX

Part VI: Services and Protocols

This part covers the services and protocols supported by ColdFusion, and includes chapters on the following topics:

- Full Text Searching
- System Integration
- Scheduling and Event Execution
- Email Integration
- LDAP
- Other Internet Protocols

Part VII: Databases

This part covers database concepts and terminology, and includes chapters on the following topics:

- Basic SQL
- Joins
- Aggregates
- Advanced Database Features
- Improving Performance

Part VIII: Tuning and Optimization

This part covers tuning and performance optimization techniques, and includes chapters on the following topics:

- Application Performance Tuning and Optimization
- Server Performance Tuning

Conventions Used in This Book

The people at Que Publishing have spent many years developing and publishing computer books designed for ease of use and containing the most up-to-date information available. With that experience, we've learned what features help you the most. Look for these features throughout the book to help enhance your learning experience and get the most out of ColdFusion.

- Screen messages, code listings, and command samples appear in `monospace type`.

- Uniform Resource Locators (URLs) used to identify pages on the Web and values for ColdFusion attributes also appear in `monospace type`.
- Terms that are defined in the text appear in *italics*. *Italics* are sometimes used for emphasis, too.

TIP

Tips give you advice on quick or overlooked procedures, including shortcuts.

NOTE

Notes present useful or interesting information that isn't necessarily essential to the current discussion, but might augment your understanding with background material or advice relating to the topic.

CAUTION

Cautions warn you about potential problems a procedure might cause, unexpected results, or mistakes that could prove costly.

→ Cross references are designed to point you to other locations in this book that will provide supplemental or supporting information. Cross references appear as follows:

→ Arrays and structures are covered in detail in Chapter 14, "Arrays," and Chapter 15, "Structures."

The Accompanying Web Site

To further assist you in preparing for the exam, this book has an accompanying Web site. This site contains the following:

- Updated exam information (should there be any)
- Links to other exam-related sites
- Any book corrections or errata (should there be any)
- A sample interactive test that you can use to help gauge your own exam readiness

The URL is `http://www.forta.com/books/0789725657/`.

Where to Go from Here

Now you're ready to get started. If you think you're ready for the exam, start with the sample questions (in the book or online) to verify this. If you're not ready (or if the same questions indicate that you might not be as ready as you thought), make sure to pay attention to the topics that need more attention by reading the documentation and actually writing appropriate applications.

When you're ready, work through this book to review the content and prepare for the exam itself as described here.

And with that, we wish you good luck!

PART 1

THE BASICS

Web Technology and Terminology

Working with Variables and Expressions

Conditional Processing

Looping

Redirects and Reuse

The Application Framework

Using Datbases

CHAPTER 1

Web Technology and Terminology

The Basics

Effective ColdFusion development requires a solid understanding of Internet and Web concepts, terms, and technologies. So, in this first chapter, we'll start with a brief review of these.

The Internet

The Internet is simply the world's biggest computer network. It connects millions of hosts (computers, servers, devices, and so on) to each other so that they can communicate and interact.

The Internet is not a physical entity, nor is it any particular host or set of hosts. You could never point to a machine and identify it as the Internet, nor could you ever turn the Internet on or off. The Internet is a living entity, and one that is evolving and changing all the time.

IP

The Internet is held together by IP, the Internet Protocol, and every host connected to the Internet must be running a copy of IP.

IP requires that every host have a unique address by which to identify it. The unique identifiers are IP addresses that (in the current version of IP) are made up of four sets of numbers separated by periods—for example, `208.193.16.250`. Some hosts have fixed (or *static*) IP addresses; others have dynamically assigned addresses. Regardless of how an IP address is obtained, no two hosts connected to the Internet may use the same IP address at any given time. (The exception to this rule is addressing used on private networks, which need just be unique within that network.)

> **NOTE**
> The IP address `127.0.0.1` always points to the local machine.

DNS

IP addresses are the only way to uniquely specify a host. When you want to communicate with a host—for example, a Web server—you must specify the IP address of the Web server you're trying to contact. Similarly, when you connect to an FTP server, or specify the SMTP and POP servers in your mail client, you must specify the name of the host to which you want to connect.

As you know from browsing the Web, you rarely specify IP addresses directly. You do, however, specify a host name, such as `www.forta.com`. If hosts are identified by IP address, how does your browser know which Web server to contact if you specify a host name?

The answer is the Domain Name Service (DNS), a mechanism that maps host names to IP addresses. When you specify the destination address of `www.forta.com`, your browser sends an address resolution request to a DNS server asking for the IP address of that host. The DNS server returns an actual IP address—in this case, `208.193.16.250`. Your browser can then use this address to communicate with the host directly.

DNS is never required. Users can always specify the name of a destination host by its IP address to connect to the host. There are, however, some very good reasons not to use the IP address:

- IP addresses are hard to remember and easy to mistype. Users are more likely to find `www.forta.com` than they are 208.193.16.250.
- IP addresses are subject to change. For example, if you switch service providers, you might be forced to use a new set of IP addresses for your hosts. If users identified your site only by its IP address, they never could reach your host if the IP address changed. Your DNS name stays the same, even if your IP address switches. You need to change only the mapping so that the host name maps to the new correct IP address.
- Multiple hosts, each with unique IP addresses, can all have the same DNS name. This allows load balancing between servers, as well as the establishment of redundant servers.
- A single host, with a single IP address, can have multiple DNS names. This enables you to create aliases if needed. For example, `ftp.forta.com` and `www.forta.com` might point to the same IP address, and thus the same server.

> **NOTE**
>
> The host name localhost always points to IP address `127.0.0.1`, the local machine.

The World Wide Web

The Web is what put the Internet on the map, and made it a household word. Many people mistakenly think the Internet is the Web. The truth, however, is that the Web is merely an application that sits on top of the Internet.

The Web is built on the Hypertext Transfer Protocol (HTTP). HTTP is designed to be a small, fast protocol that is well suited for distributed multimedia information systems and hypertext jumps between sites.

Information on the Web is stored in pages. A page can contain any of the following:

Text	Lists	Tables	Graphics
Headers	Menus	Forms	Multimedia

Each Web page is an actual file saved on a host. When a Web page is requested, the file containing the Web page is read and its contents are sent to the host that asked for it.

A *Web site* is simply a collection of Web pages along with any supporting files (such as GIF or JPG graphics). Creating a Web site thus involves creating one or more Web pages and linking them. The Web site is then saved on a Web server.

Web Servers

The Web consists of pages of information stored on hosts running Web-server software. The host is often referred to as the *Web server*, which is technically inaccurate. The Web server is actually software and not the computer itself. Versions of Web server software can run on almost all computers, and although most Web server applications do have minimum hardware requirements, no special computer is needed to host a Web server.

Originally, Web development was all performed under different flavors of UNIX. Most Web servers still run on UNIX boxes, but this is changing. There are now Web-server versions for almost every major operating system. Web servers hosted on high-performance operating systems, such as Windows NT, are becoming more and more popular because UNIX is still more expensive to run than Windows NT and is also more difficult to use for the average user. Windows NT (and especially Windows 2000) has proven itself to be an efficient, reliable, and cost-effective platform for hosting Web servers. As a result, Windows NT's slice of the Web server operating system pie is growing dramatically.

So, what exactly is a Web server? It's a program that serves up Web pages upon request. Web servers typically don't know or care what they're serving. When a user at a specific IP address requests a specific file (a Web page), the Web server tries to retrieve that file and send it back to the user. The requested file might be the HTML source code for a Web page, a GIF image, VRML worlds, .AVI files, and so on. The Web browser determines what should be requested, not the Web server. The server merely processes that request.

Pages are stored on the Web server beneath the Web *root*—a directory or folder designated to contain all the files that make up the Web site. When a request is made for a specific page within a specific directory, that page is retrieved from the appropriate directory beneath the Web root.

Web servers enable administrators to specify a default Web page, a page that is sent back to the user when only a directory is specified. These default pages are often called `index.html` or `default.htm`. If no default Web page exists in a particular directory, the server returns either an error message or a list of all available files, depending on how the server is set up.

Web Browsers

A Web browser is the program used to view Web pages. The Web browser has the job of processing received Web pages, parsing the HTML code, and displaying the page to users. The browser attempts to display graphics, tables, forms, formatted text, or whatever the page contains. The most popular Web browsers now in use are Netscape Navigator and Microsoft Internet Explorer.

Web-page designers must pay close attention to the differences between browsers because different Web browsers behave differently. Web pages are created using HTML (a language that we'll look at in a few moments). Unfortunately, no single browser supports every feature of the HTML language. Furthermore, the same Web page often looks different on two different browsers because every browser renders and displays Web page objects differently.

For this reason, most Web page designers use multiple Web browsers and test their pages in every one to ensure that the final output appears as intended. Without this testing, some Web site visitors can't correctly see the pages you published.

To request a Web page, the browser users must specify the address of the page. The address is known as a *URL*.

> **NOTE**
>
> Web browsers communicate with Web servers and provide information about themselves to the server, and that information is then made available to application servers (such as ColdFusion). Within ColdFusion code, these variables are accessed using the `CGI` scope.

URLs

Every Web page (and indeed every object, even individual graphics) on the World Wide Web has an address. This is what you type into your browser to instruct it to load a particular Web page.

World Wide Web URLs are made up of up to five parts:

- The protocol to use to retrieve the object. This is always `http` for objects on the World Wide Web (or `https` for requests over secure connections).
- The Web server from which to retrieve the object. This is specified as a DNS name or an IP address.
- The host machine port on which the Web server is running. If omitted, the specified protocol's default port is used; for Web servers, this is port `80`.
- The file to retrieve or the script to execute. The file name often includes a complete file path.
- Optional script parameters, also known as the *query string*.

There are generally two ways to go to a specific URL. The first way is by typing the URL in the Web browser's address field (or selecting it from a saved bookmark or favorite). The second way is by clicking on a link within a Web page—a link is simply a reference to another URL. When a user clicks a link, the browser requests whatever URL it references.

HTML

Web pages are plain text files constructed with HTML, the Hypertext Markup Language. HTML is implemented as a series of easy-to-learn *tags*, or instructions. Web page authors use these tags to mark up a page of text. Browsers then use these tags to render and display the information for viewing.

HTML tags are always placed between `<` and `>`. For example, to force a paragraph break, you would specify `<P>`.

> **NOTE**
>
> Even though HTML is tag based, it is not strictly typed as XML is. For example, HTML is case-insensitive, tags do not all have matching end tags, and most browsers accommodate badly formed HTML rather well.

Some tags take one or more parameters in the form of attributes. Attributes are used to specify optional or additional information to a tag. Some tags have no attributes, some have many. Attributes are almost always optional and can be specified in any order you want. Attributes must be separated from each other by a space, and attribute values should ideally be enclosed within double quotation marks.

HTML is constantly being enhanced with new features and added tags. To ensure backward compatibility, browsers must ignore tags they don't understand. For example, if you were to use the `<MARQUEE>` tag to create a scrolling text marquee, browsers that don't support this tag will still display the marquee text, but it won't scroll.

Web browsers ignore white space, so the following two lines will be displayed identically:

```
My name is Ben
My    name    is    Ben
```

Many characters have special significance to HTML. For example, the double quotation mark character is used to delimit fields and should therefore not be used in plain text. To display these characters, *entity-references* are used; for example, `"` for a double quotation mark character. Entity-references always begin with an ampersand character (`&`), so to display an ampersand, the entity-reference `&` is used. Entity-references are available for all special characters including formatting and international characters.

JavaScript

Most current Web browsers allow the execution of JavaScript within Web pages. JavaScript is used to programmatically control the Web browser and the content it displays. JavaScript cannot be used to access the file system or to perform system level operations—its scope is limited to the Web browser.

JavaScript plays an important part in usable and intuitive Web design in that it allows for more sophisticated and interactive user interface design, which in turn results in a richer and more rewarding user experience.

> **NOTE**
> JavaScript is not Java, and has nothing to do with Java. JavaScript is a scripting language, and Java is a true development language.

VBScript is another scripting language, but for the most part it is supported only by Microsoft Internet Explorer and is used far less than JavaScript.

Cascading Style Sheets

Cascading Style Sheets (often referred to as CSS) provide a mechanism by which to separate content from presentation. Instead of embedding HTML formatting in your text, you can create style definitions that the browser automatically applies when content is displayed.

Styles are associated with HTML types, so body text, links, headers, tables, and more can have associated attributes (everything from colors to fonts to spacing to special effects that are not available using inline formatting). Additional styles can be created too, so that developers can have maximum control over generated output.

All current browsers support CSS, although there are differences in the support. As such, any time CSS is used, thorough testing must be performed in as many browsers as possible.

Dynamic HTML

Dynamic HTML (or DHTML) is actually not a feature, it's a collection of features that when used together facilitate powerful browser UI control. DHTML combines HTML, scripting (usually JavaScript), CSS, and the DOM (document object model—a convention that provides naming and programmatic access to every element of every page within a browser) to enable developers to write code that can be used to create very rich and sophisticated user interfaces.

The biggest problem with DHTML is that it is dependent on all the aforementioned technologies, and their support differs dramatically from one browser to the next. As such, effective DHTML development often requires creating multiple versions of pages (or parts of pages) and intelligently including the appropriate ones as needed.

Application Servers

As explained earlier, Web servers don't do that much—they serve content that is read from disk. Application servers are software applications that extend Web servers, allowing them to do things they couldn't do on their own. These include:

- Accessing databases
- Sending and receiving email
- Personalizing content
- Building e-commerce applications
- Much more

Application servers usually rely on the underlying Web servers for all host-to-host communication (sending data to and from the browser, for example). When a request is to be processed by an application server, the Web server receives the request from the client, hands it to the application server for processing, and then returns the output from that processing to the client.

Web servers are primarily used to serve static content. Static content is usually stored in HTML files directly (and supporting image files perhaps). These files are created in editors and they are rendered and displayed just as they were created.

Application servers are used to provide dynamic content. Dynamic content is built at run-time based on external criteria. Information could be retrieved from databases, user input could be solicited, and more. All this information is then used to build an application that generates output that could be different each time it is requested.

Static content is essentially the electronic form of print-based publishing. The true power of the Web is realized in dynamic content.

ColdFusion Fundamentals

ColdFusion is an application server, and functions as described in the previous section. ColdFusion runs on several major operating systems, but regardless of the OS used, it functions the same way. The core services (or *daemons*) are always running, and requests are submitted to them for processing as they come in.

How ColdFusion Works

ColdFusion is a Web page preprocessor. It processes scripts (usually `.CFM` files) and generates output, which is then sent to the client.

ColdFusion is completely client agnostic, and thus supports every client technology (including HTML, JavaScript, and VBScript). The ColdFusion instructions within the scripts are processed on the server and are never sent to the client. The client code is sent to the client as is.

ColdFusion provides interfaces to all major backend technologies including:

- Databases (via ODBC, OLE-DB, and native drivers)
- Email (POP and SMTP)
- Internet protocols (HTTP, FTP, LDAP)
- Any other technology that can be accessed via C/C++, Java, COM, or CORBA

ColdFusion applications are made up of sets of CFM files, just like Web sites are made up of sets of HTML files. ColdFusion applications are simply sets of scripts in a directory structure of your choice (usually under the Web root).

> **NOTE**
> CFM files are plain text files and are usually stored as such. A utility named CFENCODE (provided with ColdFusion) can be used to encode the CFM files so that they are not easily readable. ColdFusion can still process encoded files, but casual browsers will not be able to see the source code. This encoding is not designed to be highly secure and hacker-proof, but it does offer some basic code protection.

CFML

ColdFusion code is written in CFML—the ColdFusion Markup Language. This is a tag-based language (much like HTML) and tags are used to perform everything from conditional processing to database integration and more. In addition, ColdFusion developers can extend the CFML language by writing their own tags.

CFML also features a rich set of functions that can be used for all sorts of data manipulation. Unlike tags, which perform specific operations, functions return data (or manipulate data).

> **NOTE**
> ColdFusion is not CFML, and CFML is not ColdFusion (although most developers equate the two). ColdFusion is an application server; CFML is a language that ColdFusion supports. Future products from Allaire will make this distinction clearer.

Summary

Effective ColdFusion development requires a solid understanding of Internet and Web-related technologies. The Internet provides the backbone on which to build Web-based applications, and ColdFusion is an application server that extends the capabilities of the Web.

Sample Questions

1. Which of the following are valid parts of a URL?
   A. Protocol
   B. Port
   C. CGI variables
   D. Query string

2. ColdFusion can access resources on the client host.
   A. True
   B. False

3. The CFML language is made up of…
   A. Tags
   B. XML
   C. Functions
   D. JavaScript

CHAPTER 2

Working with Variables and Expressions

What Are Variables and Expressions?

Simple in concept, ColdFusion variables are key to building dynamic Web pages. They provide placeholders in which to put different values. ColdFusion variables are used in expressions. Expressions are generally used in two ways: inside a `<CFOUTPUT>` block to build output on a Web page and to the right of equal signs in `<CFSET>` statements.

> **NOTE**
>
> Remember the following rules when naming ColdFusion variables:
>
> - Names must contain letters, numbers, and the underscore characters only.
> - Each name must start with a letter.
> - Spaces and any special characters besides the underscore are *not* allowed.

But what exactly is an expression? The ColdFusion documentation says that expressions are "language constructs that allow you to create sophisticated applications." The best way to define an expression is to say it is simply a combination of the following:

- Operands such as integers, strings, real numbers, arrays, query results, and variables
- Operators such as +, `MOD`, and `AND`
- Functions that return changed data such as `UCase()` and `DateFormat()`

TIP

ColdFusion variable names can be variables themselves. If you want to assign a value to a variable, simply use `<CFSET>` with the variable name to the left of the equal sign and quotation marks and # signs as follows:

```
<CFSET "#TheVar#"=15>
```

Variables and Type

ColdFusion variables are *typeless*. Unlike what you do in many other computer languages, you do not need to tell ColdFusion what type of data will be stored in the variable before it is used. So, how does ColdFusion know what type of data a variable holds? The decision is made when you use the variable in an expression.

First, consider the assignment statement

```
<CFSET TheVar="10">
```

which sets a typeless variable equal to 10. Is it the number 10 or the string 10? It does not matter at this point.

Now look at the variable in another assignment statement:

```
<CFSET TheNumber=TheVar+5>
```

The arithmetic operator + is used here. It dynamically casts the type of `TheVar` to be a number. `TheNumber` is set to equal the number 15.

Now consider the variable again in another assignment, this time concatenating strings:

```
<CFSET TheString="The number is " & TheVar>
```

This time a variable called `TheString` is set equal to the text `"The number is "` and then concatenated with `TheVar`. This assignment dynamically sets the type of `TheVar` to be a string. `TheString` is set equal to `"The number is 10"`.

NOTE

ColdFusion variables are typeless when created. The type is cast when the variables are later used with an operator.

→ Although ColdFusion expressions are typeless, not all variables in a ColdFusion template are. When writing SQL, strings must be surrounded with single quotes. For more information using SQL with ColdFusion see Chapter 7, "Using Databases."

Variable Prefixes

Many developers believe the best practice is to always use prefixes, but prefixes actually are not always required. Variables that existed in ColdFusion 2.x and earlier do not require prefixes when used. The following variables do not have to have a prefix:

Query result variables
Local variables
CGI variables
File variables
URL variables
FORM variables
COOKIE variables
CLIENT variables

> **NOTE**
> A variable's scope determines where it exists, how long it exists, and where its values are stored. The variable's prefix determines its scope.

Reason One to Use Prefixes: Performance

The first reason to use a variable prefix is for performance. Consider a variable called `TheVar` that is used in an expression and not prefixed. ColdFusion must find the value for that variable. ColdFusion must look in each variable scope for the `TheVar` variable and its associated value. The closer the variable is to the bottom of the list of order of evaluation, the longer it will take to retrieve the value of the variable.

> **TIP**
> For variable scopes that do not require prefixes, the order of evaluation is as follows:
>
> 1st: Query result variables
> 2nd: Local variables
> 3rd: CGI variables
> 4th: File variables
> 5th: URL variables
> 6th: FORM variables
> 7th: COOKIE variables
> 8th: CLIENT variables

Reason Two to Use Prefixes: Avoiding Ambiguity

Problems can arise when the same variable name is from two different scopes. Consider the following two assignment statements:

```
<CFSET TestVar="Local">

<CFCOOKIE NAME="TestVar" VALUE="Cookie">
```

The variable will be displayed using this statement:

```
<CFOUTPUT>#TestVar#</CFOUTPUT>
```

When evaluated, the value `"Local"` would be displayed. Even though the `COOKIE` variable called `TestVar` is set after the local variable `TestVar`, when the expression is evaluated, the local variable's value is displayed because of order of evaluation. If you want to display the value of the `COOKIE` variable, you have to use the `COOKIE` prefix.

A Reason *Not* to Use Prefixes: Flexibility

Consider a template that is both the action page of a form and the target of a URL. A variable of the same name is passed in from each page. In this scenario, by not using a prefix, the template would work in both cases. The nonprefixed variable could act as both a `FORM` and `URL` variable.

Creating Local Variables

As you can see from this chapter so far, `<CFSET>` is very helpful in assigning values to variables. If the variable already exists, `<CFSET>` resets the value.

A common problem in Web development is using variables when you are not sure they exist. The `<CFPARAM>` tag can assist you in this situation. If the tag

```
<CFPARAM NAME="TheVar" DEFAULT="Default Value">
```

does not exist, you could replace it with the following code:

```
<CFIF NOT IsDefined("TheVar")>
    <CFSET TheVar="Default Value">
</CFIF>
```

A lesser-known use of `<CFPARAM>` is checking the data type of a variable. The `TYPE` attribute checks the data type of the variable, and if it is not of the type specified, an error is thrown. For example, if a variable is assigned using the statement

```
<CFSET TheVar="Hello">
```

the following `<CFPARAM>` would generate an error:

```
<CFPARAM NAME="TheVar" TYPE="numeric" DEFAULT="15">
```

The following 10 different values are valid for use with the `TYPE` attribute:

Any
Array
Binary
Boolean
Date
Numeric
Query
String
UUID
VariableName

➔ Generating an error is not always a bad thing. In Chapter 21, "Error Handling," you'll see how you can catch the error and programmatically deal with it.

CAUTION

When you're using `<CFPARAM>` and no prefix is used with the variable for which you are checking existence, remember that the tag looks through all scopes that do not require a prefix for a variable of that name. You may be thinking you are checking for the existence of `VARIABLES.TheVar`, but if `FORM.TheVar` exists, `<CFPARAM>` assumes the variable exists.

Using Local Variables

In the examples shown so far in this chapter, no prefixes have been used with `<CFSET>` or `<CFPARAM>`. This creates a variable, called a local variable, whose scope is only the local page. The `VARIABLES` prefix is used with local variables.

NOTE

Remember that local variables can also be used in included templates.

When you use local variables, sometimes you must use # signs around them. The pair of # signs basically tells ColdFusion that what is inside them must be processed, or the variable needs to be distinguished from plain text. Some common uses of local variables are displaying them within `<CFOUTPUT>` tags and using them in expressions.

TIP

If you're unsure when to use or not use # signs, remember the following rules:

- # signs are always needed when ColdFusion variables are used outside or between pairs of ColdFusion tags.
- # signs are never needed when used inside ColdFusion tags, unless the variable is inside quotation marks.

Because of the ambiguity of when to use # signs in early versions of ColdFusion, they are sometimes overused.

Variables and the Request Scope

One limitation of local variables is that they can be used only on the page where they are created. An easy but not well-known remedy is to use the *request scope*. The request scope makes a variable available to the entire page request by the browser. Because the scope is the entire page request, the values are carried through to nested tags, such as custom tags. So, instead of continually passing the same value to custom tags, you put in the request scope.

> **TIP**
>
> A great place to set these request scope variables is in the `Application.cfm` template.

→ You'll see how to use custom tags and pass data to them in Chapter 22, "Custom Tags," and Chapter 23, "Advanced Custom Tags."

You therefore can set a variable using the request scope and then use that variable in custom tags. You create a variable in the request scope as shown in the following example:

```
<CFSET REQUEST.AppDSN="StoreData">
```

> **TIP**
>
> If you want to see what is in the request scope, you can look at the structure that holds all the request scope variables. Using a custom tag such as `<CF_ObjectDump>` or the Spectra tag `<CFA_DUMP>` makes seeing the entire scope simple.

Functions

Functions return manipulated values for use in, for example, expressions. The functions do not change the data they are acting on; rather, they produce a result or return a value for output.

ColdFusion functions take the form *`FunctionName(argument)`*. The argument may be nothing, like when you're using the function `Now()`, which returns the current date and time.

For a simple example, consider the assignment:

```
<CFSET Convert=UCase("hello")>
```

The function used here is `UCase()`, which converts a string into all uppercase characters. The argument is the string `"hello"`. The function does its work, and the assignment statement stores the string `"HELLO"` into the local variable `Convert`.

> **NOTE**
>
> `#` signs can sometimes be confusing when you're using functions with ColdFusion variables. The proper way to use `#` signs with a function and variable is as follows:
>
> ```
> #DateFormat(SellDate)#
> ```
>
> not
>
> ```
> #DateFormat(#SellDate#)#
> ```

Nested Functions

Functions can also be nested. This means the argument of a function can be another function itself. A very common example of nesting is using the `DateFormat()` function with the `Now()` function as follows:

```
DateFormat(Now())
```

Functions with Masks

Some functions also have another option called a *mask*. Functions that do formatting often have masks so that they can be tailored to an individual developer's needs. Again, consider the `DateFormat()` function. Say you want to change the default format to a date in the form `mm/dd/yy`. You do so as follows:

```
DateFormat(Now(),"mm/dd/yy")
```

The mask appears in quotation marks, separated from the argument by a comma.

Strings

Strings are text values, which, when used, can be surrounded by either single or double quotation marks.

> **NOTE**
> The length of a string is limited only by the amount of available memory in the ColdFusion server.

String manipulation is part of any Web developer's task. You can manipulate strings in two ways in ColdFusion: constant string manipulation and regular expression string manipulation. ColdFusion offers 40 string functions to aid in this task.

Constant String Manipulation

If you know the exact string you want to work with—even if it is part of a bigger string—you can use constant string manipulation. Constant string manipulation tasks can range from the simple, such as being sure no blank spaces are part of a string, to the complex, such as searching a page of text for the last example of an HTML table and extracting that table for use in another page.

Using the powerful string functions helps make your life simpler when you're faced with these kinds of tasks. For instance, when you're prefilling a form control, you might need to be sure that no leading or trailing spaces are included with the value put in the form control. The `Trim()` function, which follows, fits the job perfectly:

```
<INPUT TYPE="Text" NAME="FName" VALUE="#Trim(FName)#">
```

Regular Expression String Manipulation

If you know only the pattern of the string you want to work with, you need to use regular expression string manipulation. A subset of the string functions deals with regular expressions. You can recognize them by the `RE` in front of the expression names. For instance, you might see a `Replace()` function and a `REReplace()` function.

An example of regular expression string manipulation is looking for a dollar amount in some text when the exact dollar amount is not known. You need to write a regular expression and then use it with one of the appropriate functions.

> **NOTE**
> A full coverage of how to write regular expressions is not appropriate for this text, but complete books have been written on the subject. Tutorials are also available on the Web.

The appropriate regular expression to find all dollar amounts is as follows:

```
\$[0-9,\.]*
```

Then to find the location of the first instance of a dollar amount, you use the following statement:

```
<CFSET TheLocation=REFind("\$[0-9,\.]*",TheString)>
```

Summary

ColdFusion variables and expressions are the building blocks of most ColdFusion development. ColdFusion variables are typeless upon creation, and then the type is cast when used with an operator. Variable prefixes determine the scope of the variable, and using them is almost always a good idea. `<CFSET>` and `<CFPARAM>` are essential tools in creating variables. Using the request scope is a very helpful way to extend the places where local variables can be used. Functions can be used to return manipulated variable values. Both constant and regular expression string manipulation are possible in ColdFusion.

Sample Questions

1. Expressions are a combination of operands, operators, and functions. Which of the following are operands? (Choose two.)
   A. ColdFusion variables
   B. `MOD`
   C. `34`
   D. `LCase()`

2. If no prefix is used, which scope would be used if values existed in all the following for a variable of the same name?
   A. `FORM`
   B. `URL`
   C. `CLIENT`
   D. `COOKIE`

3. Which of the following is the best syntax for the assignment statement?
   A. <CFSET #PassingDate#=#DateFormat(Now())#>
   B. <CFSET PassingDate=#DateFormat(Now())#>
   C. <CFSET #PassingDate#=DateFormat(Now())>
   D. <CFSET PassingDate=DateFormat(Now())>

4. The exact string you want to replace is not known, but a general pattern can be determined. What kind of string manipulation should you use?
   A. Constant
   B. Regular expression

CHAPTER 3

Conditional Processing

What Is Conditional Processing?

Conditional processing is code that reacts to specified conditions and behaves differently based on those conditions. When application behavior depends on data that is not known at the time of development, such as user data or query information, conditional processing is an essential tool.

Performing Conditional Processing

ColdFusion employs a number of tags to implement conditional processing. The simplest is the `<CFIF>`/`<CFELSE>` tag set. In addition, the `<CFSWITCH>` tag is a better choice in some situations.

<CFIF>

The `<CFIF>` tag can take various forms. The simplest of them is as follows:

```
<CFIF expression>
       Code performed if condition true
</CFIF>
```

The expression must evaluate to true or false. Traditionally, this is some condition using an operator—for example, `TheVar IS 40`. Regardless of the outcome of the evaluation of the expression (either true or false), program flow continues after the `</CFIF>` tag.

TIP

Remember that ColdFusion does not use the normal symbols for operators. So the condition cannot use the = sign but uses the word IS. The operators are shown in the following table:

ColdFusion Operator	*Symbol*
IS, EQUAL, EQ	=
IS NOT, NOT EQUAL, NEQ	<>
GT, GREATER THAN	>
LT, LESS THAN	<
GTE, GREATER THAN OR EQUAL	>=
LTE, LESS THAN OR EQUAL	<=

Expressions to be evaluated as true or false can take many different forms, not just a condition using an operator. Many ColdFusion functions return a value that can be evaluated to TRUE or FALSE. Remember that numbers are inherently TRUE or FALSE in ColdFusion.

TIP

When ColdFusion is evaluating an expression to be TRUE or FALSE, be sure to remember the following:

Logically equivalent to TRUE:

- Any nonzero numbers (including negative numbers)
- YES

Logically equivalent to FALSE:

- 0 (Zero)
- NO

The next step in using <CFIF> is to add an else clause. The logic then becomes an either/or situation. The general format is shown here:

```
<CFIF expression>
      Code performed if expression is true
<CFELSE>
      Code performed if expression is false
</CFIF>
```

With a single else clause, still only one expression is evaluated. The <CFIF> statement can be extended in yet another way, using <CFELSEIF>. This method offers the opportunity to have multiple conditions. The general format is as follows:

```
<CFIF expression1>
      Code performed if expression1 is true
<CFELSEIF expression2>
      Code performed if expression2 is true
```

```
<CFELSE>
       Code performed if no expressions are true
</CFIF>
```

Note that the <CFELSE> is optional.

> **TIP**
>
> If you put the most common cases in the first <CFELSEIF>s, the amount of processing is minimized and performance is maximized.

<CFSWITCH>

You might be able to implement <CFIF> with multiple <CFELSEIF> clauses in a more readable and more efficient format by using <CFSWITCH>. Many languages refer to this logic as a CASE statement. The general format is as follows:

```
<CFSWITCH EXPRESSION="expression">
    <CFCASE VALUE="value" DELIMITERS="delimiters">
       HTML and CFML tags
    </CFCASE>
    additional <CFCASE></CFCASE> tags
    <CFDEFAULTCASE>
       HTML and CFML tags
    </CFDEFAULTCASE>
</CFSWITCH>
```

With this control structure, you specify the value in each <CFCASE> statement that will possibly match the expression in the <CFSWITCH> line. The following is a very simple example:

```
<CFSWITCH EXPRESSION="World">
    <CFCASE VALUE="Hello">
       Hello was matched
    </CFCASE>
    <CFCASE VALUE="World">
       World was matched
    </CFCASE>
    <CFDEFAULTCASE>
       Neither Hello nor World was matched
    </CFDEFAULTCASE>
</CFSWITCH>
```

In this case, the code would display "World was matched". If neither Hello nor World were the expression in the <CFSWITCH>, the <CFDEFAULTCASE> would apply. Just as <CFELSE> is optional in <CFIF>, so <CFDEFAULTCASE> is optional when you're using <CFSWITCH>.

NOTE

- In the <CFCASE> statement, equality is the only valid operator. You cannot use GT or LTE, for example, as the operator.
- Multiple values can be listed for one case.
- A DELIMITERS attribute with <CFCASE> specifies the character that separates multiple entries in the list of values. The default delimiter is the comma.

TIP

As with <CFIF>, it is best to put the most common cases at the top of the <CFSWITCH> to increase performance.

Nested Statements

Both the <CFIF> and <CFSWITCH> tags can be nested. In <CFIF>, one of the true conditions can be code that uses another <CFIF>. Likewise, in <CFSWITCH>, the code executed when a case is true can be another <CFSWITCH>.

More Details of Boolean Expressions

Boolean expressions are expressions that will be evaluated to either true or false. We've already discussed some details concerning evaluation of Boolean expressions, but other details are essential for understanding.

Logical Operators

ColdFusion has a set of logical, or Boolean, operators that are used with Boolean operands. They perform logical connective and negation operations. The most common of them are AND, OR, and NOT.

The operator AND returns TRUE if both operands are true; otherwise, FALSE is returned.

The operator OR returns TRUE if either operand is true. FALSE is returned only if both operands are false.

The NOT operator negates the operand. For instance, NOT FALSE returns TRUE.

Other logical operators are XOR, EQV, and IMP.

Parentheses

The standard rules for operator precedence (which operator is performed before others) are enforced in ColdFusion. If you want to change the order, you must use parentheses. For instance, AND is evaluated before OR. If you want to change this order, you could use parentheses as follows:

```
(A OR B) AND C
```

If parentheses are nested, the innermost set is evaluated first.

Short-Circuit Evaluation

When you use the logical operator AND, if the first operand is false, ColdFusion doesn't really need to do any further evaluation because FALSE joined with any operand using the AND operator is going to be false. ColdFusion realizes this and uses *short-circuit evaluation*, which means that the logical expression is evaluated only as far as necessary to determine the truth value of the whole expression.

Conditional Statements

Conditional processing occurs when one statement controls the execution of other statements. Although you might normally think of using <CFIF> and <CFSWITCH> to handle conditionals, other statements can also accomplish this task.

To set the stage for examples of these conditional statements, consider a situation often faced by Web developers—dealing with FORM variables that may or may not be passed to the action page. Unless values are supplied for check boxes, radio buttons, and select boxes, they do not pass values to the template specified in the ACTION attribute of the form.

For the following examples, consider a single check box that is used on a form to ask a user whether she wants to receive email about future product releases. The user will check the box for yes and not check it for no. The name of the form control is Email. On the action page, it must conditionally be decided whether the box was checked.

➔ For a further discussion of forms and FORM variables used with ColdFusion, see Chapter 9, "FORM Variables."

<CFPARAM>

You can use the conditional statement <CFPARAM> to provide the value "No" to the form control if it does not exist on the action page by using the following statement:

```
<CFPARAM NAME="Email" DEFAULT="No">
```

➔ For information concerning what prefix could be used with the Email variable, see Chapter 2, "Working with Variables and Expressions."

IsDefined()

You can use the IsDefined() function to do the same job as <CFPARAM> by using the following code:

```
<CFIF NOT IsDefined("FORM.Email")>
<CFSET FORM.Email="No">
</CFIF>
```

Hidden Form Controls

You can also address this problem on the actual form by including a hidden form control passing the value No associated with the form control Email. This way, you ensure that the variable will be defined on the action page.

> **CAUTION**
>
> If you use the hidden form control method, you must programmatically compensate for the event when the check box is checked. This results in both `Yes` and `No` being associated with the form control as a list of values.

➔ For more information on forms, see Chapter 9, "Form Variables."

Summary

Conditional processing is essential in development of ColdFusion applications, and several tools are available to do that. `<CFIF>` is the best tool many times, but `<CFSWITCH>` is easier to read and performs better under certain circumstances.

Sample Questions

1. Which operator is used to test for equality?
   A. `==`
   B. `IS THE SAME AS`
   C. `IS`
   D. `=`

2. Which of the following are logically equivalent to `TRUE`? (Choose all that apply.)
   A. `-45`
   B. `ON`
   C. `1`
   D. `YES`

3. The following is a valid `VALUE` attribute for a `<CFCASE>` statement:
   `VALUE="12;45;67"`

   A. True
   B. False

CHAPTER 4

Looping

What Is Looping?

Looping is using any control structure to cause a program to repeatedly execute a block of code. You can use many kinds of loops in ColdFusion. The one you choose to implement depends on both how you want to loop and whether you are looping over a data structure. Loops either repeat a specific number of times or until a certain condition is met.

Index

Index loops are used to execute a block of code a specified number of times. The loop repeats for a number of times determined by a range of numeric values. In many other languages, Index loops are referred to as `FOR` loops.

> **NOTE**
>
> If you have a condition where you want to jump out of the Index loop, using a conditional loop instead is best. Although you can use ColdFusion's `<CFBREAK>` tag, which permits jumping out of the loop, style-wise you are better off not doing so.

The Index loop has the attributes shown in Table 4.1.

Table 4.1 Index Loop Attributes

Attribute	Description
`INDEX`	The name of the variable to hold the current loop value.
`FROM`	The beginning value of the index.

Table 4.1 continued

Attribute	Description
TO	The ending value of the index.
STEP	An optional attribute that controls the increment of the index each time through the loop. The default is 1.

To create a loop that starts at 10 and steps backward to 4, you would use the following statement:

```
<CFLOOP INDEX="i" FROM="10" TO="4" STEP="-2">
     <CFOUTPUT>#i#</CFOUTPUT><BR>
</CFLOOP>
```

Conditional

You use the Conditional loop when you want to loop while a certain condition is true. In many other languages, Conditional loops are referred to as WHILE loops.

The Conditional loop has only one attribute: CONDITION. In it, you place the expression that will be evaluated by ColdFusion to be true or false, and thus determine when the loop terminates. Because the condition is checked at the entrance to the loop, the loop may not be executed at all. When you're considering how the loop will behave, it is a good idea to consider how the loop will be entered the first time, and how the loop will terminate.

→ For a complete discussion of writing expressions that will be evaluated to true or false by ColdFusion, see Chapter 3, "Conditional Processing."

A sample Conditional loop follows:

```
<!--- Set up variables for condition --->
<CFSET NumToGet="4">
<CFSET i="0">
<!--- Now loop --->
<CFLOOP CONDITION="i LTE NumToGet">
     <CFSET i=i+1>
     <CFOUTPUT>#i#</CFOUTPUT><BR>
</CFLOOP>
```

NOTE

The loop does *not* exit the instant the condition becomes false. It finishes all the statements between the <CFLOOP> and </CFLOOP> before terminating.

CAUTION

In the Conditional loop shown here, the output is from 1 to 5, not to 4 as you might expect. The reason the output goes to 5 is the order in which the increment is done versus the display. If the two lines inside the loop were reversed, the output would be 0 to 4. Be sure to consider this result when using conditional loops.

Query

The Query loop loops over a block of statements once for every record read from a query.

> **TIP**
>
> The function of the Query loop is the same as using `<CFOUTPUT>` with a `QUERY` attribute. For performance reasons, use a Query loop rather than a `<CFOUTPUT QUERY="qAny">` loop. Before ColdFusion 4.x, the `<CFOUTPUT QUERY="qAny">` query loop performed better.
>
> Generally speaking, you should use a `<CFLOOP>` with a `QUERY` attribute when doing all, or mostly, processing in the loop. If there is nothing in the loop but display, use `<CFOUTPUT>`.

The Query loop has the attributes shown in Table 4.2.

Table 4.2 Query Loop Attributes

Attribute	Description
QUERY	The name of the query to loop over
STARTROW	An optional attribute that determines the first row of the query that will be included in the loop
ENDROW	An optional attribute that determines the last row of the query that will be included in the loop

A sample Query loop follows:

```
<CFLOOP QUERY="qMyData">
    <CFOUTPUT>#qMyData.My_Column#</CFOUTPUT><BR>
</CFLOOP>
```

> **NOTE**
>
> As is the case with `<CFOUTPUT QUERY="qAny">`, the use of the query name as a prefix is optional. However, unlike `<CFOUTPUT>`, `<CFLOOP>` does not automatically act as `<CFOUTPUT>`, so those tags are required, as shown in the example.

> **TIP**
>
> ColdFusion developers often surround a block of code, or maybe even a whole page, with `<CFOUTPUT>` and `</CFOUTPUT>`. A problem arises when `<CFOUTPUT QUERY="qAny">` is needed inside the block because you cannot nest `<CFOUTPUT>` tags in this way. A simple solution is to change the inner `<CFOUTPUT QUERY="qAny">` to `<CFLOOP QUERY="qAny">`.

List

Lists in ColdFusion are simply sets of data separated by one or more delimiters. You can use a List loop to step over the elements of the list one at a time.

→ For further information on lists, see Chapter 13, "Lists."

When using a List loop, you use the attributes shown in Table 4.3.

Table 4.3 List Loop Attributes

Attribute	Description
INDEX	The name of the variable to hold the current element of the list
LIST	The list to be stepped through
DELIMITERS	An optional attribute that specifies the delimiter or delimiters used to separate items in the list

An example of a List loop follows:

```
<!--- Create a list --->
<CFSET Months="Jan,Feb,Mar,Apr">
<!--- Loop over the list --->
<CFLOOP INDEX="i" LIST="#Months#">
     <CFOUTPUT>#VARIABLES.i#</CFOUTPUT><BR>
</CFLOOP>
```

The index of the loop, here the variable `i` will assume the values of the list `Months`. Specifically `Jan`, `Feb`, `Mar`, and `Apr`, and those month abbreviations will be displayed.

Collection

Collection loops allow looping over key-value pairs in structures. Each time through the loop, the variable specified in the `ITEM` attribute takes the value of successive key names. To display the value of the key-value pairs, you use the `ITEM` with associative array notation. The following example helps clarify the situation:

```
<!--- Create and fill the structure --->
<CFSCRIPT>
     stProduct=StructNew();
     stProduct.Name="Ball";
     stProduct.Color="Red";
</CFSCRIPT>
<!--- Display the key value pairs --->
<CFLOOP COLLECTION="#stProduct#" ITEM="TheKey">
     <CFOUTPUT>#TheKey#: #stProduct[TheKey]#</CFOUTPUT><BR>
</CFLOOP>
```

The preceding code uses a `<CFSCRIPT>` block to create a structure and fill it. In the loop, the variable `TheKey` takes the values `Name` and `Color`, which are the keys in the structure. Associative array notation, `#stProduct[TheKey]#`, is used to display the values in the structure, `Ball` and `Red`.

→ You can find a complete discussion of structures in Chapter 15, "Structures."

→ For more information on using <CFSCRIPT>, see Chapter 16, "Scripting."

NOTE

In Index and List loops, the attribute that holds the current loop value is INDEX. With Collection loops, it is called ITEM.

TIP

The Collection loop is built to loop over key-value pairs of a structure. When you're looping over arrays, use an Index loop with the TO attribute set equal to #ArrayLen(aMy_Array)#.

You also can use Collection loops to loop over COM/DCOM collection objects.

Using <CFLOOP> with <CFOUTPUT>

Earlier we mentioned a solution to a very common mistake, but it is worth repeating here. When a <CFLOOP> is used in any of its variations, it does *not* preclude the need for a <CFOUTPUT> block around ColdFusion variables inside the loop. If you scan back through all the code examples in this chapter, you will see that a <CFOUTPUT> block was used.

Nested Loops

One loop placed inside another creates a *nested loop*. Generally speaking, the inside loop completely iterates for every single iteration of the outside loop. The following nested Index loops help clarify the situation:

```
<CFLOOP INDEX="Outside" FROM="1" TO="2">
    <CFLOOP INDEX="Inside" FROM="7" TO="9">
        <CFOUTPUT>
            Outside is: #VARIABLES.Outside# Inside is: #VARIABLES.Inside#<BR>
        </CFOUTPUT>
    </CFLOOP>
</CFLOOP>
```

The outside loop initializes to 1, followed by the inside loop initializing to 7; then the output is displayed. The first </CFLOOP> causes the inside, or nested loop, to increment to 8, and the output is displayed. This process continues until the inside loop terminates. Then the second </CFLOOP> is processed and increments the outer loop to 2. When the inside <CFLOOP> is seen this second time, it is as if it has not been seen before, so it initializes the variable Inside to 7. The output of the loops is as follows:

```
Outside is: 1 Inside is: 7
Outside is: 1 Inside is: 8
Outside is: 1 Inside is: 9
Outside is: 2 Inside is: 7
Outside is: 2 Inside is: 8
Outside is: 2 Inside is: 9
```

You can nest other types of loops applying the same logic.

> **TIP**
>
> You can place code between the two beginning <CFLOOP> and/or the </CFLOOP> tags that create the nested loops. This capability can be especially helpful for formatting issues such as building HTML tables.

Summary

ColdFusion can do the following: iterate through a set of numeric values; loop while a condition is true; loop over the records of a query; loop over elements of a list; and loop over key-value pairs of a collection. Loops can also be nested.

Sample Questions

1. Which one of the following is *not* true of Index loops?
   A. They can iterate over numeric values.
   B. The loop value variable is assigned using the `INDEX` attribute.
   C. They can iterate over the alphabet.
   D. They can step by negative increments.

2. What is the output from the following loop?

```
<!--- Set up variables for condition --->
<CFSET NumToGet="3">
<CFSET i="1">
<!--- Now loop --->
<CFLOOP CONDITION="i LTE NumToGet">
     <CFSET i=i+1>
     <CFOUTPUT>#i#</CFOUTPUT>
</CFLOOP>
```

   A. `1 2 3`
   B. `2 3`
   C. `1 2`
   D. `2 3 4`

3. A Collection loop is used to loop over a structure that contains key-value pairs of `Animal-Cow`, `Legs-4`, and `Tail-Yes`. What is the value of the attribute ITEM in the loop?
   A. `Animal, Legs, Tail`
   B. `Animal. Cow, Legs. 4, Tail. Yes`
   C. `Cow, 4, Yes`
   D. `Cow, 4, Tail`

4. The loops `<CFLOOP QUERY="qAny">` and `<CFOUTPUT QUERY="qAny">` are logically equivalent.
   A. True
   B. False

5. The loop variable is assigned using the `INDEX` attribute in which types of loops?
   A. Conditional
   B. Index
   C. Collection
   D. List

CHAPTER 5

Redirects and Reuse

Redirects

At some point on a page, you might want to send the user to another page. You can do so by using *redirection*. This means that although the browser requests one page, it is actually sent another. Using server-side redirection the browser never sees the requested page's HTML. This is true even if the HTML is above the tag that performs the redirection.

Using Redirection

You implement server-side redirection in ColdFusion by using the <CFLOCATION> tag. This tag has the two attributes shown in Table 5.1.

Table 5.1 <CFLOCATION> Tag Attributes

Attribute	Description
URL	The URL the browser should be redirected to.
ADDTOKEN	An optional attribute that is either Yes or No. If the value is Yes, ColdFusion appends CLIENT variable information to the URL you specify in the URL attribute. This assumes that CLIENT variables are turned on using the CLIENTMANAGEMENT attribute of the <CFAPPLICATION> tag. The default value is Yes.

→ See Chapter 6, "The Application Framework," and Chapter 11, "Session State Management," for further information on CLIENT variables and the <CFAPPLICATION> tag.

The URL attribute is simply set equal to the HTML file or CFML template the browser should be redirected to.

> **TIP**
>
> A query string is allowed at the end of the URL listed in the TEMPLATE attribute. This permits variables and their associated values to be passed to the redirection page.

The ADDTOKEN attribute needs further explanation. A CLIENT variable called CLIENT.URLToken automatically exists in the Client scope. This variable is the CFID set equal to its value and the CFTOKEN set equal to its value concatenated with an ampersand (&). An example would be CFID=1&CFTOKEN=69684259. If the ADDTOKEN attribute is set to Yes or is not used (in which case, it defaults to Yes), the CLIENT.URLToken variable is appended to the URL listed for redirection.

Why would you need to append the CFID and CFTOKEN variables to the URL? The answer is that when you're using redirection, cookies sent by the browser to the first page requested are not automatically sent to the redirection page. So, if CFID and CFTOKEN are needed on the redirection page, they must be appended to the URL.

> **CAUTION**
>
> Because <CFLOCATION> does not send data to the client, cookies created in the page (before the redirection) are not registered with the browser.
>
> Three solutions to this problem are shown below. All three basically do the same thing, insure the page was sent to the browser so the cookies are set, but display the page for zero seconds before the redirection takes place.
>
> Solution 1: You could use an HTML META tag for redirection and set the time to wait on the requested page to zero seconds using the following code:
>
> ```
> <META HTTP-EQUIV="REFRESH" CONTENT="0;URL=SomePage.cfm">
> ```
>
> Solution 2: You also could use JavaScript as follows:
>
> ```
> <script language="javascript">
>     location.href = "SomePage.cfm"
> </script
> ```
>
> Solution 3: You could also use a ColdFusion solution, which leads nicely into the next topic of the chapter:
>
> ```
> <CFHEADER NAME="Refresh" VALUE="0; URL=SomePage.cfm">
> ```

HTTP Headers

An HTTP header passes information about requests by the browser and responses from the server. The information needed for the exchange to take place, without being displayed, is included in the header.

The response header is most interesting for this discussion because you have some control over it using ColdFusion. The general format of the response header includes, as its first line, what version of HTTP it is speaking (such as 1.1) and a status code (such as 200 for OK or 404 for File Not Found). Separate lines of attribute/value pairs follow the first line. A colon and then a space separate the attributes and values.

When a page that contains this line of code is browsed

```
<CFCOOKIE NAME="Chap5Cookie" VALUE="Test" EXPIRES="1/1/2002">
```

the first line of the response header would look something like

```
HTTP/1.1 200 OK
```

followed by the attribute/value pairs. The following are some examples:

```
Date: Fri, 24 Nov 2000 17:41:31 GMT

Set-Cookie: CHAP5COOKIE=Test; expires=Tue, 01-Jan-2002 00:00:00 GMT; path=/;
```

You see a default attribute/value pair concerning the date, as well as the pair created by setting the cookie.

Using HTTP Headers

The <CFHEADER> tag sets attribute/value pairs in the response header. The attributes of the tag are shown in Table 5.2.

Table 5.2 <CFHEADER> Tag Attributes

Attribute	Description
NAME	The name of the attributes to set
VALUE	The value associated with the corresponding NAME

A common use of the <CFHEADER> tag is to prevent a Web page from being cached by the browser. This caching can cause a problem if the Web page is used to display data that is being updated in some way. If database data is inserted, updated, or deleted and the page to display that data is cached by the browser, the database records might not be shown accurately on the page. The Web browser has an EXPIRES attribute, which you can set to some time in the past so that the page will always be expired. The code to do so is as follows:

```
<CFHEADER NAME="Expires" VALUE="#Now()#">
```

The entry created in the header would look something like this:

```
Normal Expires: {ts '2000-11-24 19:34:42'}
```

> **TIP**
>
> If you run into a situation in which you need to prevent a page from being cached, you must take into account different browsers and browser versions. The one example shown here may not cover all possibilities. You might also want to test

the following to be sure you get the best results for the range of browsers you are considering:

```
<meta http-equiv="Pragma" content="No-Cache">
<meta http-equiv="Expires" content="0">
<cfheader name="Pragma" value="no-cache">
<cfheader name="cache-control" value="no-cache, no-store, must-revalidate">
```

Be sure to check the support forums when you need this functionality to see whether new browser versions require different code.

Reuse

Imagine building a Web site with thousands of pages and a copy of the header on each page. Sometime during the life of a successful Web site, changes will be wanted or needed. The developers must go in and change the header code on every page. Obviously, this is not a position in which you want to find yourself.

Code reuse has many benefits, one of the most important of which occurs when you need to change code that is viewed on many pages. Other obvious benefits include using code that is already written, tested, and debugged.

Reuse and Including Files

One way to implement reuse in ColdFusion is to use the `<CFINCLUDE>` tag. In essence, this tag takes code from one page, called the *included page*, and puts it into the page that contains the `<CFINCLUDE>` tag, called the *calling page*. Therefore, the code for a header could be stored in a central location and included in every page where it is needed. The `<CFINLCUDE>` tag has only one attribute, `TEMPLATE`, which is the path to the page to include.

The path can be specified either as a relative path or as a ColdFusion mapping. If the first character after the quotation mark in the `TEMPLATE` attribute is a forward slash (/), the path uses a ColdFusion mapping.

The included page assumes the directory of the calling page. This means that you must be very careful using relative paths in the included code because they are often used at many different directory levels in the Web site. You can find solutions to this issue in the next two sections of this chapter.

Variables are not protected in the calling or included pages. This means that a variable in the calling page can be directly displayed and manipulated in the included page. Conversely, any variables from the included code can later be displayed and manipulated in the calling page after the `<CFINCLUDE>`. Later in this chapter, you will see that this capability can work to your advantage.

ColdFusion Mappings

ColdFusion mappings are directory aliases created in the ColdFusion Administrator. A virtual directory name can be associated with an actual physical directory path.

For example, a ColdFusion mapping called `templates_mapping` can be mapped to the physical directory `c:\inetpub\wwwroot\templates\`. You then could write a `<CFINCLUDE>` tag as follows:

```
<CFINCLUDE TEMPLATE="/templates_mapping/header.cfm">
```

The use of ColdFusion mapping offers some advantages. No matter where in the directory structure of your Web site the header is called, the path specified in the template attribute of the `<CFINCLUDE>` can be the same. You don't need to worry about a relative path to the header. If the Web page is moved in the directory structure, you don't need to change the path to the header.

If a mapping isn't used and a major overhaul of the site is made, changing the actual directory where the templates are stored, you would have to edit every `<CFINCLUDE>`. If a mapping is used, you would need to make only one change in the ColdFusion Administrator.

Web Server Mappings

Earlier in this chapter, you learned that the included page assumes the current directory of the calling page. You also learned about the advantages of having code stored centrally and reused in many places throughout the Web site. A problem can arise when you're using this method if it is not planned for. Consider a header that is included in many different pages throughout a Web site's directory structure. Almost assuredly, some images used in the header will be called with an `<IMG SRC>` tag. If relative paths are used in this tag, broken links will occur. So, if you are reusing code with `<CFINCLUDE>`, part of the solution is to use Web server mappings. Just as ColdFusion mappings allow a virtual name for a physical directory that can be used in ColdFusion tags, so can Web server mappings be used with HTML tags where needed.

Consider a Web server mapping, or *virtual directory* as it is called in some Web server software, named `images_mapping`. Say it is mapped to the physical directory of `c:\inetpub\wwwroot\images\`. You then can use this mapping in the header code where needed to be sure the images are correctly found and no broken links appear. For example, you could use the following:

```
<IMG SRC="/images_mapping/car.gif">
```

If this tag is used in the header, it does not matter where it is included; the link will function correctly.

Variable Scoping and `<CFINCLUDE>`

Remember that variables are not protected either in calling or included pages, meaning that a variable from one can be displayed or manipulated by the other. At first, this capability may seem like a negative factor, but sometimes it is just what you need.

Some search engines use the HTML title as part of the search report. If you include the header as suggested earlier, every title will be the same. Remember that variables set in the calling page can be used in the included page. So you could build the header something like this:

```
<HTML>
<HEAD>
    <TITLE>
        <CFOUTPUT>#VARIABLES.TheTitle#</CFOUTPUT>
    </TITLE>
</HEAD>
```

Then, when you're building the home page, you could use this code:

```
<CFSET TheTitle="PassThatTest.com Home Page">
<CFINCLUDE TEMPLATE="/templates_mapping/header.cfm">
```

So every page would simply set the title before using the `<CFINCLUDE>` tag.

If many parts of the header are changeable, like a navigation system, a query could be performed before the include and the information from the database used in the header.

> **CAUTION**
>
> When you include a page, the `<CFOUTPUT>` block does *not* carry into the included page. This means that if the `<CFINCLUDE>` is inside a `<CFOUTPUT>` block, any ColdFusion variables to be displayed on the included page must be surrounded with another `<CFOUTPUT>` block.

Generating Non-HTML Content

Using `<CFCONTENT>`, you can send documents to the client browser. The attributes you use with this tag are shown in Table 5.3.

Table 5.3 `<CFCONTENT>` Tag Attributes

Attribute	Description
TYPE	The MIME type of the document being sent. This attribute is mutually exclusive with the RESET attribute.
FILE	The file to be sent to the browser.
DELETEFILE	An optional attribute, which defaults to NO, that controls whether the file should be deleted after the download operation.
RESET	An optional attribute, which defaults to NO, that determines whether any output before the <CFCONTENT> tag should be discarded. This attribute is mutually exclusive with the FILE attribute.

> **CAUTION**
>
> The RESET attribute should be set to NO if the `<CFCONTENT>` tag is used in a custom tag. If this attribute is not set, all output from the page before the custom tag call will be discarded.

This example sends a Word document to a browser:

```
<CFCONTENT TYPE="application/msword" FILE="C:\MyWork.doc" DELETEFILE="No">
```

In addition to sending a file that is already created, you can send a document that is built on-the-fly. For instance, you might want to build an Excel spreadsheet to send to users, but with the absolutely latest data. You could use the following example. Assume that the ColdFusion variables `Test.Name` and `Test.Price` are read from the query:

```
<cfcontent TYPE="application/vnd.ms-excel" RESET="Yes">"Name"	"Price"
<CFOUTPUT QUERY="Test">"#Test.Name#"	"#Test.Price#"
</CFOUTPUT>
```

TIP

The `RESET` attribute is very helpful in this example because it cleans up any text that might exist on the page before you start the spreadsheet. It is also helpful in cases in which XML packets are being produced and sent.

Also, the lack of a carriage return after the `<CFOUTPUT QUERY="Test">` is intentional. All characters after `<CFCONTENT>` are used in the file, so a carriage return in this location would have put a blank line between each row of data in the spreadsheet. Tabs separate the two labels that are the column heading names. Tabs also separate the two actual data column names.

NOTE

You can turn off the `<CFCONTENT>` tag's functionality in the ColdFusion Administrator.

Summary

To have the browser request one page but redirected to another page, you can use `<CFLOCATION>`. When you're using `<CFLOCATION>`, you must take special care when dealing with cookies. `<CFHEADER>` enables ColdFusion to create attribute/value pairs in HTTP's response headers. You might practice code reuse for many reasons, and using the `<CFINCLUDE>` tag is a way to do so in ColdFusion. `<CFCONTENT>` sends non-HTML files, either existing or built dynamically, to a browser.

Sample Questions

1. Why do you sometimes need to use the `ADDTOKEN="Yes"` attribute with `<CFLOCATION>`?
   - A. To set cookies on the browser
   - B. To send the `CFID` variable to the server
   - C. To send the `URLToken` variable to the redirection page
   - D. To send the `CFTOKEN` variable to the redirection page

2. Which of the following are true about `<CFHEADER>`? (Choose two.)
   A. It creates attribute/value pairs in the request header.
   B. It creates attribute/value pairs in the response header.
   C. It can be used to prevent a browser from caching a page.
   D. It can be used to prevent a server from caching a page.

3. The following `<CFINCLUDE>` tag uses what kind of path?

```
<CFINCLUDE TEMPLATE="/templates_mapping/header.cfm">
```

   A. Relative
   B. ColdFusion mapping

4. What is displayed from the following line of code?

```
ABC<CFCONTENT TYPE="text/html" RESET="Yes">DEF
```

   A. `ABC`
   B. `ABCDEF`
   C. `ABEF`
   D. `DEF`

CHAPTER 6

The Application Framework

What Is the Application Framework?

The ColdFusion development environment provides a framework for combining application pages or templates into a single coherent application. This "application framework" is based on three basic components:

- Application-wide variables and code
- Client and application state management
- Error handling services

The topmost parent in the application directory tree is known as the *application root*. This directory is located within a branch of the Web document root. The subdirectories below this are typically used to separate code templates and other media based on their functionality. For example, included files such as headers might be found in an `../includes` directory and images in a separate `../images` directory, depending on your development methodology.

> **NOTE**
>
> The Web document root is the directory that has been mapped to the base Web site URL, such as `http://www.allaire.com/`. The location of this directory is configured in the Web server administration interface and can be different for each Web site hosted on your server. For example, the default Web document root for Internet Information Server is `c:\inetpub\wwwroot\`.

Global variables and application-wide functionality can be implemented within an application by the use of two special code templates: `Application.cfm` and `OnRequestEnd.cfm`. For example, a variable assignment for the application datasource or debugging directives.

→ Client state management is covered in detail in Chapter 10, "`APPLICATION` and `SERVER` Variables," and Chapter 11, "Session State Management." Error handling is covered in Chapter 21, "Error Handling."

Application.cfm

When any ColdFusion application page is called, the application server checks the page's local directory for an `Application.cfm` file. If one doesn't exist, the server looks in the parent directory, and then the parent's parent, and so on up the directory tree until it either finds an `Application.cfm` file or reaches the root directory of the hard drive.

> **CAUTION**
>
> Many developers incorrectly assume that the ColdFusion application server searches only to the document root of the Web server for an `Application.cfm` file. In fact, the server searches all the way up the directory tree to the root directory of the hard drive.

After an `Application.cfm` file is found, it is automatically included at the top of the code template and executed first. If more than one `Application.cfm` file exists in the directory tree, ColdFusion uses only the first one it finds. If there is no `Application.cfm` file, the template page executes as per normal.

The `Application.cfm` file behaves in the same way as a standard `<CFINCLUDE>` in that the code is run as if it were cut and pasted into the top of the executing template. Local variables defined in the `Application.cfm` file are unprotected and are available to the rest of the code template. An `Application.cfm` file placed in the application root is implicitly included at the top of every page in the application. Therefore, it is an ideal place to assign global variables such as file paths and datasource names, and to implement application-wide functionality such as security authentication.

→ Included files are covered in detail in Chapter 5, "Redirects and Reuse."

It is worth noting that it is impossible to prevent the `Application.cfm` file from being included. If the file exists in the directory tree of the application, the `Application.cfm` code will be executed.

Typical application uses of the `Application.cfm` file include:

- The application name and other state management variables through `<CFAPPLICATION>`
- Default variables and global constants such as datasource names, and absolute file paths for image and file libraries

- Custom error handling for general exceptions using <CFERROR>
- Default style settings such as fonts or colors using the local or request scope (perhaps saved into structures for simplified organization and management)
- Application-wide security code (such as requiring logins and redirecting to a login page if needed)

The following example shows an Application.cfm file for the CoffeeValley application:

```
<!--- Set application name and enable session variables --->
<CFAPPLICATION NAME="CoffeeValley"
    SESSIONMANAGEMENT="Yes"
    SETCLIENTCOOKIES="Yes">
<!--- Check to see if the user has logged in --->
<CFIF NOT IsDefined("SESSION.loggedin")>
     <CFLOCATION URL="../login/login.cfm">
</CFIF>
<!--- Install custom error pages --->
<CFERROR TYPE="REQUEST"
    TEMPLATE="error.cfm"
    MAILTO="webmaster@coffeevalley.com">
<!--- Set global variables --->
<CFSET FileLibrary="d:\secure\files\">
<CFSET DataSource="CoffeeValley">
```

In this example, the application is defined using the <CFAPPLICATION> tag, which is also used to enable session-state management. After this is done, access control and security are implemented using SESSION variables (if one does not exist, the user has not logged in). The rest of the code block defines a custom error page and two variables for use within the application.

> **CAUTION**
>
> Presentation code such as HTML, JavaScript, and other client-side technologies should not be placed in the Application.cfm. Application.cfm is designed specifically as a globally included template for application-wide logic, and is not appropriate for any aspect of your application's presentation layer.

Local or request-scope variables that are set in the Application.cfm are available in all pages that include the file. Such variables do not need to be locked. However, Application.cfm is often used for the setting of SERVER, APPLICATION, and SESSION variables and careful consideration must be given to the appropriate locking of these shared variable types.

→ Client state management is covered in detail in Chapter 10, "Application and Server Variables," and Chapter 11, "Session State Management." The importance of locking in ColdFusion is discussed in Chapter 12, "Locking."

> **NOTE**
> As a security measure, neither `Application.cfm` nor `OnRequestEnd.cfm` can be called directly from a URL on the Web browser. They can be executed only in the context of another page in the application.

OnRequestEnd.cfm

In the same way that `Application.cfm` is executed at the beginning of every page in the application, you can create a file called `OnRequestEnd.cfm` that is executed at the end of every page. However, unlike `Application.cfm`, `OnRequestEnd.cfm` must be located in the same directory as the calling page's `Application.cfm`. It will not be executed if it is placed in another directory. If you choose to use `OnRequestEnd.cfm` files in your application, they are in effect linked to the `Application.cfm` file residing in the same directory.

`OnRequestEnd.cfm` can be useful in a multitude of ways for more advanced ColdFusion implementations. For example, to control debugging directives or to manage the logging of code that responds to specific page settings.

```
<!--- OnRequestEnd.cfm example --->
<!--- suppress debugging output --->
<CFSETTING showdebugoutput="No">

<!--- activate logging module --->
<CFIF REQUEST.logpage>
   <CF_LOG_MODULE>
</CFIF>
```

> **CAUTION**
> On UNIX operating systems (such as Solaris, Linux, and HP-UX), filenames are case sensitive. Therefore, `Application.cfm` and `OnRequestEnd.cfm` must be named with exactly the right casing; capital `A` for `Application.cfm` and capital `O`, `R`, and `E` for `OnRequestEnd.cfm`. Although Windows NT and Windows 2000 have case insensitive file systems, it is good practice for portability of the code to stick to the correct casing when you create these files.

Multiple Application.cfm Files

Although you can use a single `Application.cfm` file to govern an entire application, it is often useful to break up an application into individual sections or modules. In these instances, you might need to define a different `Application.cfm` for each section of code in order to provide different global variables and functions. Figure 6.1 illustrates this concept.

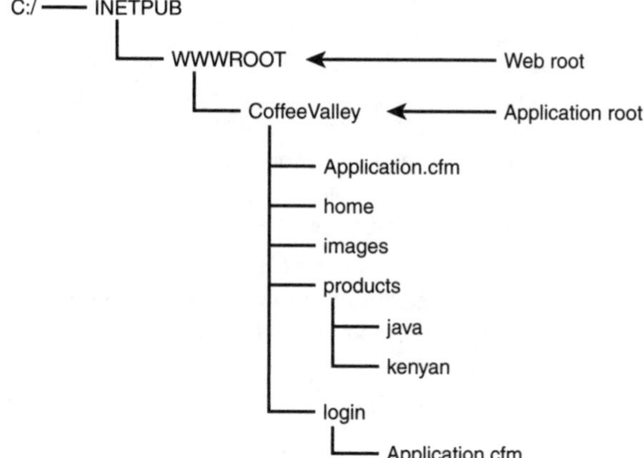

Figure 6.1

More than one `Application.cfm` *file may be used in an application, in which case the one used will be the first one found while moving up the directory tree.*

If you place an `Application.cfm` file in the application root of your web application this file will be automatically included in all the files throughout the branches of the sub directory tree. However, by placing an `Application.cfm` file in a subdirectory below the application root it is possible to define different parameters and functionality for all the pages in that specific branch of the directory structure. Remember that ColdFusion will only execute one `Application.cfm` file per page and will look in the current directory first.

For example, in the `Application.cfm` code listing shown earlier in this chapter, the following block of authentication code checks whether the user has logged in to the application:

```
<CFIF NOT IsDefined("SESSION.loggedin")>
     <CFLOCATION URL="../login/login.cfm">
</CFIF>
```

`SESSION.loggedin` is set after a successful login. Any user who does not have the session variable `SESSION.loggedin` in his session scope will be rejected and relocated to the login page. Unfortunately, the login page must include an `Application.cfm` itself and the same authentication code sends the application into an infinite loop preventing the user from ever logging in.

This problem can be easily resolved if you place another `Application.cfm` file in the login subdirectory with exactly the same code as the original `Application.cfm` in the application root minus the authentication routine. Now when the user is relocated to the `login.cfm` page, the `../login/Application.cfm` page is included instead and the rest of the `login.cfm` page is executed. In fact, any application page in the login directory is effectively isolated from the security that has been applied to the rest of the application.

TIP

Sometimes you might want to define additional Application.cfm files that simply include all the code from the Application.cfm file placed in the application root plus a few additional variables and/or functions specific to that section or branch of the application. If you need to make a change to the common code between these files, you have to make changes to all the Application.cfm files, which makes maintenance of code more cumbersome.

If the common code is identical, you can <CFINCLUDE> the application root Application.cfm at the top of the section or branch Application.cfm, effectively tricking ColdFusion into executing both Application.cfm files.

```
<!--- Include the application root Application.cfm --->
<CFINCLUDE template="../Application.cfm">

<!--- set section specific variables --->
<CFSET sectionvar1="something interesting">
<CFSET sectionvar2="something fascinating">
```

A ColdFusion application using state management is given a unique name on the server. This is defined using the NAME attribute of the <CFAPPLICATION> tag. Any code that needs to share APPLICATION and SESSION variable scopes must also share the same application name.

<CFAPPLICATION> is always defined in the Application.cfm file as it must be specified for every code template in a particular application on the server. Because you can run multiple applications on a single ColdFusion server, each independent application requires a unique NAME attribute to make it distinct from the others. However, if you are referring to multiple Application.cfm files within the same application, each <CFAPPLICATION> tag must refer to the same unique application name.

→ Client state management is covered in detail in Chapter 10, "APPLICATION and SERVER Variables," and Chapter 11, "Session State Management."

Summary

The Application.cfm file and, to a lesser extent, the OnRequestEnd.cfm file are integral parts of the ColdFusion development environment application framework. As such, they play a role in many different aspects of ColdFusion development. Certain features and services of ColdFusion require that supporting code be placed into these files so that it is globally accessible. It is important to understand the ramifications of placing code in either the Application.cfm or OnRequestEnd.cfm file because that code may effectively run every time a page executes within your application.

Sample Questions

1. ColdFusion will search the directory tree only as far as the Web document root for an Application.cfm file.
   A. True
   B. False

2. OnRequestEnd.cfm must have the active Application.cfm in the same directory in order to function.
   A. True
   B. False

3. Application.cfm should not be used for which of the following tasks?
   A. Defining the application using <CFAPPLICATION>
   B. Assigning default variables and global constants
   C. Including a generic HTML header file to maintain a standard look and feel across the application
   D. Implementing error handling using <CFERROR>

4. An Application.cfm file cannot be included in a page using <CFINCLUDE>.
   A. True
   B. False

CHAPTER 7

Using Databases

How to Connect to Databases

To access a database, you need a datasource. A datasource is a logical name for the database you need to work with. The database may be located on the same server as ColdFusion or on another server elsewhere in the network.

The connection behind the datasource acts as a gateway or translator to the database servicing the application. All databases have their own particular format and mechanisms for storing and retrieving data. So, to make application development easier, we set up an interface to the application that is standard and on the other side, we allow the interface to the database to be unique. These gateways are commonly known as *drivers*. Database connectivity in ColdFusion is possible through ODBC (Open Database Connectivity), OLE DB, or Native Driver support.

ODBC is perhaps the most common type of connectivity used in ColdFusion applications. ODBC is a very popular standard for database connectivity and most modern databases provide an ODBC driver for access to their system. It allows programs to use SQL requests that will access databases without having to know the proprietary interfaces to the databases. ODBC handles the SQL request and converts it into a request that the individual database system understands.

NOTE

SQL (Structured Query Language, often pronounced "sequel") is a standard programming language for interacting with a database. Interactions include retrieving, adding, updating, and deleting information. SQL can also be used for restructuring or modifying the schema and indexing properties of a database.

Although SQL is an ANSI standard, many database products support SQL with proprietary extensions to the standard language, known as a dialect. Examples include Oracle's PL-SQL and MS SQL Server's Transact-SQL.

ODBC is designed to provide access primarily to SQL data in a multiplatform environment. OLE DB, on the other hand, is designed to provide access to all types of data in an OLE Component Object Model (COM) environment. OLE DB includes the SQL functionality defined in ODBC but also defines interfaces suitable for gaining access to data other than SQL data. OLE DB connectivity on Windows is generally considered to be more reliable than ODBC.

➔ For more information on OLE DB check the Microsoft Web site, `http://www.microsoft.com/data/oledb/`.

The Allaire Knowledge Base contains some detailed references to installing and configuring OLE DB connections:

- Article 14632, "Configuring OLE DB Data Sources in ColdFusion"
- Article 564, "Using Microsoft Access Databases in a Production Environment"

NOTE

OLE DB connections from ColdFusion are available in the Professional and Enterprise Editions of ColdFusion, but not in the Express Edition.

Native drivers are specific to a particular database. These are often supported directly by the database vendor and can provide increased performance, stability, and functionality. The particular features of a native driver will be described by the vendor.

➔ For Windows-based datasource connectivity, make sure that you have the very latest data access components (MDAC) installed on your server:

`http://www.microsoft.com/downloads/release.asp?ReleaseID=10730`

These do change slightly from version to version. Make sure that any previously written applications will work on a development or staging environment before upgrading these services on your production server.

Adding a Datasource

Datasources can be added to your system in a variety of ways. The type of datasource you require often dictates the various methods available to set things up. You can add ODBC and OLE DB datasources through the ColdFusion Administrator or, alternatively, through the ODBC applet in the Control Panel on Windows platforms. Native drivers often require the installation of database-specific client utilities on the ColdFusion server. The native driver effectively provides communication between ColdFusion and these so called database client libraries.

In any event, the ColdFusion Administrator can be used to view and modify details of the datasource connections registered for your server. The type of datasource will determine what options are available and to what extent they can be modified through the ColdFusion Administrator interface.

A logical name is assigned to a datasource so that you can refer to it within tags such as <CFQUERY>. During a query, the datasource informs ColdFusion which database to connect to and what default attributes to use for the connection.

ColdFusion datasources should abide by the following naming conventions:

- As with other ColdFusion variables, datasource names should always begin with a letter.
- Datasource names can contain any combination of letters, numbers, and underscores.
- Datasource names should not contain any special characters (including spaces and periods).

Obviously, a datasource must be visible in the ColdFusion Administrator before attempting to reference it within an application page.

The datasource configuration options make reference to the location of the underlying database. In addition, they provide the Administrator with the capability to set a series of default values for connection parameters. Several of these parameters are specific to the driver in question and can be used to tweak performance and reliability of the database connection.

Username and password details define a default authentication for the ColdFusion server in the absence of any other instructions. It is worth noting that a default password can be defined at the level of the driver, which is superceded by anything placed in the ColdFusion Login fields of the Administrator. The Administrator is, in turn, overridden by the use of a USERNAME or PASSWORD attribute in the <CFQUERY> tag itself.

CAUTION

Do not specify the database admin password as the authentication used for the datasource. If a malicious developer were able to modify code on the ColdFusion server, he would have total control of the database.

The best practice is to set up a user account for ColdFusion on the database with specific permissions for your application. These permissions should enable your code to perform only the required database operations on the application database and nothing more.

SQL operations can be restricted through the datasource. This enables administrators to grant access to the database but to restrict the types of SQL statements that can be passed. For example, you could enable SELECT statements for retrieving information but not allow any updates or deletions. Security-conscious DBAs might prefer to implement these types of restrictions at the database level instead.

By default, the standard ODBC/OLE DB connection allows only 64KB worth of SQL statement through the driver. This seems like a lot, but if you consider building a content management system you might easily exceed that limit with Web page content.

Through the ColdFusion Administrator, you can enable the long text retrieval settings, and increase the size of the long text buffer size to something just bigger than the largest data packet you expect your system to handle. Unfortunately, long text retrieval has a significant performance hit on the database connection that isn't desirable on a high-traffic site.

TIP

To overcome the performance hit for long text retrieval settings, you can set up multiple datasources.

Typically, long text retrieval settings are only required to perform administrative tasks in the system. Consider setting up two datasources pointing to the same database but with different connection settings; one running with long text and the other without. The administration section of the application uses the long text option while the high volume, user-facing section takes advantage of the datasource that is optimized for better data access speed.

Connecting to the Database

<CFQUERY> is used to prepare and submit a SQL statement to a datasource. <CFQUERY> and its attributes can also be used to override the default settings on the datasource connection to the database. Any SQL statement that can be interpreted by the database and its driver can be sent, including SELECT, UPDATE, and INSERT statements.

```
<CFQUERY NAME="qHorses"
         DATASOURCE="Equitation"
         DBTYPE="ODBC"
         USERNAME="#request.username#"
         PASSWORD="#request.password#">
SELECT HorseID, StableName, ShowName, Breeding, Height, Colour
FROM Dressage
</CFQUERY>
```

The SQL language is used to communicate with the database through the datasource. ColdFusion does not perform SQL validation, so you are able to use any syntax that is supported by your datasource. Check your database documentation for details on the usage of non-standard SQL.

→ Interactions with the database are covered in detail throughout Part VII, "Databases." Chapter 32, "Basic SQL," offers an introduction to SQL.

→ The <CFQUERY> attributes BLOCKFACTOR, CACHEDWITHIN, and CACHEDAFTER are used to improve query performance and implement dynamic caching. These attributes are covered in detail in Chapter 36, "Improving Performance."

When <CFQUERY> performs a SELECT operation on the database, a record set is returned (assuming that records have been found). This recordset is converted into a ColdFusion query object. The query object is neither an array nor a structure but a special variable in its own right. Although it does exhibit array-like properties, the query object has its own set of ColdFusion functions such as `QueryAddColumn()` and `QueryAddRow()`.

➔ Arrays are discussed in Chapter 14, "Arrays," and structures are covered in Chapter 15, "Structures."

A query object is referenced by the `NAME` specified in the `<CFQUERY>` tag. It stores the complete record set returned by the SQL statement and several additional variables that might be of use as shown in Table 7.1.

Table 7.1 <CFQUERY> Variables

Variable Names	Description
`RecordCount`	The total number of records in the query. If no records were returned, this is `0`.
`ColumnList`	A comma-delimited list of all the column names in the query, returned in no particular order.
`CurrentRow`	The current row of the query. This is relevant when the result set is being processed by a tag like `<CFOUTPUT>` that loops over the rows in the recordset.
`ExecutionTime`	The time taken to execute the query on the database and return the results to ColdFusion in milliseconds.

NOTE

To reference a specific record in the recordset of a query object, you can use the row number in the same way as an array position. For example, to reference the `ShowName` column of the tenth record of the query `qHorses` with array syntax, try this:

```
#qHorses.ShowName[10]#
```

Dynamic queries can be generated within `<CFQUERY>` by the use of variables and conditional logic. `<CFQUERY>` will process any ColdFusion code or variables first before submitting the resulting SQL to the database.

```
<CFQUERY NAME="qHorses"
        DATASOURCE="Equitation">
SELECT HorseID, StableName, ShowName, Breeding, Height, Colour
FROM Dressage
<CFIF FORM.Breeding IS NOT "">
WHERE Breeding = '#FORM.Breeding#'
</CFIF>
</CFQUERY>
```

➔ Conditional processing is covered in Chapter 3, "Conditional Processing."

Simplified Database Connectivity

<CFINSERT> and <CFUPDATE> are tags that simplify the process of database inserts and updates, respectively. They effectively build a dynamic SQL statement based on the form variable structure and submit this like a standard <CFQUERY> with the appropriate SQL statement. Consequently, they are easier to use than <CFQUERY> and SQL, but they are less flexible and have certain limitations. Only DATASOURCE and TABLENAME are required attributes.

```
<!--- inserting a record --->
<CFINSERT DATASOURCE="Equitation"
          TABLENAME="Horses"
          DBTYPE="ODBC"
          FORMFIELDS="StableName, ShowName, Breeding, Height, Colour">

<!--- updating a record --->
<CFUPDATE DATASOURCE="Equitation"
          TABLENAME="Horses"
          DBTYPE="ODBC"
          FORMFIELDS="HorseID, StableName, ShowName, Breeding, Height, Colour">
```

<CFINSERT> and <CFUPDATE> have the following restrictions:

- The tags will only submit form variables.
- The form field names must be the same as the corresponding column names in the database table.
- <CFUPDATE> must include values for all the columns that make up the table primary key.

The FORMFIELDS attribute acts as a mask, allowing only those form fields that are specified to be included in the operation. If FORMFIELDS is not present, all the form fields will be submitted. Other tag attributes are available in order to override default settings in the datasource connection.

Displaying Data

<CFOUTPUT> is used to resolve and display dynamic ColdFusion variables. Coupled with a query object such as the results of a <CFQUERY> and SELECT statement, <CFOUTPUT> can be used to loop over results, once per record in the recordset.

```
<CFQUERY NAME="qHorses" DATASOURCE="Equitation">
SELECT HorseID, StableName, ShowName, Breeding, Height, Colour
FROM Dressage
</CFQUERY>

<TABLE>
<TR BGCOLOR="cccccc">
    <TH>Horse</TH>
    <TH>Breeding</TH>
    <TH>Height</TH>
```

```
</TR>
<CFOUTPUT QUERY="qHorses">
<TR BGCOLOR="#IIF(qHorses.CurrentRow MOD 2, DE("ededed"), DE("ffffff"))#">
    <TD>#qHorses.ShowName#</TD>
    <TD>#qHorses.Breeding#</TD>
    <TD>#qHorses.Height#</TD>
</TR>
</CFOUTPUT>
</TABLE>
```

<CFOUTPUT> loops over the block of code contained within the opening and closing tag once per record in the recordset of the query nominated in the QUERY attribute. The column name in the query is prefixed with the name of the query itself to define the variable. The value of the variable changes with each iteration to reflect the value of the column for the current row in the record set. The dynamic IIf() function uses the qHorses.CurrentRow variable of the query to alternate the background color of the table rows as the qHorses.CurrentRow variable changes with every iteration to reflect the current record number.

→ <CFOUTPUT> is also covered in Chapter 2, "Working with Variables and Expressions."

→ IIf() and DE() are covered in Chapter 17, "Dynamic Functions."

NOTE

Query variables don't always need the query name prefix. If the variable is referenced inside a <CFOUTPUT> with the same query object specified in the QUERY attribute, you do not need the query name as a prefix. The <CFOUTPUT> query variables are the first to be resolved so there is no chance of a variable name conflict. However, it is still recommended best practice to prefix all variables with their appropriate scope.

Referencing a query variable from within a <CFOUTPUT> without a QUERY attribute specified or indeed with a different query name nominated, is still possible.

```
<CFOUTPUT>#qHorses.Breeding#</CFOUTPUT>

<CFOUTPUT QUERY="qHorses">#qEvent.EventName#</CFOUTPUT>
```

The variable resolves the value of the first record in the query only.

Grouping Data with <CFOUTPUT>

<CFOUTPUT> can also be used to group data together by a specific column for reporting purposes by using the GROUP attribute. <CFOUTPUT> does not provide any kind of sort function, so the data in the query object must already be appropriately ordered. After GROUP is specified, the <CFOUTPUT> statement will loop only once per distinct value in the grouped column. A second, nested <CFOUTPUT> statement can be used to loop over every record in a particular group, including the first record in the group.

```
<!--- order results by Breeding --->
<CFQUERY NAME="qHorses" DATASOURCE="Equitation">
SELECT HorseID, StableName, ShowName, Breeding, Height, Colour
FROM Dressage
ORDER BY Breeding
</CFQUERY>
```

The preceding qHorses query might generate a recordset similar to the one that follows. It is important to note that the recordset has been ordered by the Breeding column.

```
Breeding, HorseID, StableName, ShowName, Height, Colour
Thoroughbred, 234, James, Cannasson, 16.3, Chestnut
Thoroughbred, 345, Harry, Daemon, 16.2, Bay
Thoroughbred, 357, Bobby, Pharlap, 17.3, Chestnut
Warmblood, 567, Aaron, LL Daemon, 16.2, Black
Arabian, 456, Symie, Symphony, 15.2, Chestnut
Arabian, 789, Shim, Chamonix, 15.3, Bay
```

This next report uses the Breeding column in the GROUP attribute of <CFOUTPUT> to generate an HTML table:

```
<TABLE>
<CFOUTPUT QUERY="qHorses" GROUP="Breeding">
<TR>
    <TD COLSPAN="3" BGCOLOR="cccccc"># qHorses.Breeding#</TD>
</TR>
<CFOUTPUT>
<TR>
    <TD># qHorses.ShowName#</TD>
    <TD># qHorses.Colour#</TD>
    <TD># qHorses.Height#</TD>
</TR>
</CFOUTPUT>
</CFOUTPUT>
</TABLE>
```

The first <CFOUPUT> tag loops once only for each distinct value in the Breeding column. In this example, the recordset is ordered by breeding and the first three records share the same value. Therefore, although there are three "Thoroughbred" entries, the first <CFOUTPUT> loops only once. The second, nested <CFOUTPUT> statement then loops three times, once for each record that lists "Thoroughbred" as the value for the Breeding column. The resulting HTML output is as follows:

```
<TABLE>
<TR>
    <TD COLSPAN="3" BGCOLOR="cccccc">Thoroughbred</TD>
</TR>
<TR>
    <TD>Cannasson</TD>
```

```
    <TD>Chestnut</TD>
    <TD>16.3</TD>
</TR>
<TR>
    <TD>Daemon</TD>
    <TD>Bay</TD>
    <TD>16.2</TD>
</TR>
<TR>
    <TD>Pharlap</TD>
    <TD>Chestnut</TD>
    <TD>17.3</TD>
</TR>
<TR>
    <TD COLSPAN="3" BGCOLOR="cccccc">Warmblood</TD>
</TR>
<TR>
    <TD>LL Daemon</TD>
    <TD>Black</TD>
    <TD>16.2</TD>
</TR>
.....
```

In the latter example, <CFOUTPUT> with GROUP avoids the need to repeat the breeding column for each record. Without this feature a developer might have to resort to more complicated conditional logic and looping to determine when and when not to display the output. Overall the technique is ideal for reporting when you have results that our grouped by a category heading of some kind.

> **NOTE**
>
> The GROUP attribute of <CFOUTPUT> is quite distinct from the SQL GROUP BY command. SQL GROUP BY is used to provide for a variety of aggregate functions on sets of records in a database query result. By comparison, GROUP in <CFOUTPUT> is only used to modify the output and looping behavior of the ColdFusion query object.

→ GROUP BY and aggregate functions are discussed in Chapter 34, "Aggregates."

Summary

A datasource is needed for ColdFusion to communicate with a database. The datasource is effectively a driver that acts as a translator communicating SQL statements to the database backend. <CFQUERY> is used to prepare the SQL statements and send them through to the datasource with the appropriate connection settings. <CFQUERY> can pass any SQL statement that the datasource can handle.

A recordset passed back to <CFQUERY> is converted into a query object. The query object can be looped over for each individual record and the values of the various columns outputted using <CFOUTPUT>. <CFOUTPUT> has a group function that provides additional output options for recordsets ordered by a particular column.

Sample Questions

1. What variables does a <CFQUERY> query object contain?
   A. `RecordCount`
   B. `ColumnList`
   C. `ExecutionTime`
   D. `MaxRows`

2. <CFOUTPUT> with the `GROUP` attribute requires which SQL clauses in the SQL query?
   A. `WHERE 0=0`
   B. `ORDER BY columnname`
   C. `GROUP BY columnname`
   D. `GROUP BY columnname and ORDER BY columnname`

3. Which of the following SQL operations can be performed using <CFQUERY>?
   A. `SELECT`
   B. `INSERT`
   C. `UPDATE`
   D. Stored procedure

PART 2

VARIABLES AND EXPRESSIONS

CHAPTER 8

URL Variables

What Is a URL Variable?

URL variables are variables that are created by passing data on the end of a hypertext link.

Earlier, you learned how to create local variables by declaring name=value pairs. URL variables are created in much the same way, except with a slightly different syntax and purpose.

→ Local variables were introduced in Chapter 2, "Working with Variables and Expressions."

How Are URL Variables Created?

To create a URL variable, you must first create a hypertext link like so:

```
<A HREF="index.cfm">Click Me</A>
```

You add URL variables to the link by first typing a question mark (?) and then adding the name=value pair as follows:

```
<A HREF="index.cfm?FName=Emily">Click Me</A>
```

Now when the link is clicked, a variable called FName, with a value of Emily, is passed to the index.cfm page.

> **NOTE**
>
> You can make images into hypertext links as easily as you can with text. The same rules for creating URL variables apply to links around images. Just add the name=value pairs to the HTML <A> tag as shown in the preceding example. When the image is clicked, the variables are passed as normal.

Passing Multiple Variables at Once

You can pass multiple variables on the end of one link by separating each name=value pair with an ampersand (`&`). The following code passes three variables to the `index.cfm` page:

```
<A HREF="index.cfm?FName=Emily&MInit=B&LName=Kim">Click Me</A>
```

Everything after the question mark in a URL is called the *query string*.

> **CAUTION**
>
> You can pass a lot of information in a query string; however, a length limitation is associated with URLs for each browser. Typically, older browsers allow approximately 254 characters to be passed in a URL; newer browsers have a higher limit. You should use this variable type with care because URLs can become unsightly if used excessively.

Passing Complicated Strings

Sometimes you need to pass URL-unfriendly characters in your `URL` variables. For instance, spaces are not allowed in a URL. A ColdFusion function called `URLEncodedFormat()` is very useful in such a scenario.

`URLEncodedFormat()` takes one parameter, which can be either a string or variable, as shown in the following code snippet:

```
<!--- using URLEncodedFormat() with a string --->
<CFOUTPUT>
<A HREF="index.cfm?Name=#URLEncodedFormat("Emily Kim")#">Click Me</A>
</CFOUTPUT>
<!--- using URLEncodedFormat() with a variable --->
<CFSET MyName="Emily Kim">
<CFOUTPUT>
<A HREF="index.cfm?Name=#URLEncodedFormat(Variables.MyName)#">Click Me</A>
</CFOUTPUT>
```

> **NOTE**
>
> The `<CFOUTPUT>` tags are necessary in either case because `URLEncodedFormat()` is a ColdFusion function that must be evaluated by the ColdFusion server even if its parameter is a string.
>
> Also note that quotation marks appear around the string but not the variable name in the function parameter. Quotation marks denote a string, whereas the lack of quotation marks in this case tells the ColdFusion server to evaluate the variable.

In either case, the function takes the space and converts it into its ASCII equivalent (in this case, `%20`), which allows the variable's value to be passed successfully. Without this function, the part of the string after the space would be lost.

NOTE

When working with some of the newer browsers, you will often find that the string is passed successfully whether or not you use the function URLEncodedFormat() because the browsers are being forgiving and converting the special characters for you automatically. However, you should not depend on this feature unless you are sure that your Web audience will be using such browsers.

TIP

When you're passing URL variables, using URLEncodedFormat() is usually a good idea even if you don't think doing so is necessary. Later, we will discuss dynamically created URL variables whose values can often be unpredictable.

What Is the Scope of a URL Variable?

Unlike local variables, URL variables are not available for use on the page in which they are first declared. Rather, they are available on the page to which the link points.

Because of this fact, using URL variables is the simplest way of maintaining state on a Web site. *State* refers to the capability of a Web server to remember things from one page to the next. For instance, local variables do not help the programmer maintain state because they are available only locally on the page in which they are created; they are not available on any other page in the Web site. URL variables allow you to pass information from one page to another when the user clicks a link.

URL variables do not provide a total solution to the state problem because they have a limited scope. They are available only on the page to which they have been passed. After that page is processed by the ColdFusion server, the variables expire. However, while they exist, they can be used like local variables.

NOTE

It is always a good idea to scope a URL variable, like any other variable in ColdFusion, when you are using it. You do so by typing URL. in front of the name of the variable. You should not scope the variable when you are declaring it.

TIP

You can also create URL variables by using the <CFPARAM> tag. You usually do so on the page to which the link points in order to create a default value for a URL variable that is expected for the processing of the page. You can create URL variables by using <CFPARAM> in one of the following ways:

```
<!--- without scoping the variable --->
<CFPARAM FName="Emily">
<!--- scoping the variable --->
<CFPARAM URL.FName="Emily">
```

The first method creates a generic variable, but ColdFusion treats it as a URL variable if no local variables of the same name are present on the page.

→ <CFPARAM> was introduced in Chapter 3, "Conditional Processing."

Using URL Variables

So far, we have passed only *static* URL *variables*. The values of static variables remain constant. What is far more useful to you as a ColdFusion developer is to create *dynamic* URL *variables*, which are usually generated from the results of a database query.

> **NOTE**
>
> URL variables can be accessed as structures in ColdFusion 4.5. FORM, APPLICATION, SERVER, SESSION, COOKIE, REQUEST, CGI, and ATTRIBUTES variables are also available as structures. Chapter 15, "Structures," reviews structures in detail.

Dynamic

In this section we will create a page that queries all of the countries from the database. We will then print out each country name and turn it into a link. When the link is clicked, the user will be sent to the target page, which will display all employees in that country.

The following query pulls all the countries out of the database:

```
<CFQUERY NAME="GetCountries" DATASOURCE="Employees">
SELECT *
FROM Countries
</CFQUERY>
```

> **TIP**
>
> When you pull information out of the database for use in your dynamic URL variables, you may encounter an interesting characteristic of some databases. Many databases often pad data with extra whitespace. Often you need to remove it before using the data in your ColdFusion code. The `Trim()` function has been built to do just that. When used on a string like `"   Emily Kim    "`, the `Trim()` function gets rid of the extra whitespace to the left and right of the string, but not the whitespace in the middle. The resulting string would read `"Emily Kim"`. You can use the `Trim()` function with `URLEncodedFormat()` to get rid of the white space and prepare the string for use in a URL variable. The code would look like this:
>
> ```
> <A HREF="index.cfm?Name=#URLEncodedFormat(Trim("   Emily Kim    "))#">Click
> Here</A>
> ```
>
> A more realistic example would not be using a static variable, but a dynamic variable from a query resultset:
>
> ```
> <A HREF="index.cfm?Name=#URLEncodedFormat(Trim(GetEmployees.Name))#">Click Here</A>
> ```

You can then use the results of this query to print all the countries as HTML links:

```
<CFOUTPUT QUERY="GetCountries">
<A HREF="index.cfm?CID=#GetCountries.CountryID#">#GetCountries.CountryName#
➥</A><BR>
</CFOUTPUT>
```

> **TIP**
>
> Long documents often use *URL bookmarks,* which are links presented in a list at the top of a document. When clicked, these bookmarks jump the user down the page to a specific location on the page. Creating these bookmarks involves first naming the points to which you would jump by using the `<A NAME="somename">` syntax. To create the URL bookmark to reference that location, you use the syntax `<A HREF="#somename">`. Note the use of the `#` sign to tell the browser to jump to the spot on the page with the specified name. If you were dynamically generating this list of URL bookmarks, the `#` sign would be located inside the `<CFOUTPUT>` tags and would cause the ColdFusion server to throw an error message essentially stating that it doesn't understand the use of the `#` sign. To correct this syntax, you would have to *escape* the `#` sign, thereby rendering it usable by the ColdFusion server. To escape a pound sign, you double it. The correct code would read `<A HREF="##somename">`.

As each country name is printed, its associated country ID is coded as a `URL` variable called `CID`. When the user clicks any of the links, the country ID associated with the country name on which he clicked is passed to the target page. That target page can now use the country ID to query the database for more specific information.

The following query uses the country ID, passed in the variable `URL.CID`, to query the database for all the employees in that country:

```
<CFQUERY NAME="GetEmployees" DATASOURCE="Employees">
SELECT *
FROM Employees
WHERE CountryID = #URL.CID#
</CFQUERY>
```

Passing the primary key field of a database table is very useful for affecting the results of the target page.

> **CAUTION**
>
> Passing primary key values as `URL` variables could possibly open your database to a security hole. ODBC 2.0 introduced the capability to append multiple SQL statements to one request by using a semicolon to separate the statements. Review the following code:
>
> ```
> <CFQUERY NAME="GetCountries" DATASOURCE="Employees">
> SELECT *
> FROM Countries
> WHERE CountryID = #URL.CID#
> </CFQUERY>
> ```
>
> Now, imagine that some unsavory character decided to modify your URL to read as follows:
>
> ```
> http://www.somedomain.com/index.cfm?CountryID=3;drop%20table%20countries
> ```

Keeping in mind what you learned from the discussion of `URLEncodedFormat()`, remember that `%20` is the ASCII equivalent for a space. This means that the SQL statement would end up as follows:

```
<CFQUERY NAME="GetCountries" DATASOURCE="Employees">
SELECT *
FROM Countries
WHERE CountryID = 3;drop table countries
</CFQUERY>
```

This statement might cause your database to immediately delete the `Countries` table!

You could avoid this potential headache by running a check of your `URL` variable before you run your query to ensure that it is a number, not a string.

Two functions could help you in this scenario. The `Val()` function tries to convert the value to a number. If the value is already a number, the function just returns that number to you. If the value is a not a valid number, the function returns `0`. The `IsNumeric()` function returns either a Boolean yes or no value if the variable in question is a number or not, respectively.

Chapter 35 discusses using bind paramenters and the `<CFQUERYPARAM>` tag. This tag will also help you avoid the potential security issue mentioned above.

Summary

Using `URL` variables is the easiest method for maintaining state in a Web environment. However, their scope is limited because they can pass variables only from one page to a specific target page. Nevertheless, they give you some level of interactivity with the Web visitor by allowing you to present the visitor with a list of dynamically generated hypertext links that are coded to pass information on to the target page. The variables being passed can then direct the target page to display information about the item selected by the visitor.

Sample Questions

1. Which function should you use to ensure that extra whitespace is removed around a string?
   A. `Val()`
   B. `Trim()`
   C. `URLEncodedFormat()`
   D. `StripSpaces()`

2. Which statement is true?
   A. The scope of a `URL` variable is the target page.
   B. You can pass only one `URL` variable on the end of a link.
   C. Everything after the question mark (`?`) in a link is referred to as the *variable list.*
   D. Like local variables, `URL` variables are usually created by using the `<CFSET>` tag.

3. Which of the following is a valid method of creating URL variables?

   A. <A HREF="index.cfm?#URLEncodedFormat("Emily Kim")#">

   B. <CFSET URLVar.FName="Emily">

   C. <CFPARAM name="URL.FName" default="Emily">

   D. <A NAME="index.cfm?#URLEncodedFormat("Emily Kim")#">

CHAPTER 9

FORM Variables

What Is a FORM Variable?

URL variables allow you to interact with Web visitors in a limited fashion. However, the most common and useful method for providing visitors with an interactive experience is through HTML forms. Examples of the usefulness of forms include collecting user information, allowing users to enter criteria to search a database, giving users the option to respond to polls, presenting visitors with options for printing reports, and allowing users to select personalization requirements.

It's important to remember that two pages are involved in using FORM variables: FORM and ACTION. The *FORM page* has the HTML form elements on it. After a user enters or chooses her information in the form and submits it, all this information is passed on to the *ACTION page,* which then performs some actions based on that information.

> **NOTE**
>
> In concept, working with FORM variables is the same as working with URL variables. Both have a display page and processing page. In a URL scenario, the display page lists all the hypertext links. In a form scenario, the display page is the HTML form. The action page in both scenarios merely takes the variables that are passed to it and uses them to perform some action.

➔ URL variables were introduced in Chapter 8, "URL Variables."

How Are FORM Variables Created?

Unlike local and URL variables, FORM variables are not created by explicitly declaring name=value pairs. To create a FORM variable, you must first create an HTML form, name all the controls in that HTML form, and then submit it. The data entered or selected on a form by the Web visitor are the values for the FORM variables.

→ Local variables were introduced in Chapter 2, "Working with Variables and Expressions."

> **NOTE**
>
> This tutorial is written to help you brush up on your ColdFusion knowledge and to fill in some of the gaps. In other words, we are assuming that you are a seasoned developer and have a good working knowledge of ColdFusion and Web development. Therefore, we will assume you know how to create HTML form controls and will not discuss them in detail.

The following sample code creates a short form:

```
<FORM ACTION="actionpage.cfm" METHOD="post">
First Name: <INPUT TYPE="text" NAME="FName"><BR>
Favorite Color: <INPUT TYPE="checkbox" NAME="FavColor" VALUE="R">Red
           <INPUT TYPE="checkbox" NAME="FavColor" VALUE="G">Green
           <INPUT TYPE="checkbox" NAME="FavColor" VALUE="B">Blue<BR>
<INPUT TYPE="submit">
</FORM>
```

> **NOTE**
>
> You can have multiple forms on the FORM page, but only one can ever be submitted. As soon as you click a submit button, the FORM variables are passed on to the action page referenced in this form's ACTION attribute.
>
> You can also have more than one submit button per form. If you click either of the submit buttons, the FORM variables are passed on to the action page. The trick here is to give each submit button a unique name. Only the name of the submit button you clicked is ever passed. You can check for it in your conditional statements.

→ Conditional processing was introduced in Chapter 3, "Conditional Processing."

Be sure to note these important points about the code:

- The ACTION attribute of the FORM tag specifies to which page the information from the form will be submitted.
- The text box is named FName.
- The check boxes are all named FavColor.
- No ColdFusion functions or tags appear in this code.

> **CAUTION**
>
> When you're working with HTML forms and ColdFusion, it's a good idea to always make sure that the `METHOD` attribute is set to `POST`, not `GET`. By HTML rules, if `METHOD` is not declared, its value defaults to `GET`. You will find that (you can verify this by looking in your server debugging information) if you have `METHOD="GET"`, your `FORM` variables are actually sent as URL variables instead. Additionally, if you misspell the words `METHOD` or `POST`, you will find that the form submission will automatically default to `GET`.

➔ Debugging is discussed in Chapter 20, "Debugging."

In this section we describe how to create `FORM` variables, but while you've created HTML form elements, you have not yet actually created any FORM variables. `FORM` variables don't exist until they get to the action page. Really, you're just naming the variables when you create the form element. A user enters the values when she types into the form fields. It's not until she submits the form that the values she entered are matched up with the name of the field, and then the name=value pairs are actually created as `FORM` variables and passed on to the action page.

So, in the preceding example, if the user entered the name `Emily` into the text box, selected the `Blue` check box, and clicked the submit button, the `FORM` variable name=value pairs passed on to the ACTION page would be `FName=Emily`, `FavColor=B`.

> **NOTE**
>
> Because the submit button was not named, it is not passed as a `FORM` variable.

> **NOTE**
>
> What you name a form control is very important. When many form controls on a page have the same name (as in the case of check boxes or radio buttons), the browser collects all the values the user selected and passes them on to the action page in the form of a list. Consider the following code:
>
> ```
> <INPUT TYPE="checkbox" NAME="FavColor" VALUE="R">Red
> <INPUT TYPE="checkbox" NAME="FavColor" VALUE="G">Green
> <INPUT TYPE="checkbox" NAME="FavColor" VALUE="B">Blue
> ```
>
> If the user checked the check box for Red and Blue, the ACTION page would receive the name=value pair `FavColor=R,B`.
>
> You can use what you know about ColdFusion lists to work with this data.

➔ You'll learn about lists in Chapter 13, "Lists."

> **TIP**
>
> When you create a form, you are usually creating it to gather information that will be inserted into a database. Therefore, it is a recommended practice to name your form fields with the same name as the corresponding database column.

As we just discussed, the name=value pair for each form element is passed to the action page. However, if you just want a list of all the names of all the form elements passed to the action page, you can access the list using the variable `FORM.FIELDNAMES`. The ColdFusion application server automatically generates this variable for you when the form is submitted. It is a very useful variable for dynamically determining the name of all the form elements. Again, you can use what you know about lists to manipulate this information.

> **TIP**
>
> In chapter 22, "Custom Tags," you are introduced to a custom tag called `<CF_EmbedFields>` which makes good use of `FORM.FIELDNAMES`.

Building Database-Driven Form Elements

Earlier you saw that the FORM page didn't have any ColdFusion functions or tags in it. That's not because it can't. In this section, you'll see how to use ColdFusion to dynamically generate a `SELECT` (drop-down list) form control from a database query to display a list of colors.

The first step in this process is to perform the query on the FORM page to grab the color information that you want displayed in the drop-down list:

```
<CFQUERY NAME="GetColors" DATASOURCE="MyDSN">
SELECT ColorID, ColorName
FROM Colors
ORDER BY ColorName
</CFQUERY>
```

After you have the query, you just need to loop over the query result to print the variables in place of the hard-coded elements:

```
<SELECT NAME="ColorID">
<CFOUTPUT QUERY="GetColors">
<OPTION VALUE="#GetColors.ColorID#">#GetColors.ColorName#</OPTION>
</CFOUTPUT>
</SELECT>
```

> **TIP**
>
> If you find that the dynamically generated form elements are not being created properly, you can always run the page in your browser and view the source. That way, you can see the generated HTML code. Looking at it should help you figure out what is wrong.

Server-Side Validation

After you create a form, you should validate the information the user submits to ensure that it fits within expected parameters. For instance, the following code prompts the user to enter her first name. The user must enter her name, or she should not be allowed to proceed.

```
<FORM ACTION="actionpage.cfm" METHOD="post">
First Name: <INPUT TYPE="text" NAME="FName"><BR>
<INPUT TYPE="submit">
</FORM>
```

To ensure that the user properly fills out the form, you can add the following line of code anywhere inside the form:

```
<INPUT TYPE="hidden" NAME="FName_Required" VALUE="You must enter your name to
➥proceed.">
```

You add `TYPE="hidden"` because you don't want to display the validation as a form control on the page. It should work without the Web visitor seeing it.

`NAME="FName_Required"` uses a server-side validation suffix. Note that the name in front of the underscore is exactly the same as the name of the field you are trying to validate. You merely add the proper suffix behind the name to force ColdFusion to validate the field. All the suffixes are listed in Table 9.1.

> **CAUTION**
>
> Make sure that you don't name your regular form fields with any of the reserved suffixes if you don't mean for ColdFusion to perform validation on them.

Table 9.1 Server-Side Validation Suffixes

Suffix	Description
`_date`	Makes sure the field contains a date in the most common format; for instance, 11/27/00 or November 27, 2000
`_eurodate`	Validates dates as above, but in European format; for instance, 27/11/00 or 27 November 2000
`_float`	Checks whether the value of the field is a number (decimal points allowed)
`_integer`	Checks whether the value of the field is a number (no decimal points allowed)
`_range`	Ensures that the value is within a minimum and maximum
`_required`	Makes sure that a field is not left empty
`_time`	Validates time in the most common time formats

`VALUE="You must..."` is used for your validation error message. ColdFusion displays this message to your user when her input is invalid.

> **TIP**
>
> You can customize the look and feel of the server-side validation results by using `<CFERROR>`, which is introduced in Chapter 21, "Error Handling."

Client-Side Validation

In server-side validation, when the user clicks the submit button, the FORM variables are actually sent to the server for processing. If the values are okay, ColdFusion just continues processing. If, however, the values are not okay, ColdFusion returns a validation error message to the user. Although this process ensures that only good data will pass validation, it requires an extra trip to the server.

With client-side validation, ColdFusion generates JavaScript code in your FORM page to perform the validation in the browser. When the user clicks the submit button, the validation is performed immediately without having to make a trip all the way to the server.

You implement client-side validation by changing <FORM> tags to <CFFORM> tags and <INPUT> tags to <CFINPUT> tags like this:

```
<CFFORM ACTION="actionpage.cfm" METHOD="post">
First Name: <CFINPUT TYPE="Text" NAME="FName" MESSAGE="You must
➥enter your name to proceed." REQUIRED="Yes"><BR>
<INPUT TYPE="submit">
</CFFORM>
```

> **NOTE**
>
> When you implement client-side validation, you can still use the standard attributes for the <INPUT> tag with the <CFINPUT> tag. If you look at the HTML source that is produced for the browser, you will see that the ColdFusion server returns the <CFINPUT> and <CFFORM> tags back into their HTML equivalents.

As the ColdFusion server processes the preceding code, it sees the <CFFORM> tag and immediately begins to generate a JavaScript validation script on the page. When it processes the <CFINPUT> tag, it adds JavaScript code to specifically perform the validation for that field. When this script is called, the user sees a pop-up dialog box showing the error message you defined with `MESSAGE="You must..."`.

`REQUIRED="Yes"` ensures that the form is not processed without adding data to the field.

You can also add another attribute called `VALIDATE`. You can set it to the following values:

- DATE
- EURODATE
- TIME
- FLOAT
- INTEGER
- TELEPHONE
- ZIPCODE
- CREDITCARD
- SOCIAL_SECURITY_NUMBER

Most of these values were introduced earlier. However, note that the telephone, ZIP code, credit card, and Social Security number options are called *masks*. A mask ensures that the data entered into the field fits into the standard format for each category.

> **TIP**
>
> Client-side validation is browser-specific so it should not be used if your target audience does not have JavaScript-enabled browsers or if the users are prone to turning off JavaScript. Such users will be able to submit your form without any problems since they will never be prompted with the JavaScript alert message.
>
> Server-side validation ensures that your data is fully validated but requires a full round trip to the server to display error messages to the user.
>
> SOLUTION: You can use server-side and client-side scripting together. The client-side scripting helps you avoid having to make a round trip to the server, and if JavaScript is not available or is disabled in the browser, the server-side scripting serves as backup.

> **NOTE**
>
> If server-side or client-side validation do not meet your validation needs, you can always use what you have learned about conditional processing to perform your own custom validation on the ACTION page.

> **NOTE**
>
> You can also implement client-side validation for <SELECT> drop-down lists. You use the <CFSELECT> tag to accomplish this, similar to the use of the <CFINPUT> tag. The following example prints out all the colors from the query GetColors but also makes sure that a value is passed:
>
> ```
> <CFSELECT NAME="Color_ID" MESSAGE="Select a color."SIZE="1"
> ➥QUERY="GetColors" VALUE="Color_ID" DISPLAY="Color" REQUIRED="Yes">
> <OPTION value="">Select All</OPTION>
> </CFSELECT>
> ```
>
> Each color is displayed in the drop-down list with the Color_ID listed as the <OPTION> tag's VALUE attribute and the Color itself listed in the display.
>
> The additional <OPTION> tag between the <CFSELECT> tags displays a default message in the drop-down list.

What Is the Scope of a FORM Variable?

As stated earlier in this chapter, FORM variables are very similar to URL variables. That means they can be used as a short-lived method of maintaining state on a Web site.

The scope of FORM variables is the ACTION page, and, also like URL variables, they expire after the page is processed.

TIP

You can pass URL variables at the same time you pass FORM variables. Just add them to the end of the ACTION attribute of your FORM tag.

NOTE

Now that you've reviewed both FORM and URL variables, you should keep in mind that, between the two types of variables, you could implement your own poor man's state maintenance. Between the two methods, you could pass necessary variables page to page throughout your site if you needed to. This method is used for SESSION variables when cookies are turned off.

→ You'll review SESSION and COOKIE variables in Chapter 11, "Session State Management."

The Action Page

After the form data is entered and validated, it is pushed to the ACTION page for processing. You can use FORM variables on the ACTION page in much the same way that you would use URL or even local variables. Consider this example:

```
<CFQUERY NAME="GetEmployees" DATASOURCE="MyDSN">
SELECT *
FROM Employees
WHERE EmployeeID = #FORM.EmployeeID#
</CFQUERY>
```

FORM variable name=value pairs for text boxes, text areas, and drop-down lists always exist on the ACTION page even if the user didn't enter any information. For instance, if a text box named FName was left empty upon form submission, the ACTION page would get FName=.

This point is important because some form controls—namely, check boxes, radio buttons, multiple select controls, and submit buttons that are not clicked—are not passed at all if they are not selected. So, if a form has a set of check boxes named FavColor and the user doesn't check any of those check boxes, *nothing* is sent to the ACTION page.

It is very important that you do the following on your action page:

- Set default values for form controls that could potentially not exist by using <CFPARAM>

or

- Use the IsDefined() function in your conditional statements to perform validation to ensure that a variable exists before you use it

→ <CFPARAM> was introduced in Chapter 2, "Working with Variables and Expressions."

> **TIP**
>
> We've stated before that it is always a good idea to prefix your ColdFusion variables. However, it's okay *not* to prefix your variables if you want to intentionally leave your code flexible. For instance, review this code:
>
> ```
> <CFQUERY NAME="GetEmployees" DATASOURCE="MyDSN">
> SELECT *
> FROM Employees
> WHERE EmployeeID = #EmployeeID#
> </CFQUERY>
> ```
>
> If this code were in the ACTION page, it could use either a `FORM` variable or `URL` variable in the `WHERE` statement.

Summary

HTML forms are the most powerful tool available to you for interacting with Web visitors. In this chapter, you reviewed the concepts necessary for creating, validating, and using `FORM` variables. Once FORM elements are named, and the user fills in the value and submits the form, you can have the ColdFusion application server perform either server-side or client-side validation on the entries. You also have the option of creating your own custom validation before performing any other processing on the ACTION page.

Sample Questions

1. What two pages are necessary for working with `FORM` variables in ColdFusion?
   A. DISPLAY and PERFORM
   B. HTML and COLDFUSION
   C. FORM and METHOD
   D. FORM and ACTION

2. Which of the following is an example of a form control that does *not* pass a value to the ACTION page by default?
   A. Text box
   B. Text area
   C. Check box
   D. Drop-down select control

3. Consider the following check boxes:
   ```
   <INPUT TYPE="checkbox" NAME="FavCountry" VALUE="US">United States
   <INPUT TYPE="checkbox" NAME="FavCountry" VALUE="CAN">Canada
   <INPUT TYPE="checkbox" NAME="FavCountry" VALUE="ENG">England
   <INPUT TYPE="checkbox" NAME="FavCountry" VALUE="FRA">France
   ```
   If you check France and Canada, what would your `FORM` variable look like?

   A. `FavCountry=CAN,FRA`
   B. `FavCountry=CAN`
   C. `FavCountry=FRA`
   D. `FavContry=CAN&FRA`

CHAPTER 10

APPLICATION and SERVER Variables

Understanding APPLICATION and SERVER Variables

This chapter discusses both APPLICATION and SERVER variables. Both types of variables are very important to maintaining state on a server.

→ State maintenance was discussed in Chapter 8, "URL Variables."

Using these variables, you can "remember" things on a Web site over multiple pages and multiple applications because they are stored in memory on the ColdFusion server.

APPLICATION variables can be set for one application on a server. By doing so, you can create variables that are universal to your one application but that cannot be used by other applications.

SERVER variables are set for the entire server and are available to every application on that server. You can add to the server scope or use variables that are already available in the scope.

→ Some default variables that are available in the server scope are listed in Table 10.1 later in this chapter.

APPLICATION Variable Scope

After you create an APPLICATION variable, it is immediately available to every page in your application. You can store simple variables or complex data types such as structures and arrays in it. Query recordsets can also be stored in APPLICATION variables.

TIP

APPLICATION variables are great places to store queries that are used in many pages of your Web site. For instance, many forms that collect user information have a drop-down list of states. Querying the database every time you want to display this list can be a waste of valuable resources. Instead, write the query directly to the APPLICATION scope, and it will be stored in memory.

➔ You will see an example of the code to put a query recordset into the APPLICATION scope in the next section, "Creating APPLICATION Variables."

By default, APPLICATION variables are stored in the ColdFusion server's memory for two days. You can see and change the default and maximum timeout for these variables by looking in the ColdFusion Administrator. After you log in to the Administrator, look in the `Server` section at the top and find a link called `Variables`. The APPLICATION variables settings are toward the bottom of the screen.

TIP

If you're worried about APPLICATION variables gobbling up all your extra RAM, you can always turn them off using the ColdFusion Administrator. On the `Variables` page of the ColdFusion Administrator, you will see a check box labeled `Enable Application Variables`. If you uncheck it, your developers will be restricted from using these variables.

Creating APPLICATION Variables

If you plan to use APPLICATION variables, each page of your Web site must belong to a specific application. Coding this information on each individual page can be time intensive and a maintenance headache. Therefore, the `Application.cfm` page is the perfect location to put this information. Because every page within the directory runs the `Application.cfm` file first, before it runs itself, you can be sure that the page will be declared a part of the application.

➔ `Application.cfm` was discussed in Chapter 6, "The Application Framework."

Inside the `Application.cfm` file, you should place the following code:

```
<CFAPPLICATION NAME="MyApplicationName">
```

This code simply states the name of the application to which the page belongs.

CAUTION

Be careful when naming your application. If you give the same name to two different applications on the same server, the server will treat them as if they were the same application and will allow one to see the other's APPLICATION variables.

TIP

On the converse of that caution, you can use the naming of your application to your advantage. If the framework of your application requires that you put associated files in widely separated directories, you can still treat the files as part of the same application by naming them accordingly.

We mentioned earlier that the maximum and default timeout values of the APPLICATION variables are set in the ColdFusion Administrator. However, you can also set a value in the <CFAPPLICATION> tag by using the attribute APPLICATIONTIMEOUT like this:

```
<CFAPPLICATION NAME="MyApplicationName"
➥APPLICATIONTIMEOUT="#CreateTimeSpan(3,0,0,1)#">
```

The preceding code sets the APPLICATION variables to expire in three days AND ONE SECOND using the CreateTimeSpan() function. The numbers used in the function represent days, hours, minutes, and seconds, respectively.

NOTE

Using the APPLICATIONTIMEOUT attribute of the <CFAPPLICATION> tag, you can set how long you want your APPLICATION variables to persist. However, using this attribute, you can never exceed the maximum time limit set in the ColdFusion Administrator.

Now that you have enabled the use of APPLICATION variables, you can create them. Creating APPLICATION variables is very similar to creating local variables. The only addition that is required is the proper scope, as shown here:

```
<CFSET APPLICATION.FNAME="Emily">
```

This code creates a variable called FNAME with a value of Emily and places it in the APPLICATION scope. Now it can be used everywhere in your application until it hits its time limit.

CAUTION

Because APPLICATION variables are stored in the ColdFusion server's memory, misusing them can cause serious stability problems on your server. You can avoid these problems by using the <CFLOCK> tag.

➔ You can learn more about <CFLOCK> and why it's so important to the health of your ColdFusion server by reading Chapter 12, "Locking."

Complex data can also be stored in APPLICATION variables. In the following code, the query is created as normal but placed into the APPLICATION scope by prefixing it:

```
<CFQUERY NAME="APPLICATION.GetStates" DATASOURCE="Employees">
SELECT StateAbbreviation, StateName
FROM States
</CFQUERY>
```

Now the query resultset will be available in memory. You can use the query as usual, but with the addition of the scope as shown here:

```
<CFOUTPUT QUERY="APPLICATION.GetStates">
#StateAbbreviation#
#StateName#<BR>
</CFOUTPUT>
```

> **CAUTION**
>
> Although APPLICATION variables are great places to store some query recordsets, others should not be placed in them. For instance, personalized user information should not be stored in APPLICATION variables. Because APPLICATION variables are available to the entire application, they transcend all users. Personalized information is better stored in COOKIE, CLIENT, or SESSION variables.

→ COOKIE, CLIENT, and SESSION variables are discussed in Chapter 11, "Session State Management."

Because APPLICATION variables stay in memory for the specified period of time, it doesn't make sense for you to run the query against the database every time the page is accessed. You should run the query only if it has expired in memory.

In the following code, a conditional statement is placed around the query. This statement causes the query to run only if it has been expired in memory:

```
<CFIF NOT IsDefined("APPLICATION.States")>
     <CFQUERY NAME="APPLICATION.GetStates" DATASOURCE="Employees">
     SELECT *
     FROM States
     </CFQUERY>
</CFIF>
```

→ <CFIF> was discussed in Chapter 3, "Conditional Processing."

> **CAUTION**
>
> APPLICATION variables persist for a given time on the server and are not refreshed until their time limit has been reached. Therefore, if you need to refresh the APPLICATION variables, you must do so programmatically using conditional processing.

> **TIP**
>
> Checking for the existence of APPLICATION variables before you use them is always a good idea. Besides the fact that they expire naturally, they also are lost if the server is ever rebooted.

Creating SERVER Variables

Much of what you know about APPLICATION variables can be applied to SERVER variables. The most obvious deviation, however, is the fact that you do not require the use of the <CFAPPLICATION> tag to enable them. SESSION variables are automatically available to any page in any application on the server.

Table 10.1 lists some default SERVER variables for the Windows NT and Solaris operating systems.

Table 10.1 Default SERVER Variables

SERVER Variable	Description
Server.ColdFusion.ProductName	Contains the name of the ColdFusion product
Server.ColdFusion.ProductVersion	Holds the ColdFusion version information
Server.ColdFusion.ProductLevel	Stores the ColdFusion Product level, such as Express, Professional, or Enterprise
Server.ColdFusion.SerialNumber	Holds the ColdFusion server serial number
Server.OS.Name	Stores the name of the operating system
Server.OS.Version	Stores the version information for the operating system

As you can see in the following code, you can use SERVER variables like any other variable type:

```
<!--- display server variables --->
<CFOUTPUT>#SERVER.OS.Name#</CFOUTPUT>
<!--- rename server variables --->
<CFSET SERVER.OS.Name="Emily's Personal Operating System">
```

CAUTION

Overwriting default system SERVER variables is a bad idea. Usually, the manipulation of SERVER variables is only performed during debugging.

NOTE

Like APPLICATION variables, SERVER variables can store complex data, require the use of <CFLOCK>, and are lost when the server is restarted. However, since placing exclusive locks on APPLICATION or SERVER variables can be a drain on the server resources, it is recommended that you try to use read locks rather than exclusive locks, if possible.

NOTE

APPLICATION and SERVER variables are structures. Therefore, you can also use the structure functions to manage them.

➔ Structures and their functions are discussed in Chapter 15, "Structures."

Summary

APPLICATION and SERVER variables are wonderful tools for making information widely available throughout an application or server. Although they do take up space in memory, they can decrease the need for calls to the database, which is often the most taxing function of your application.

Sample Questions

1. What is the best way to ensure that code to put a query recordset into an APPLICATION variable is run only when that query doesn't already exist?
   A. <CFSET TMP=RunWhenExpired(APPLICATION.QueryName)>
   B. <CFIF TMP=StructIsEmpty(APPLICATION.QueryName)>
   C. <CFSWITCH EXPRESSION="#APPLICATION.QueryName#">
   D. <CFIF NOT IsDefined("APPLICATION.QueryName")>

2. Where are APPLICATION variables stored?
   A. The ColdFusion server's memory
   B. In cookies on the server
   C. In cookies on the client
   D. In a database

3. Which of the following is a way of setting the default application timeout value?
   A. Setting the value of SERVER.APP to the timeout value
   B. Passing the value in a FORM or URL variable
   C. Using the ColdFusion administrator settings
   D. Declaring it each time you create an APPLICATION variable

CHAPTER 11

Session State Management

What Is Session State Management?

Earlier in the book, you learned about how FORM and URL variables can be used to pass variables from one page to another. Later, in the chapter on custom tags, you will learn of a tag called <CF_EmbedFields>, which allows you to simulate the passing of form variables across multiple pages. Although these techniques leave the impression of state maintenance, they are, at most, a poor man's version of it.

→ URL and FORM variables were discussed in Chapters 8 and 9, respectively. Custom tags are discussed in Chapter 22, "Custom Tags."

True state maintenance requires that information is stored in a way such that it exists outside the scope of variables that must be manually passed from page to page.

In the previous chapter, you learned about APPLICATION and SERVER variables. These are true state maintenance variables that are saved in the server's memory.

→ APPLICATION and SERVER variables were discussed in Chapter 10, "APPLICATION and SERVER Variables."

In this unit we learn about three more state maintenance variables: COOKIE, SESSION, and CLIENT. The difference between these variables and APPLICATION and SERVER variables is that these are used specifically to maintain state about one user, rather than just information global to the application or the server.

Cookies

Cookies are simply variables. Their main difference from ColdFusion variables is that they are saved on the client machine. The ColdFusion server writes cookies to the browser, which then saves them to specific files in the browser's file system.

> **NOTE**
> Each browser has a unique location where it saves cookies. In Netscape Navigator, all cookies from all domains are usually stored in a file called `cookies.txt`. In Internet Explorer, each domain's cookies are saved in a separate file, but usually in a directory called `Cookies` in either the user's profile or the `Windows` directory.

Making Cookies

Cookies are domain specific—they can be retrieved only by the domain server that set them.

Within your application, you can create cookie variables by using the `<CFCOOKIE>` tag, as shown here:

```
<CFCOOKIE NAME="FirstName" VALUE="Emily" EXPIRES="10">
```

The preceding code creates a cookie called `FirstName` with a value of `Emily`. It is set to expire in `10` days.

The `EXPIRES` attribute can be set as shown in Table 11.1.

Table 11.1 Values for the* `<CFCOOKIE>` `EXPIRES` *Attribute

Attribute Values	Description
`EXPIRES="5"`	Cookie will expire in five days.
`EXPIRES="1/1/2001"`	Cookie will expire on January 1, 2001.
`EXPIRES="never"`	Cookie will never expire.
`EXPIRES="now"`	Cookie will expire immediately. Use this setting to delete a cookie.
No `EXPIRES` attribute	Without an `EXPIRES` attribute in the `<CFCOOKIE>` tag, you are creating a browser *session cookie,* which will expire when the browser is closed.

Cookies are not actually set in the browser until after the entire page is done processing. The reason you can use cookies on the same page on which you create them is because the ColdFusion application server creates temporary cookies for the first page process.

> **CAUTION**
> Because a page must finish processing before a cookie is set in the browser, you will find that if you set a cookie and then use the `<CFLOCATION>` tag to go to a different page, the cookie will never be set.

Using Cookies

A cookie can be used like any other variable in ColdFusion. To use a cookie, you simply call it with the `COOKIE.` prefix like so:

```
<CFOUTPUT>#COOKIE.FirstName#</CFOUTPUT>
```

Depending on your browser, you might be limited to 20 cookies per domain or 4KB worth of information. Twenty cookies is very limiting. Just collecting the user's first name, last name, email address, phone number, and other personal information can easily use up half of your cookie allotment very quickly.

You can bypass this limit with a little creativity and by employing *cookie crumbs*, or *cookie chips*, which take multiple name=value variable pairs, combine them into one variable, and use a delimiter to separate them:

```
<CFCOOKIE NAME="ContactInfo" VALUE="firstname=emily;lastname=kim;
➥email=emily@trilemetry.com">
```

There is nothing exceptional about this technique. When you want to use this cookie, you just access it and parse out the values using list techniques. Lists are introduced in Chapter 13, "Lists."

A Cookie's Scope

Cookies are available as long as the browser is set to use them and they have not expired or been deleted.

> **TIP**
>
> Some Web visitors set their browsers not to accept cookies. If you depend upon cookies in your application, you should use a detection script to display a message to such visitors. Depending on your application, it might not actually break without cookies enabled—it might merely act weird. Don't ever assume that a cookie will be present just because you set it.

The files in which cookies are stored are just plain text files and can be easily deleted. So, to ensure that they are actually there before you use them, be sure to check that they exist:

```
<CFIF IsDefined("COOKIE.FirstName")>
    <CFOUTPUT>#COOKIE.FirstName#</CFOUTPUT>
</CFIF>
```

> **CAUTION**
>
> Cookies have always received a bad rap in the media. They are seen as a threat to the safety of the public because they can store personal information about the user and can be retrieved by servers. Much of this fear is unfounded because only servers that set the cookie can retrieve it. However, some of this fear is reasonable because cookies are just text files on the client machine, and they can be opened easily.

> Some responsibility lies in the hands of the programmer. If the programmer stores credit card or password information in cookies, he or she is actually putting the user at risk and risking the reputation of cookies.

SESSION Variables

SESSION variables are memory-resident variables that are saved in the server's memory, as with APPLICATION and SERVER variables. However, although SESSION variables maintain information about one user rather than an entire application or server, they are still tied to one application.

Preparing to Use SESSION Variables

Because SESSION variables track a user through an application, their use is intrinsically tied to the application. Therefore, you turn them on using the <CFAPPLICATION> tag as follows:

```
<CFAPPLICATION NAME="MyApplicationName" APPLICATIONTIMEOUT=
➥"#CreateTimeSpan(3,0,0,1)#" SESSIONMANAGEMENT="Yes"
SESSIONTIMEOUT="#CreateTimeSpan(0,0,20,0)#">
```

By setting the SESSIONMANAGEMENT attribute to yes, you tell the ColdFusion server to allow you to use SESSION variables. The SESSIONTIMEOUT attribute uses the CreateTimeSpan() function to declare how long you want SESSION variables to stay in the server's memory. In this example, the SESSION variables are set to expire in 20 minutes.

> **NOTE**
> Using the SESSIONTIMEOUT attribute of the <CFAPPLICATION> tag, you can set how long you want your SESSION variables to persist. However, using this attribute, you can never exceed the maximum time limit set in the ColdFusion Administrator.

When the <CFAPPLICATION> tag is first encountered by the ColdFusion application server with SESSIONMANAGEMENT set to yes, two variables are automatically created: CFID and CFTOKEN. Both these variables are used to track and authenticate the user.

Copies of CFID and CFTOKEN are saved as SESSION variables in the server's memory. Second copies are saved on the client machine as cookies. When a user accesses an application, a copy of these cookies are sent to the server, as all cookie variables would be. The ColdFusion server then attempts to match the CFID and the CFTOKEN from the cookies with those set as SESSION variables. If they match, the user is authenticated. If not, the user is rejected.

> **NOTE**
> SESSION variables use cookies to store copies of the CFID and CFTOKEN in order to track the user to one particular browser. However, no other information is stored in cookies.

Using cookies to store the CFID and CFTOKEN is the preferred and easiest way of creating an application to store SESSION variables. However, some applications are built for an audience whose browsers do not accept cookies. In that case, you will have to pass both variables manually using URL and FORM variables.

NOTE

If you use <CFLOCATION>, you can have ColdFusion pass the CFID and CFTOKEN for you by using the attribute ADDTOKEN and setting it to yes.

TIP

If you are working with multiple subdomains and need the SESSION variables to be available to all of them, you can set the SETDOMAINCOOKIES attribute of the <CFAPPLICATION> tag to yes. This attribute creates a CFMAGIC cookie that tells the server that this user's information is available to all subdomains on the server. This is especially useful when working within an e-commerce site.

As your users shop, they might be on a nonsecure server called shop.domainname.com. However, when they go to check out, they should be moved to a secure server for credit card transactions. This server could be named secure.domainname.com. The session information will be lost when you move the users to the new server because the browser will recognize the subdomains as different machines.

The SETDOMAINCOOKIES attribute tells the server to allow the CFID and CFTOKEN to be recognized by both subdomains. This attribute is also useful in a clustered environment.

Creating SESSION Variables

After you have prepared the environment to use SESSION variables, you create them using <CFSET>, just as with local variables, except that you add the prefix SESSION. to them:

```
<CFSET SESSION.FirstName="Emily">
```

After you create the SESSION variable, it is available until the session expires.

TIP

You can also use <CFPARAM> to create and set default values for SESSION variables.

➔ <CFPARAM> was introduced in Chapter 2, "Working with Variables and Expressions."

Because SESSION variables are stored in the ColdFusion server's memory, they can cause serious stability problems on your server if they are accessed improperly. You can avoid these problems by using the <CFLOCK> tag. This tag should be placed around every use of SESSION variables, whether you are reading or writing them.

➔ <CFLOCK> is discussed in detail in Chapter 12, "Locking."

The ColdFusion server stores all SESSION variables in structures. Therefore, you should use the structure functions to maintain your SESSION variables.

> **NOTE**
> COOKIE variables are also stored as structures.

➔ Structures are discussed in Chapter 15, "Structures."

Using SESSION Variables

Although they are useful for many tasks, SESSION variables are most often used for authentication purposes because they are automatically associated with one user within an application.

The following example shows how SESSION variables can be used for the authentication of users. In this example, a user has typed his username and password into a form. When he submits the form, his login information is checked against the database to make sure that he is a valid application user.

```
<CFQUERY NAME="CheckLogin" DATASOURCE="HR">
SELECT FirstName, LastName
FROM Employees
WHERE username='#FORM.username#'
    AND password='#FORM.password#'
</CFQUERY>
<!--- if the user logged in successfully... --->
<CFIF CheckLogin.RecordCount>
    <CFLOCK SCOPE="SESSION" TIMEOUT="10" TYPE="EXCLUSIVE">
        <!--- set the user's name in session variables for easy access --->
        <CFSET SESSION.FirstName=CheckLogin.FirstName>
        <CFSET SESSION.LastName=CheckLogin.LastName>
        <!--- set a flag that the user has logged in succesfully --->
        <CFSET SESSION.LoggedIn="1">
        <CFLOCATION URL="homepage.cfm">
    </CFLOCK>
<!--- if the user did not log in successfully... --->
<CFELSE>
<!--- send them back to login again --->
        <CFLOCATION URL="login.cfm">
</CFIF>
```

If the user logs in successfully, the number of records being returned from the database is 1. You determine this using the special query variable Query.RecordCount.

➔ Query variables were introduced in Chapter 7, "Using Databases."

If the user enters the correct login information, set two session variables for his first and last name. This information can be used for personalized messages. You also set a flag called SESSION.LoggedIn, which declares that the user has logged in successfully to the session and is used to authenticate him for access to other pages in the application.

You can check for this variable on every page by placing code in the `Application.cfm` file.

```
<CFLOCK SCOPE="SESSION" TIMEOUT="10" TYPE="EXCLUSIVE">
<CFIF NOT IsDefined("SESSION.LoggedIn")>
    <CFLOCATION URL="login.cfm">
</CFIF>
</CFLOCK>
```

→ The `Application.cfm` file was discussed in Chapter 6, "The Application Framework."

This code checks for the existence of the session variable, `LoggedIn`. If it exists, the user is allowed to continue unhindered. If it does not exist, the user is forced back to the login page.

Even if a user has logged in successfully, he will be forced back to the login page if his session expires. By default, a session is set in the ColdFusion Administrator for 20 minutes. That does not mean that the user has 20 minutes to complete his task; it means that the user cannot be idle for 20 minutes.

TIP

After `SESSION` variables have been enabled, they persist for at least the 20-minute timeout period. If you close your browser before the 20-minute period is up and then open your browser again to access the site, you will find that the session is still active. This could be a problem if there is a chance that another user could access the program within the timeout period. You can rectify this problem by converting the `CFID` and `CFTOKEN` variables into browser session cookies.

```
<CFIF IsDefined("Cookie.CFID")>
<CFLOCK SCOPE="SESSION" TIMEOUT="10" TYPE="EXCLUSIVE">
        <CFCOOKIE NAME="CFID" VALUE="#SESSION.CFID#">
    </CFLOCK>
</CFIF>
```

The `CFID` and `CFTOKEN` cookies are now session cookies, so when the browser is closed, the cookies will expire immediately. The next time the user opens the browser and goes to the web site, he will not have any cookies to use for the authentication and will be forced to log back in.

CLIENT Variables

Like `COOKIE` and `SESSION` variables, `CLIENT` variables are specific to one user. However, rather than being stored on the client machine or in the server's memory, `CLIENT` variables are stored elsewhere.

Preparing CLIENT Variable Storage

`CLIENT` variables, like `SESSION` variables, are also tied to an application. Therefore, we must use `<CFAPPLICATION>` again, to prepare the ColdFusion application server for their use.

```
<CFAPPLICATION NAME="MyApplicationName" CLIENTMANAGEMENT="Yes"
➥CLIENTSTORAGE="HR">
```

The attribute CLIENTMANAGEMENT declares that this application should allow the use of CLIENT variables. The CLIENTSTORAGE attribute declares that the CLIENT variables should be stored in the HR datasource. CFID and CFTOKEN are also used to recognize the user's browser.

> **CAUTION**
>
> Although CFID and CFTOKEN are used to recognize a user's browser, you should not assume that, because of their presence, the user is authenticated. Authentication against an authentication source such as a database should still be performed.

There are three locations where you can store CLIENT variables. They are discussed in Table 11.2 and can be set in the VARIABLES page of the ColdFusion Administrator's SERVER section.

Table 11.2 Storage Locations for* CLIENT *Variables

Storage Location	Description
Datasource	A specific datasource can be used to store client variable data.
Registry	Client variables can be stored in the system registry.
Cookie	Client variables can be stored in cookies.

The default location for the storage of CLIENT variables is the system registry. Although the registry is fine for storing a limited amount of data, you should avoid storing large amounts of data in it.

> **CAUTION**
>
> Your system can become unstable or unusable if your registry becomes too full of data. It is always a good idea to monitor registry size and usage and to increase its size as needed.

If you set CLIENT variable storage to a datasource, you will find that the ColdFusion application server creates two tables called CDATA and CGLOBAL in the datasource for this purpose.

Cookies can be a good place to store CLIENT variable IDs, but all the limitations you have learned about cookies remain true in this case.

Creating CLIENT Variables

CLIENT variables are the only way to reliably store information about one user over multiple sessions. Although you can do this with cookies, the fact that COOKIE variables can be easily deleted or modified makes them less reliable.

You create CLIENT variables using <CFSET> and prefixing the variable name with CLIENT.:

```
<CFSET CLIENT.FirstName="Emily">
```

You can also use <CFPARAM> to set default values for this variable, but you do not have to use <CFLOCK> because client variables are not memory-resident variables.

Using CLIENT Variables

To use CLIENT variables, you just prefix them appropriately:

```
<CFOUTPUT>#CLIENT.FirstName#</CFOUTPUT>
```

The output of the preceding line will display the name Emily.

Which Variables Should I Use?

In this chapter you reviewed COOKIE, SESSION, and CLIENT variables. They overlap in some uses, but there is also a specific time and place for each.

COOKIE variables are often used for nonsecure data that can be lost without consequence to the application. Also, because they are tied to one particular browser, if a user were to use the same application at home and at work, his data would have to be recreated in both places.

SESSION variables are usually used for sensitive information because that information remains on the server and is never transmitted to the client machine. As mentioned earlier, SESSION variables are often used for authentication as well.

CLIENT variables are usually used for site personalization efforts. Although the CFID and CFTOKEN variables are used to recognize a browser, if cookie storage is not declared, the actual data about the user is stored either in a database or in the system registry. In either case, it is on the server and available to the user from any computer.

Remember that within one application, you might find it useful to use more than one of these types of variables to accomplish your tasks.

Summary

Session state management takes advantage of COOKIE, SESSION, and CLIENT variables, which are essential to an application that needs to track individual visitors.

Sample Questions

1. What value would you assign to the EXPIRES attribute of the CFCOOKIE tag if you wanted to create a browser session cookie?
   A. Session
   B. browser
   C. now
   D. Don't set the EXPIRES attribute

2. Which is not an optional storage location for client variables?
   A. Database
   B. Registry
   C. Cookies
   D. Session

3. Which cookie is set by the ColdFusion application server when the attribute SETDOMAINCOOKIES is set to yes in the <CFAPPLICATION> tag?

   A. CFID

   B. CFTOKEN

   C. CFMAGIC

   D. CFDOMAIN

CHAPTER 12

Locking

Understanding Locking

The concept of locking is well established in multi-user environments. File locking prevents multiple users from editing a single file. Database management systems also use locking by allowing different users to access the same records without interference. In a ColdFusion environment, locking must be taken into consideration to stop multiple requests from accessing code that cannot be accessed concurrently (for example, accessing shared variables).

Any application logic that uses `SERVER`, `APPLICATION`, or `SESSION` variables must use ColdFusion's locking features. Because Windows and UNIX are multithreaded operating systems, any ColdFusion page request could be interrupted by another request. This can lead to stability problems when a requested page sets a variable and is interrupted by a page that resets the same variable to a different value. The idea is a lot like using database locks in which users can lock certain rows to prevent other users from making changes simultaneously.

Code blocks that need to be locked are those involving variables that persist beyond a single request. Code blocks that utilize `APPLICATION` and `SERVER` variables are shared among multiple users (requests) and must be locked. SESSION variables also persist across requests when a single browser demands the same page multiple times. Inherent to the Web's architecture, a single browser tends to open two to four connections to every HTML template. Additionally, the user could click Refresh, which requests the same page and causes potential threading conflicts in the operating system. Or you could be using frames that always open multiple requests for the same client.

NOTE

Locking must also be used for CFX calls when the C++ library is not thread-safe. This is typically an issue with novice C++ developers who have not considered threading or would rather use ColdFusion to ensure that conflicts do not occur.

In addition, it is possible to lock access to a file system procedure such as `<CFFILE>` to provide synchronous file access.

Locking Strategies

You lock `SESSION`, `APPLICATION`, or `SERVER` scopes directly by using the `<CFLOCK>` tag. New to ColdFusion is the capability to lock variables without using `<CFLOCK>`, but you may have to use certain coding practices.

TIP

These new features may have implications on upgrading, but Allaire has provided a migration wizard at `ftp://ftp.allaire.com/kbftp/coldfusion/lockmigrationtool.zip` (these implications will be discussed later in the chapter).

NOTE

Locking is further covered in a KnowledgeBase article at Allaire's Web site at `http://www.allaire.com/Handlers/index.cfm?ID=14165&Method=Full`

<CFLOCK> Attributes

The `<CFLOCK>` tag has two mutually exclusive attributes: `NAME` and `SCOPE`. The `NAME` attribute was the only option in ColdFusion 4.0, and although this attribute still functions, you might need to use the `SCOPE` attribute instead. The migration wizard searches and replaces this attribute within a given .CFM template. See the preceding section for the upgrade wizard's URL.

In addition to the `NAME` and `SCOPE` attributes, two other attributes also need attention. The first is the `TIMEOUT` attribute, which throws a lock error if a procedure exceeds the value or if two locks are contentious. Contentious locks, which are also known as *deadlocks*, will be reviewed later in this chapter.

The other `<CFLOCK>` attribute is `TYPE`, which specifies whether the lock is `READONLY` or `EXCLUSIVE`. `EXCLUSIVE` locks are required if a variable is set and provides single-threaded access to the code block. A `READONLY` lock is for reading the value of a variable and is multithreaded. `READONLY` locks are faster than `EXCLUSIVE` ones.

Using the NAME Attribute

The `NAME` attribute of the `<CFLOCK>` tag uniquely identifies a lock around a specific variable, file system, or custom tag call. This `NAME` is referenced in all locations where the lock needs to be obeyed. The `NAME` attribute is useful for custom tag calls that are not thread-safe or file access locks. Specific SESSION, APPLICATION, or SERVER variables can also be locked using the NAME attribute.

The following code locks a custom tag call using the NAME attribute:

```
<CFLOCK NAME="myCfxLock" TIMEOUT="15" TYPE="exclusive">
     <CFX_CREATEGIF IMAGENAME="blue.gif" TEXT="Test" BACKGROUNDCOLOR="Blue">
</CFLOCK>
```

By locking this block of code, all subsequent requests will wait until the initial request finishes running the custom tag. Because the TIMEOUT attribute was set for fifteen seconds, an error will be thrown if the lock exceeds this period of time.

> **TIP**
>
> You should use EXCLUSIVE locks whenever custom tags or file access is locked. This makes the lock a single-threaded operation. And all calls to the same tag should use the same lock NAME.

Using the SCOPE Attribute

The SCOPE attribute is the alternative to the NAME attribute. This attribute has three possible values: SESSION, APPLICATION, or SERVER. Setting one of these values through the SCOPE attribute locks all the variables of that scope at the same time. A locked SESSION scope automatically applies to a single SESSION and does not lock any other sessions.

Using the SCOPE attribute gives you additional functionality. As of ColdFusion 4.5, new lock settings can be toggled through the browser-based ColdFusion Administrator. Almost all these settings are available only when the SCOPE attribute is used instead of NAME.

> **NOTE**
>
> The SCOPE attribute is more robust than the NAME attribute. The server settings available to this attribute allow for comprehensive lock checking by the ColdFusion server.

READONLY Locks

The alternative to using an EXCLUSIVE lock is to use a READONLY lock. READONLY locks should be used within code blocks that access but do not set shared variables. A READONLY lock will permit two requests to run simultaneously as though no lock existed. But if an EXCLUSIVE lock is active any READONLY locks will wait until that lock is released.

Server-Based Settings

As of version 4.5, ColdFusion's browser-based Administrator offers lock settings. To get to these settings, open the ColdFusion Administrator and click the LOCKING link under the SERVER section.

After the settings page is loaded, a list of descriptive explanations appears next to each setting check box and radio button.

The first option to appear enables single-threaded sessions. You use this option when ColdFusion session is enabled. When it is enabled, using `<CFLOCK>` with `SESSION` variables becomes unnecessary. ColdFusion automatically locks each variable based on each user's unique session ID.

> **CAUTION**
>
> Enabling single-threaded sessions may affect the performance of your ColdFusion application. You should load-test an application to ascertain the degree of impact.

The following options change how ColdFusion checks locks on each scope. Under each scope are three radio buttons you can choose to select the degree of lock checking. The three lock check options are as follows:

- No Automatic Checking or Locking—Enabling this option for a given scope means that no checking is performed on any shared variable. It is completely up to you to use `<CFLOCK>` around all shared variables.
- Full Checking—Enabling this option for a given scope means that any missing `<CFLOCK>` will be found automatically by the ColdFusion server. The result of a missing `<CFLOCK>` is an intelligible error message indicating that all shared variables must be locked. Using this option degrades performance.
- Automatic Read Locking—Enabling this option for a given scope means that every shared variable will be checked for a `<CFLOCK>` if that shared variable is being set. If the variable is being read instead of set, ColdFusion automatically locks it without the need for a `<CFLOCK>`. This means you don't need to use `<CFLOCK>` with a `TYPE` attribute set to `READONLY` because ColdFusion will enforce read locks on its own. Manual `EXCLUSIVE` locks are still required. This option is the best in terms of flexibility and the worst in terms of performance.

> **NOTE**
>
> The second and third options in this list require the use of the `SCOPE` attribute rather than the `NAME` attribute.

Some examples of using the server-based options with the `<CFLOCK>` tag are shown next.

Option 1 (No Checking Done by ColdFusion Server)

```
<!--- ColdFusion is not checking anything, do it manually --->
<CFLOCK TYPE="exclusive" SCOPE="session" TIMEOUT="15">
     <CFSET SESSION.firstName=FORM.firstName>
</CFLOCK>
```

```
<CFLOCK TYPE="readonly" SCOPE="session" TIMEOUT="15">
    <CFOUTPUT>Welcome to the site #SESSION.firstName#!</CFOUTPUT>
</CFLOCK>

<!--- no possible problems so far --->
<!--- if I forgot to use CFLOCK as I do below, collisions are possible: --->

<CFOUTPUT>We have entered your name #SESSION.
➥firstName# into our user database!</CFOUTPUT>

<!--- the above line could be problematic since it is not locked --->
```

Option 2 (Full Checking Done by ColdFusion Server)

```
<!--- ColdFusion is checking everything,I still need to lock manually --->
<CFLOCK TYPE="exclusive" SCOPE="session" TIMEOUT="15">
    <CFSET SESSION. firstName=FORM.firstName>
</CFLOCK>

<CFLOCK TYPE="readonly" SCOPE="session" TIMEOUT="15">
    <CFOUTPUT>Welcome to the site #SESSION.firstName#!</CFOUTPUT>
</CFLOCK>

<!--- no errors so far --->
<!--- I forgot CFLOCK below, COLDFUSION THROWS AN ERROR-I am protected --->

<CFOUTPUT>
We have entered your name #SESSION.firstName# into our user database!
</CFOUTPUT>
<!--- the above line would not run - forcing me to fix things --->
```

Option 3 (Automatic Read Locking)

```
<!--- ColdFusion checks exclusive locks, if I forgot CFLOCK, I am ok --->
<CFLOCK TYPE="exclusive" SCOPE="session" TIMEOUT="15">
    <CFSET SESSION.firstName=FORM.firstName>
</CFLOCK>
<CFOUTPUT>
    Welcome to the site #SESSION.firsName#!
    We have entered your name #SESSION.firstName# into our user database!
</CFOUTPUT>
<!--- above is ok- ColdFusion locks it for me --->
```

Dealing with Deadlocks

One potential hazard of using `<CFLOCK>` is that nested locks can lead to a *deadlock*. A deadlock occurs when two or more locks are initiated on separate templates. Say that you have two pages that lock both the `APPLICATION` and `SESSION` scope. The first page, named `login.cfm`, records a user's name in a `SESSION` variable and then appends the user's name to an `APPLICATION` variable. The `APPLICATION` variable contains an embedded structure of users who are currently logged in. A second page, `logout.cfm`, clears the `SESSION` structure and removes the user's name from the embedded structure in the `APPLICATION` scope.

These pages behave perfectly if the scopes are locked and nested in the same order. If, however, the locks are nested in a different order, the potential for a deadlock exists. The following code causes a deadlock:

`login.cfm`:

```
<CFLOCK SCOPE="session" TYPE="exclusive" TIMEOUT="15">
     <!--- locked the session scope - now set a session variable --->
     <CFSET SESSION.userName=FORM.userName>
     <CFLOCK SCOPE="application" TYPE="exclusive" TIMEOUT="15">
     <!--- a nested lock since we are dealing with both scopes at once --->
     <!--- note that this structure was defined on another page somewhere --->
     <CFSET APPLICATION.loggedInUsers[SESSION.userName] = SESSION.userName>
     </CFLOCK>
</CFLOCK>
```

`logout.cfm`:

```
<CFLOCK SCOPE="application" TYPE="exclusive" TIMEOUT="15">
     <!--- locked the application scope FIRST, opposite of the login page!!!
➥--->
     <!--- then we nest a second lock since the session scope is used --->
<CFLOCK SCOPE="session" TYPE="exclusive" TIMEOUT="15">
          <!--- get rid of the user from the application scope--->
                 <CFSET StructDelete(APPLICATION.SESSION.userName)>
          <!--- kill the session --->
          <CFSET structClear(SESSION)>
     </CFLOCK>
</CFLOCK>
```

Although this code may appear to be sound, it is not. If the `login.cfm` page runs and is then interrupted by another thread that runs the logout page, a fatal deadlock may occur. The `login.cfm` page could lock the `SESSION` scope at the same time the `logout.cfm` page locks the `APPLICATION` scope. Then the nested locks will demand exclusive access to the nested scopes. `login.cfm` will wait for `logout.cfm` to release the application scope, while `logout.cfm` will wait for `SESSION` scope to be released. Both would wait forever if there were not a timeout, but because there is a timeout, a fatal error will occur instead. Regardless, the deadlock causes one of the pages to fail.

TIP

According to Allaire's official recommendations, you should manage deadlocks by locking scopes in a certain order. This order is not arbitrary and is based on the underlying architecture of the ColdFusion engine. Locks should be declared in terms of specificity, moving from least specific (SERVER scope) to most specific (SESSION scope).

You need to declare nested locks in this order:

1. SERVER scope
2. APPLICATION scope
3. SESSION scope

To solve the deadlock in the previous code example, you could simply reverse the order of locking in the login.cfm page so that the APPLICATION scope is locked first rather than second. Finally, you could place all the <CFSET> tags on login.cfm in the nested lock.

Summary

Locking is an essential element to any production application. Because ColdFusion is a multithreaded server, exclusive locks must be enforced whenever a shared variable is set, an unsafe custom tag is called, or a file access operation is performed. READONLY locks are available when shared variables are read and not written to. This improves performance over exclusively locking a variable to print it. The NAME and SCOPE attributes are mutually exclusive and have various pros and cons, but some of ColdFusion's new server settings work only when the SCOPE attribute is used. Server settings can affect performance but make an application safer by automatically locking SESSION variables or checking to make sure certain scopes are locked before honoring a <CFLOCK>. Deadlocks can occur if the locks are nested and not locked in a specific order.

Sample Questions

1. Choose the legal <CFLOCK> statement.
   A. `<CFLOCK TIMEOUT="16">`
   B. `<CFLOCK NAME="myLock" SCOPE="session" TIMEOUT="16">`
   C. `<CFLOCK SCOPE="myLock" TIMEOUT="16" TYPE="readonly">`
   D. `<CFLOCK NAME="myLock" TIMEOUT="16">`

2. What do server-based locking settings include? (Choose all that apply.)
   A. Single-threaded SESSION variables
   B. Single-threaded APPLICATION variables
   C. Single-threaded SERVER variables
   D. Automatic read locking for SERVER variables

3. When does using <CFLOCK> throw an error? (Choose all that apply.)
   A. When a timeout is reached during a deadlock
   B. When a timeout is reached outside a deadlock

C. When read locks are missing and no read checking was set
D. When read locks are not missing and read checking was set

4. When can deadlocks occur? (Choose two.)
   A. When locks are nested
   B. When locks are in a different order on different pages
   C. When locks wait for each other and are not nested
   D. When `READONLY` locks are declared against the `CLIENT` scope

PART 3

DATA TYPES

Lists

Arrays

Structures

CHAPTER 13

Lists

Understanding Lists

A list is one of the most basic variable types in ColdFusion—although, in truth, a list is not a type per se. A list is a simple set of data separated by one or more delimiters. The following is a simple list of six American states (in this example, the list is delimited by commas):

```
CA,FL,MA,MI,NY,WA
```

The individual items in a list are known as *elements*, and unless a list is an empty string, it always has at least one element in it. By default, lists are delimited by commas, but ColdFusion allows you to specify any character (or multiple characters) as the delimiter. The following is the same list, this time separated by spaces:

```
CA FL MA MI NY WA
```

In fact, any variable that is not an array or a structure is a list (whether you use it that way or not). Unlike an array or a structure, a list is not actually a data type. Rather, it is nothing more than simple strings, and internally ColdFusion treats it as such. When you access a specific element in a list (we'll get to that topic in a moment), ColdFusion performs basic string processing for you because that's all lists are—strings.

→ Arrays and structures are covered in detail in Chapter 14, "Arrays," and Chapter 15, "Structures."

> **NOTE**
>
> ColdFusion stores arrays and structures in memory in special formats designed especially for structured data. This makes accessing and manipulating arrays and structures far quicker than accessing and manipulating lists that are simply strings. List processing is essentially string and substring processing.

Working with Lists

Lists are extremely easy to use and even easier to create. For this reason, many of ColdFusion's internal data sets are stored as lists, and several CFML functions (and variables) return data in this format too.

Lists are accessed via a set of special CFML functions, all beginning with the word *List*, and all of which take a list as the first attribute.

Creating Lists

CFML functions are generally not used to create a list (this is in contrast to arrays and structures, both of which require the use of special functions). The following `<CFSET>` statement creates the list of states shown at the beginning of the chapter:

```
<!--- States list --->
<CFSET states="CA,FL,MA,MI,NY,WA">
```

> **TIP**
>
> You also can use `<CFPARAM>` to create lists; you can use the assignment operator in a `<CFSCRIPT>` block as well.
>
> You can also create lists using any of the functions that update lists (for example, `ListAppend()`) by passing an empty string to the function as the existing list.

Accessing List Elements

You access and manipulate lists by using the list functions. For example, to determine the number of elements in a list, you can use the `ListLen()` function as follows:

```
<!--- Display number of states in list --->
<CFOUTPUT>#ListLen(states)#</CFOUTPUT>
```

> **NOTE**
>
> Empty elements are ignored by the list functions, so list `a,,b` contains just two elements (not three). However, whitespace is not ignored, so list `a, ,b` contains three elements.

To access a specific list element, use the `ListGetAt()` function as follows:

```
<!--- Display the third State --->
<CFOUTPUT>#ListGetAt(states, 3)#</CFOUTPUT>
```

ColdFusion provides special functions to quickly access the first and last elements in a list (the `ListFirst()` and `ListLast()` functions, respectively), as well as to return all the elements after the first element (the `ListRest()` function).

> **CAUTION**
>
> Be careful never to refer to an element that does not exist (for example, trying to retrieve the sixth element in a five-element list) because doing so throws an error. Always checking the length of a list (using `ListLen()`) before accessing specific elements is good practice.

> **NOTE**
>
> List elements are numbered starting from `1` (not `0`, as in other development languages and platforms).

You also can search lists to find the first element that matches or contains specific text. Use `ListFind()` to perform an *element match* (the element matches if it is the exact search text and nothing more) and `ListContains()` to perform a *contains match* (the element matches if it contains the search text). Both functions return the position of the first matching element (not the element itself) and `0` if no match is found. The following code snippet checks to see whether a state is in a list (using the `ListFind()` function) and displays one of two messages based on the result:

```
<!--- Is user's State in the taxable State list? --->
<CFSET match=ListFind(states, user.state)>
<!--- "match" will be greater than 0 (TRUE) if in "states" list --->
<CFIF match>
 <!--- Yes, tell user that it is taxable --->
 <CFOUTPUT>Sales to #user.state# residents are taxable</CFOUTPUT>
<CFELSE>
 <!--- No, tell user that tax will not be added --->
 <CFOUTPUT>No tax is added for #user.state# residents</CFOUTPUT>
</CFIF>
```

> **TIP**
>
> List searches (both exact or partial matches) are case sensitive. To perform searches that are not case sensitive, use the `ListFindNoCase()` and `ListContainsNoCase()` functions.

Modifying Lists

You can modify lists as you create them—directly using standard CFML assignment tags and operators. A more efficient way to modify them is to use functions designed for just this purpose. To update an element in a list, for example, use the `ListSetAt()` function, and to delete an element from a list, use `ListDeleteAt()`.

You can add new elements to a list at any time. The `ListPrepend()` function inserts an element at the beginning of a list, `ListAppend()` adds an element at the end of a list, and `ListInsertAt()` inserts an element at a specific location.

> **NOTE**
>
> The list functions do not modify lists; rather, they return modified lists. If you want to modify a list, you must use that same list as the list parameter and as the variable being assigned, as follows:
>
> ```
> <CFSET states=ListAppend(states, "WY")>
> ```
>
> Here, an element is added to the `states` list, so the value returned by `ListAppend()` (the new list) is assigned to `states`.

Specifying Delimiters

By default, lists use commas for delimiters, as you saw in the previous examples. But as we explained at the beginning of this chapter, ColdFusion allows you to use any characters as list delimiters. You therefore can use list functionality in interesting ways. For example, to determine how many words are in a string, you could treat that string as a list delimited by spaces, as follows:

```
<!--- How many words in "text"? --->
<CFOUTPUT>#text# contains #ListLen(text, " ")# words</CFOUTPUT>
```

Because the default delimiter is a comma, alternative delimiters must be explicitly specified. Every list function takes an optional last attribute—the delimiter to be used. If you specify `" "` (a string containing only a space) as the delimiter, the elements in the preceding list are the words in the variable `text` (words separated by a space).

You can specify multiple delimiters, in which case *any* of the specified characters acts as a delimiter (not all). In other words, to count the number of words in a string separated by either spaces, periods, commas, or hyphens, you could do the following:

```
<!--- How many words in "text"? --->
<CFOUTPUT>#text# contains #ListLen(text, " .,-")# words</CFOUTPUT>
```

> **NOTE**
>
> To change the delimiter used in a list (returning a copy of the list using the new delimiter), use the `ListChangeDelims()` function.

Using Lists

As you have seen thus far, lists are very easy to use and are well suited for simple access to grouped data. Lists were designed to be simple; they were not designed to be efficient. Therefore, it is important to know when to use lists and when not to.

When to Use Lists (and When Not To)

Lists are primarily designed to be used with data that is already in list format. Two primary examples are as follows:

- HTML form field values are returned in list form when multiple values exist for the same field name (for example, two HTML form controls have the same name, or a control that allows multiple selections is used).
- SQL uses the list format for sets of values (for example, in an `IN` clause).

➔ Form controls and variables are covered in detail in Chapter 9, "`FORM` Variables." The SQL `IN` clause is covered in Chapter 32, "Basic SQL."

When data is already in a list format, or needs to be, you should use lists and lists functions.

Lists are not designed for complex or frequent processing; they just don't perform well enough for that. Arrays and structures are far better suited for that task.

> **TIP**
>
> You can convert lists into arrays and back again by using the `ListToArray()` and `ArrayToList()` functions.

Sorting Lists

You can sort lists by using the `ListSort()` function, and you must specify one of three sort types:

- `NUMERIC` should be used for lists containing just numbers (and should never be used if any elements are not numeric).
- `TEXT` performs case-sensitive alphabetical sorting (`A` before `a`, `1` before `10`, `2` after `10` but before `20`, and numbers before letters).
- `TEXTNOCASE` performs an alphabetical sort that is not case sensitive.

An optional sort order may also be specified; the default is `ASC` (ascending).

Looping Through Lists

In addition to accessing lists via functions as shown previously, you also can use CFML to loop through lists with `<CFLOOP>`. Like the list functions, `<CFLOOP>` supports alternative (and multiple) delimiters. The following code snippet displays the list of `states` in an HTML unordered list:

```
<!--- Start unordered list --->
<UL>
<!--- Loop through "states" --->
<CFLOOP INDEX="i" LIST="#states#">
 <!--- Write this element --->
 <CFOUTPUT><LI>#i#</LI></CFOUTPUT>
</CFLOOP>
<!--- End unordered list --->
</UL>
```

The list must be passed to `<CFLOOP>` in the `LIST` attribute, and the variable name specified in the `INDEX` attribute will contain the appropriate element in each loop iteration.

➔ Looping and the `<CFLOOP>` tag were covered in detail in Chapter 4, "Looping."

> **TIP**
>
> Another way to apply formatting to list elements (without needing to loop through them) is to use the `Replace()` and `ReplaceList()` functions to replace all delimiters with appropriate HTML code.

Nested Lists

Although the ColdFusion documentation states that lists cannot be nested, technically they actually can. The trick is to use different delimiters for the inner and outer lists. For example, the following list has three elements if the default delimiter is used and seven elements if a space is the delimiter:

```
<CFSET list="a b c,1 2 3,x y z">
```

But accessed within nested `<CFLOOP>` tags, the same list can be used as a nested list—three lists each with three elements. The outer list is delimited by commas, and each inner list is delimited by spaces.

> **TIP**
>
> This kind of list processing is especially useful when you're working with comma-delimited imported data files (sometimes called CSV files). A file can be read into a variable (using `<CFFILE>`), and the entire file can be treated as a list delimited by carriage-return and line-feed characters (ASCII characters 13 and 10, respectively). This way, each line in the file can be accessed individually as a list element. The data format within each line is comma delimited, so the list functions can be used to process and extract the individual elements easily.

Special Lists

Several CFML functions return data in list format (comma delimited). They include `ValueList()` and `QuotedValueList()` (which return query columns in list form so that they can be easily used in additional SQL statements) and functions such as `GetClientVariableList()` (which returns a list of all `CLIENT` variables for the current user) and `GetFunctionList()` (which returns a list of all supported CFML functions).

In addition, several variables are always formatted as lists (again, for simplicity's sake). They include `query.ColumnList` (which lists the columns returned in a query) and `Server.ColdFusion.SupportedLocales` (which lists the locales supported by ColdFusion).

You can manipulate all these lists by using the functions and loops discussed earlier.

> **TIP**
>
> Lists that need to be accessed frequently (particularly ones that persist across requests) should be converted into arrays (or structures) to improve performance.

Summary

Lists are an important and highly flexible ColdFusion data type. Lists are very well suited for use with HTML form fields, SQL statements, and any other data that is delimited by common characters. But lists should not be overused because they do not perform as well as more advanced data types (specifically arrays and structures).

Sample Questions

1. Which of the following are lists?
   A. Dates
   B. Arrays
   C. Structures
   D. Strings

2. Which of the following are valid list delimiters?
   A. `","`
   B. `" "`
   C. `"#Chr(13)##Chr(10)#"`
   D. `"-"`

3. How many elements are in the list `"Ben Forta"`?
   A. 0
   B. 1
   C. 2
   D. 3

CHAPTER 14

Arrays

Understanding Arrays

Arrays, like lists, store multiple values within a single variable. Arrays differ from lists in two ways:

- ColdFusion stores arrays in memory using a special format known as *Complex Data*.
- Although arrays can be used to store multiple strings or numbers (like lists), they can also be used to store multiple arrays, queries, or structures.

In most of this chapter, the array `aFlightInfo` is used. This array holds multiple levels of information about airline flights. Because one airline flight can have multiple stops, the sequence of destinations must be numbered. Flight information may also include descriptions of the flight crew on board. The first, second, and third officers are known by their order. Arrays are used when order matters, and in these two cases, it does. Arrays are also used for their capacity to store multiple sets of ordered data, such as destinations and flight crews. Because arrays are complex, you can store as many sets of data in one array as you need.

> **NOTE**
>
> ColdFusion stores queries, structures, and arrays as Complex Data. ColdFusion stores strings and numbers as Simple Data.

When to Use Arrays

You should use arrays when the order of something is crucial. A shopping cart, for example, is the perfect candidate for an array because each item is referenced according to the order in which the buyer chose it. Arrays should also be used where descriptive statistics (average, sum, min/max, count) need to be performed on a series of values.

When Not to Use Arrays

Arrays are not appropriate to use in some circumstances. Because arrays are complex data, a complete array can't be printed or passed without the use of `<CFLOOP>`. In situations in which you need to pass a set of data between HTML form pages or print it on an HTML page, lists are preferred.

In situations in which the order of values does not matter and simple calculations such as averaging or summation are not necessary, a structure is a better alternative.

> **CAUTION**
> Allaire's documentation and course material contain references to *associative arrays*. They are not arrays but are a technique for using structures.

➔ Structures will be covered in detail in Chapter 15, "Structures." `<CFLOOP>` was described in Chapter 4, "Looping," and lists were discussed in Chapter 13, "Lists."

Using Arrays

Arrays are easy to use, but like all complex data, they must be created and initialized before they can be accessed. The array function `ArrayNew()` creates an array and takes one required argument. After you create the array, you must initialize it.

> **NOTE**
> According to Allaire's documentation, initialization occurs at the point when a value is placed into the array or the array is resized. As of ColdFusion 4.5, however, ColdFusion behaves as though initialization occurs at the same time as creation. Although this point may seem unimportant, the potential exists for Allaire certification exams to use the terms *initialization* and *creation* interchangeably. As long as you understand this point, you will not be misled by ambiguous certification questions.

Creating Arrays

The `ArrayNew()` function creates an array and specifies how many dimensions the array can hold. Passing an argument of `1` to `ArrayNew()`, as shown in the following example, creates a one-dimensional array. Multidimensional arrays will be discussed later in this chapter. After you create an array, you can access it by using functions or setting values directly.

```
<!--- create a one dimensional array --->
<CFSET aFlightInfo = ArrayNew(1)>
```

> **TIP**
>
> Allaire's training material and documentation recommend that arrays be prefaced with a lowercase *a* followed by a mixed-case variable name. The sample array in this chapter has been named `aFlightInfo`.

Populating Arrays

You can populate an array in a number of ways. The most specific way is to reference the index directly:

```
<!--- setting the first couple of indexes of an array --->
<CFSET aFlightInfo = ArrayNew(1)>
<CFSET aFlightInfo[1] = "Flight 2833 to Burlington, Vermont">
<CFSET aFlightInfo[2] = "Flight 7074 to Albany, New York">
```

> **TIP**
>
> Array indexes may consist of any ColdFusion expression. For instance, you can reference an element at index `[Q+1]` by using `aFlightInfo[Q+1]`. To append a value to an array, you could use `aFlightInfo[arrayLen(aFlightInfo)+1]`.

The problem with directly referencing a static index is that you must know ahead of time where each value belongs within the array. A better way of populating an array would be to use the `ArrayAppend()` or `ArrayPrepend()` functions, which place values at the beginning or end of the array. Note that these functions, like most array functions, return `TRUE` in the variable at the left-hand side of the equal sign but perform their task against the array referenced in the array function. Much of Allaire's documentation uses a temporary variable named `tmp` for this useless return code:

```
<CFSET aFlightInfo = ArrayNew(1)>
<CFSET tmp = ArrayAppend(aFlightInfo,"Flight 7074 to Albany, New York")>
```

> **NOTE**
>
> As of ColdFusion 4.5, you don't need to use an equal sign for functions that return `TRUE`. Therefore, you now can set array values by using the following syntax:
>
> ```
> <CFSET ArrayAppend(aFlightInfo,"Flight 7074 to Albany, New York")>
> ```

After you create an array, you must access it according to its indexes. Therefore, printing the array causes an error:

```
<!--- This will cause an error since aFlightInfo is not a simple value --->
<CFSET aFlightInfo = ArrayNew(1)>
<CFSET aFlightInfo[1] = "Flight 1867">
<CFOUTPUT>#aFlightInfo#</CFOUTPUT> <!--- OUCH!!! Ugly error --->
```

Converting Between Arrays and Lists

Because HTML forms and `URL` variables frequently pass lists to the Web server, being able to switch back and forth between complex data (arrays) and simple data (lists) is handy. The functions `ArrayToList()` and `ListToArray()` achieve these goals.

> **NOTE**
>
> Older versions of ColdFusion would fail if a newly created array were converted to a list before initialization. As of ColdFusion 4.5, the initialization is unnecessary, so conversion of a new (empty) array creates an empty list. This is one reason that Allaire seems to use *initialize* and *create* interchangeably.

Printing Array Values

Printing one value of an array is straightforward. Simply reference the index you want to print in brackets after the array name:

```
<CFOUTPUT>#aFlightInfo[1]#</CFOUTPUT>
```

Because it is illegal to print the contents of an entire array by putting # signs around it and omitting the index reference, you need to loop through the indexes of the array to print each value individually.

Printing all values in the array requires that you use the `ArrayLen()` function. The loop is a standard `<CFLOOP>` using the attributes `FROM`, `TO`, and `INDEX`. Because `ArrayLen()` returns the highest index in the array, this combination renders each value for every index:

```
<CFLOOP FROM="1" TO="#arrayLen(aFlightInfo)#" INDEX="i">
     <CFOUTPUT>#aFlightInfo[i]#</CFOUTPUT><BR>
</CFLOOP>
```

> **NOTE**
>
> Although most programming languages start arrays at position `0`, ColdFusion begins at array position `1`. Attempting to loop, set, or read from position `0` throws an error.

Empty Array Indexes

Empty array indexes can be hazardous. For example, if you place values in the first and third indexes while skipping the second, `<CFLOOP>` still loops three times, but ColdFusion throws an error on the second loop stating that no index was defined at location `2`. The following example illustrates this scenario:

```
<CFSET aFlightInfo = ArrayNew(1)>
<CFSET aFlightInfo[1] = "Flight 2833 to Burlington, Vermont">
<!--- setting the 3rd index and skipping the 2nd --->
<CFSET aFlightInfo[3] = "Flight 7074 to Albany, New York">
```

```
<CFLOOP FROM="1" TO="#arrayLen(aFlightInfo)#" INDEX="i">
     <CFOUTPUT>#aFlightInfo[i]#</CFOUTPUT><BR> <!--- ERROR on 2nd LOOP! --->
</CFLOOP>
```

An easy way around this problem is to use the `ArraySet()` function to give "empty" values to any array where the problem could occur. `ArraySet()` takes a start index, an end index, and a value to repeatedly set within the span. The problem of empty indexes will be discussed more in the next section.

Arrays and Memory

In ColdFusion, as with any server-side scripting language, performance is always a consideration. In most languages—Java, for example—arrays must be given a certain size before they are populated. ColdFusion does not require that a size be given because the array is dynamically resized. As data is placed into the array, ColdFusion appropriates memory along the way. Although this is a friendly feature of the ColdFusion server, it is also a performance risk if arrays keep growing past a certain threshold.

It is recommended that the array be sized ahead of time to instantly allocate the memory that will be needed. To perform this task, you should use the `ArrayResize()` function. Resizing the array, as shown here, is not deleterious to the data within it:

```
<!--- the values in the array do not change, but the array size does --->
<CFSET aFlightInfo = ArrayNew(1)>
<CFSET aFlightInfo[1] = "Flight 2833 to Burlington, Vermont">
<CFSET arrayResize(aFlightInfo,600)>
```

> **TIP**
>
> Allaire recommends that an array be resized if it is likely to hold more than 500 indexes.

A resized array actually has multiple empty values in it. This means that a resized array should be implemented in conjunction with `ArraySet()` if looping is likely to occur. This strategy would require much more memory than if you had used a `<CFTRY>/<CFCATCH>` block to suppress errors during the loop.

→ `<CFTRY>/<CFCATCH>` will be discussed in Chapter 21, "Debugging."

Compressing Arrays

The solution for getting rid of empty values within an array is to compress the array by using the `ArrayDeleteAt()` function. This function not only deletes any value within a given index, but also compresses the array so that its length decrements by one. Compressing an array is a good practice to avoid some of the problems with empty values. It is also a good practice for the purpose of releasing memory.

> **NOTE**
> As of ColdFusion 4.5, resizing works only to grow an array. Attempting to shrink an array through `ArrayResize()` has no effect on the array or the memory it occupies.

Multidimensional Arrays

Although one-dimensional arrays are adequate for most ColdFusion tasks, multidimensional arrays are more robust. Multidimensional arrays contain other arrays. This is what separates a multidimensional array from a one-dimensional array: One-dimensional arrays hold simple data in each index, whereas multidimensional arrays are arrays combined with other arrays.

Two-Dimensional Arrays

Two-dimensional arrays provide a means to capture more data per index. So far, you have been capturing only one value in a single dimension. Now you will capture multiple values using a second dimension. By increasing the `ArrayNew()` argument to `2`, you can store a second set of values within the indexes of the first dimension:

```
<!--- now we pass "2" to the ArrayNew() function --->
<CFSET aFlightInfo = ArrayNew(2)>
<!--- we can place more data in each index --->
<CFSET aFlightInfo[1][1] = "Flight 2833 to Burlington, Vermont">
<CFSET aFlightInfo[1][2] = "Captain Alicia Ouellette on duty">
<!--- now some info about the Albany flight --->
<CFSET aFlightInfo[2][1] = "Flight 7073 to Albany, New York">
<CFSET aFlightInfo[2][2] = "Captain Brian Smith on duty">
```

> **CAUTION**
> When an array is two-dimensional, it must be referenced using both indexes. If the second index is omitted in `<CFOUTPUT>`, an error occurs.

Allaire product and training materials often compare two-dimensional arrays to database tables. The reasoning behind this analogy is sound: Two-dimensional arrays can be represented as rows and columns. The first index of `aFlightInfo` in the preceding example could represent a database table column named Destination, and the second index could represent a column named Flight Crew. Although this analogy is useful, it may be misleading for the certification exam. The database table analogy begins to fall apart as soon as you build `ArrayDeleteAt()` into the equation:

```
<CFSET ArrayDeleteAt(aFlightInfo[2],1)>
```

This line of code would shift the Flight Crew information into the Destination column, which shatters the database table analogy. For this reason, it is best to think of a two-dimensional array as an array containing another array and leave it at that. The following example does the same thing as a two-dimensional array using `ArrayNew(2)`, but better illustrates this point:

```
<!--- instead of passing "2" to arrayNew(), let's do this another way --->
<CFSET aFlightInfo = ArrayNew(1)>
<!--- now put another array inside the first index --->
<CFSET aFlightInfo[1] = ArrayNew(1)>
<CFSET aFlightInfo[1][1] = "Flight 2833 to Burlington, Vermont">
```

NOTE

Although the preceding example is almost the same as declaring a two-dimensional array using `ArrayNew(2)`, it is a bit different in practice. `ArrayNew(2)` creates the second dimension in `aFlightInfo[2]` automatically, whereas the preceding example would require that you create a second array manually. Consider the following:

```
<!--- this would print a "yes" --->
<CFSET aFlightInfo = ArrayNew(2)>
<CFOUTPUT>#IsArray(aFlightInfo[2])#</CFOUTPUT>
```

The preceding works whereas the following fails:

```
<!--- this would throw an error aFlightInfo[2] not created --->
<CFSET aFlightInfo = ArrayNew(1)>
<CFSET aFlightInfo[1] = ArrayNew(1)>
<CFOUTPUT>#IsArray(aFlightInfo[2])#</CFOUTPUT>
```

Three-Dimensional Arrays

With two-dimensional arrays defined as arrays of arrays, three-dimensional arrays are arrays of arrays of arrays. In the previous example, the `aFlightInfo` array had destination and crew information and therefore required two dimensions. For destination information, a third dimension would make it possible to list all the flight's destinations in the order they occur each day. For crew information, a third dimension would enable you to list the captain and second and third officers on the flight deck. You could do so by manually creating new arrays in each index or by passing a `3` to the `ArrayNew()` function:

```
<CFSET aFlightInfo = ArrayNew(3)>
<!--- the first index is for flight 2833 Destinations --->
<CFSET aFlightInfo[1][1][1] = "Burlington, VT">
<CFSET aFlightInfo[1][1][2] = "Lebanon, NH">
<CFSET aFlightInfo[1][1][2] = "Springfield, MA">
<!--- we're still on flight 2833 --->
<!--- now we're on [1][2] which represents flight crew --->
<CFSET aFlightInfo[1][2][1] = "Alicia Ouellette">
<CFSET aFlightInfo[1][2][2] = "Sampson Reider">
```

> **TIP**
>
> `ArrayNew()` supports only three dimensions. For four-dimensional arrays and higher, you must manually declare new arrays for each index. You can quickly create a six-dimensional array by using `ArrayNew(3)` twice as follows:
>
> ```
> <CFSET aBigArray = ArrayNew(3)>
> <!--- now we'll make a 3 dimensional array in aBigArray --->
> <CFSET aBigArray[1][1][1] = ArrayNew(3)>
> <CFSET aBigArray[1][1][1][1][1][1] = "I am the 6th dimesion ">
> ```

Looping Over and Printing Multidimensional Arrays

To present the values in a multidimensional array, you need to nest loops. Because each embedded array has a different length, the length of each must be obtained using `ArrayLen()`. Because the complex data elements are not printable, you use loops to access the simple data elements individually as follows:

```
<CFSET aFlightInfo = ArrayNew(2)>
<CFSET aFlightInfo[1][1] = "Flight 2833 to Burlington, Vermont">
<CFSET aFlightInfo[1][2] = "Captain Alicia Ouellette on duty">
<CFSET aFlightInfo[2][1] = "Flight 7073 to Albany, New York">
<CFSET aFlightInfo[2][2] = "Captain Brian Smith on duty">
<CFLOOP FROM="1" TO="#ArrayLen(aFlightInfo)#" INDEX="i">
     Flight Info:
     <CFLOOP FROM="1" TO="#ArrayLen(aFlightInfo[i])#" INDEX="j">
     <CFOUTPUT>#aFlightInfo[i][j]#</CFOUTPUT>
     </CFLOOP> <BR>
</CFLOOP>
```

> **NOTE**
>
> Arrays of arrays are otherwise known as multidimensional arrays. It is important to understand that arrays can also contain other types of complex data such as queries and structures. Because structures have not been covered yet, this topic will be revisited in Chapter 15, "Structures."

> **TIP**
>
> Arrays can hold complex data, and complex data can also contain arrays. The `SESSION`, `APPLICATION`, and `REQUEST` scopes can hold arrays through the following statement:
>
> ```
> <CFSET Session.aFlightInfo = ArrayNew(1)>
> ```
>
> It is illegal to declare arrays in the `CLIENT` scope.

→ `SESSION` and `CLIENT` scopes were covered in Chapter 11, "Session State Management."

Summary

Arrays are an important type of complex data. They allow you to order data and do easy calculations on data sets. Arrays are useful for embedding other arrays and complex data. Arrays can also be combined with `SESSION` or `APPLICATION` scopes. Special attention must be given to resizing arrays and empty values within them.

Sample Questions

1. What function do you use to create an array? (Choose one.)
   A. `ArrayNew()`
   B. `ListToArray()`
   C. `ArrayCopy()`
   D. Both A and B

2. The following code produces an error.

```
<CFSET aThat = ArrayNew(1)>
<CFSET aThat[1] = ArrayNew(1)>
<CFSET aThat[2][1] = "test">
<CFSET aThat[3] = "test">
<CFOUTPUT>#aThat[3]#</CFOUTPUT>
```

   Why does the error occur?
   A. Index 3 cannot hold a simple value.
   B. Index 2 does not contain an array.
   C. Both A and B.
   D. None of the above.

3. Why will this code fail? (Choose two.)

```
<CFSET aThis = ArrayNew(1)>
<CFSET ArrayResize(aThis,400)>
<CFSET LoopUntil = ArrayLen(aThis)>
<CFLOOP FROM="1" TO="#LoopUntil#" INDEX="i">
<CFSET ArrayDelete(aThis,i)>
</CFLOOP>
```

   A. `<CFSET>` requires an equal sign.
   B. An array must be resized to a size greater than 500.
   C. `ArrayDelete()` will fail.
   D. The loop will go past the array's length.

4. Which two of the following statements are false?
   A. An associative array is a form of array.
   B. Multidimensional arrays are "arrays in arrays."
   C. Arrays can have a maximum of three dimensions.
   D. One-dimensional arrays can contain simple values.

CHAPTER 15

Structures

Structures Defined

Like arrays, structures are complex variables capable of holding multiple values simultaneously. One of the big differences between structures and arrays is that arrays are ordered, whereas structures are not. Another major difference is that arrays are indexed, whereas structures are accessed by a *key*. A key is more flexible than an array index because it can be any combination of numbers, letters, or special characters.

In thinking about the `aFlightInfo` array from Chapter 14, "Arrays," you were concerned about the order of flight destinations. Because order mattered, you used an array. Yet you may need to look up plenty of things about a flight without worrying about order, such as the flight number or equipment type. For these values, you will switch from an array to a structure and thereby rename the example `stFlightInfo`.

> **NOTE**
> Allaire documentation and training materials recommend prefixing structures with a lowercase *st,* such as `stFlightInfo`. This is not required, but it does help in that, when you're reading the code, you'll know that the variable is a structure.

When to Use Structures

Almost any ColdFusion task could be accomplished without structures, but the programming logic would not be as readable or concise. Structures are capable of some things, however, that simple variables are not.

- Structures can send complex data to different scopes such as a custom tag.

- With structures, you can specify two values in a single <CFSET> statement. You do so by using a special kind of structure known as an *associative array*, which will be described later in this chapter.
- Many things in ColdFusion are exposed as structure variables. If you don't have a firm grasp of structures, it is impossible to work with advanced custom tags, thorough error handling, and numerous other features.

→ Custom tags will be discussed in Chapters 22, "Custom Tags," and 23, "Advanced Custom Tags." Error handling is the focus of Chapter 21, "Error Handling."

Creating Structures

You create structures by using the function `StructNew()`. This function, shown here, takes no arguments:

```
<CFSET stFlightInfo = StructNew()>
```

After you create the structure, you can assign values based on certain keys. You can place the keys after the structure using a period (this is sometimes called *dot notation* or *object/property syntax*) or place them inside brackets much like an array (known as *array syntax*), as follows:

```
<CFSET stFlightInfo = StructNew()>
<!--- this key is called 'equipment' and uses dot notation --->
<CFSET stFlightInfo.equipment = "Boeing 777">
<!--- this key is called 'flight number' and uses array syntax --->
<CFSET stFlightInfo["flight number"] = "7050">
```

Notice that quotation marks surround the key `"flight number"` in the example. Without the quotation marks, ColdFusion would attempt to evaluate the key as an expression:

```
<CFSET stFlightInfo = StructNew()>
<!--- this key is called 'equipment' and uses dot notation --->
<CFSET stFlightInfo.equipment = "Boeing 777">
<!--- the key will be a variable instead of a literal --->
<CFSET newKey = "flight number">
<CFSET stFlightInfo[newKey] = "7050">
```

NOTE

Using array syntax is preferable to using dot notation when keys start with numbers or contain special characters. If dot notation is used, the variable must adhere to ColdFusion's variable naming restrictions. `stFlightInfo.flight info` would throw an error because the key name contains a space.

You can make the key dynamic by piecing the variable together using # signs, but this approach is not as clear-cut as using array syntax.

You will not notice any measurable performance differences between array syntax and dot notation.

➔ Variables and expressions were discussed in Chapter 2, "Working with Variables and Expressions" and Dynamic variable naming will be covered in Chapter 17, "Dynamic Functions."

Types of Structures

Officially, structures do not have different types at all. Allaire documentation, however, makes a distinction between a standard structure and an associative array. Associative arrays store two values at once, whereas standard structures store property/value pairs.

To understand this concept, think about an `"equipment"` key in `stFlightInfo`. This key is a property of the flight. But what if you added a key called `"Boeing 757"`? It would not be a property per se, but more of a value for an implicit property (the equipment property). The `"Boeing 757"` key would be associated with another value: `"December 22, 1994"` (the date the Boeing 757 was manufactured). When you associate two values together as follows, the `stFlightInfo` structure becomes an associative array:

```
<CFSET stFlightInfo = StructNew()>
<!--- the first example uses a key as a property --->
<CFSET stFlightInfo["equipment"] = "Boeing 757">
<!--- start over with the array for example 2 --->
<CFSET stFlightInfo = StructNew()>
<!--- the second example uses a key as a value: the equipment --->
<!--- the date is associated with the equipment value --->
<!--- associating two values is known as an associative array --->
<CFSET stFlightInfo["Boeing 757"] = "Manufactured on December 22, 1994">
```

TIP

Associative arrays are frequently used to look up one value based on another.

Looping Over Structures

When looping over a structure using `<CFLOOP>`, you have no control over the order of the structure's keys. If order were an important factor, an array would be used instead. To loop over a structure, `<CFLOOP>` requires the attributes `COLLECTION` and `ITEM`. The `ITEM` attribute steps through the keys of the structure with each loop as follows:

```
<!--- create a structure and put some key / values in it --->
<CFSET stFlightInfo = StructNew()>
<CFSET stFlightInfo["flight number"] = "7010">
<CFSET stFlightInfo["destination"] = "Albany, NY">

<!--- now loop through the structure --->
<!--- this will print 'the FLIGHT NUMBER is 7010' and --->
<!--- this will also print 'the DESTINATION is Albany, NY'--->
<!--- note that FLIGHT NUMBER and DESTINATION are uppercase! --->
<!--- This will print DESTINATION first - no control over key order --->
```

```
<CFLOOP COLLECTION="#stFlightInfo#" ITEM="i">
     <CFOUTPUT>The #i# is #stFlightInfo[i]#</CFOUTPUT><BR>
</CFLOOP>
```

Some important aspects of this example will further define a structure's behavior. When you're defining the collection attribute of `<CFLOOP>`, you must use quotation marks and `#` signs to surround the structure's name. The variable `i` changes from `"flight number"` to `"destination"` as the loop repeats. Using `i` as the key of `stFlightInfo` alternates the output from `"7010"` to `"Albany, NY"`. But what is not obvious here is that printing `#i#` alone will be uppercase, but printing `#stFlightInfo[i]#` will be its original case. ColdFusion saves a structure's keys as uppercase and preserves the original case of a structure's value.

As discussed earlier, structure keys are not ordered. So, even though `"Flight Number"` is placed in the structure prior to `"Destination"`, it is actually printed second.

> **NOTE**
>
> Although it may seem like unordered and uppercase keys would be problematic, this is the sacrifice you must pay for performance. Accessing data within a structure is incredibly fast.

> **TIP**
>
> Keys are rarely printed. Instead, you use keys to access or print values. Also, you rarely loop through a collection to print data but rather to find a certain key or value. For these reasons, you should not feel any pain from the unordered, uppercase nature of a structure's keys.

Internal Structures

Due to their speed and versatility, structures are employed by ColdFusion for their internal data. The following variable prefixes are structures in ColdFusion:

- `SESSION`
- `APPLICATION`
- `COOKIE`
- `URL`
- `REQUEST`
- `ATTRIBUTES`
- `FORM`
- `CGI`
- `CFCATCH`
- `CFERROR`
- `THISTAG`

As of ColdFusion 4.5, the following variable prefixes are not structures in ColdFusion:

- `SERVER`
- `CLIENT`
- `FILE`
- `CFHTTP`
- `CFFTP`

> **TIP**
>
> Knowing about structures translates into your having a stronger grasp of ColdFusion in general. You can flush `SESSION` variables, for example, by issuing `StructClear(session)`.

➔ `SESSION` variables were covered in Chapter 11, "Session State Management."

Combining Complex Data

As was the case with multidimensional arrays, you can combine complex data with itself. Rather than make arrays of arrays, as detailed in the preceding chapter, you can combine arrays with structures and structures with themselves.

Arrays of Structures

Combining structures with arrays supplies you with a perfect combination. You use arrays for their capability to maintain order. You use structures for their capability to store information by logical key names rather than numbers. By combining the two, you can create an ordered array of structures.

Looking back at the preceding chapter's array examples, you can see that two-dimensional arrays have certain drawbacks that could be solved by swapping a structure for the array in the second dimension. Imagine taking a trip from San Francisco to Burlington, Vermont. The trip involves changing planes in Chicago. The order of the flights is important, so you want to store the flights in an array. But a lot of other pertinent information about each flight does not need to be ordered at all, such as the flight number, destination, equipment, and crew. Using an embedded array for this information would be illogical and potentially hazardous.

Example 1 uses a two-dimensional array and is flawed. Example 2 uses an array of structures and is the preferred method.

Example 1

```
<CFSET aFlightInfo = ArrayNew(2)>
<!--- the first flight --->
<!--- second index stores info about the flight --->
<CFSET aFlightInfo[1][1] = "Flight Number 48">
<CFSET aFlightInfo[1][2] = "Chicago, Illinois">
<CFSET aFlightInfo[1][3] = "Boeing 737">
<CFSET aFlightInfo[1][4] = "Captain Alicia Ouellette">
```

```
<!--- the second flight --->
<!--- flight numbers in [1], destinations in [2] etc--->
<!--- if destination were deleted from [2]...--->
<!--- it would shift the equipment into [2] BAD! --->
<CFSET aFlightInfo[2][1] = "Flight Number 3022">
<CFSET aFlightInfo[2][2] = "Burlington, Vermont">
<CFSET aFlightInfo[2][3] = "Boeing 737">
<CFSET aFlightInfo[2][4] = "Captain Charlotte Rose">
```

Example 2

```
<CFSET aFlightInfo = ArrayNew(1)>
<!--- the first flight --->
<!--- the second index allows us to store information about the flight --->
<CFSET aFlightInfo[1]= StructNew()>
<CFSET aFlightInfo[1]["flight number"] = "48">
<CFSET aFlightInfo[1]["destination"] = "Chicago, Illinois">
<CFSET aFlightInfo[1]["equipment"] = "Boeing 737">
<CFSET aFlightInfo[1]["captain"] = "Captain Alicia Ouellette">
<!--- the second flight --->
<!--- now we see the advantages...--->
<!--- deleting "destination" has no impact on other keys --->
<CFSET aFlightInfo[2]["flight number"] = "3022">
<CFSET aFlightInfo[2]["destination"] = "Burlington, Vermont">
<!--- etc... --->
```

> **NOTE**
>
> Example 1 is flawed for the following reason: If you remove an index from the second dimension, you are disorganizing your data. For example, by deleting `aFlightInfo[1][2]`, you push what was once in `[1][3]` down to `[1][2]`. This change seems to conflict with how each array is organized because the second index of the second dimension always holds destinations. Example 2 does not have such a problem because you can reference the data by what it is rather than how it is ordered.

Structures of Arrays

Arrays of structures fit the bill when order is primary (first dimension of `aFlightInfo`) and logic is secondary (second dimension of `aFlightInfo`). Turn these two priorities around, and the result is a structure of arrays. Rethinking the flight information data would require a new scenario. Perhaps each flight has certain destinations during the course of a day. In this case, the flight number is primary, and the destinations are secondary, as shown here:

```
<CFSET stFlightInfo = StructNew()>
<CFSET stFlightInfo["Flight 54"] = ArrayNew(1)>
<CFSET stFlightInfo["Flight 54"][1] = "Washington DC">
<CFSET stFlightInfo["Flight 54"][2] = "Boston MA">
<CFSET stFlightInfo["Flight 54"][3] = "Burlington VT">
```

TIP

Looping over data such as this would involve nesting loops much like a multidimensional array:

```
<!--- an extension of the structure of arrays example above... --->
<!--- This will print all flights and their destinations in order --->
<CFLOOP COLLECTION="#stFlightInfo#" ITEM="i"><P>
     <CFLOOP FROM="1" TO="#arrayLen(stFlightInfo[i])#" INDEX="j">
     <CFOUTPUT>#stFlightInfo[i][j]#</CFOUTPUT><BR>
     </CFLOOP>
</CFLOOP>
```

Structures of Structures

You can place structures inside other structures when information is hierarchical. Keys are used to store the topmost element such as the flight number. A structure is declared for this key, and another key is defined. This second key could be either a property of that flight (destination) or another structure containing further details (crew names), as shown here:

```
<CFSET stFlightInfo = StructNew()>
<CFSET stFlightInfo["54"] = StructNew()>
<CFSET stFlightInfo["54"]["destination"] = "Chicago, Ill">
<CFSET stFlightInfo["54"]["crew"] = StructNew()>
<CFSET stFlightInfo["54"]["crew"]["captain"] = "Jacob Reider">
<CFSET stFlightInfo["54"]["crew"]["purser"] = "John Sampson">
```

NOTE

Because structures can use dot notation *or* array syntax, you can mix the two. You could write the preceding structure `stFlightInfo["54"].crew.purser` if you prefer. The first structure would have to stay in array syntax because `"54"` is not a legal variable name.

Structures as Pointers

In many programming languages, the term *pointer* signifies that multiple variables can all share the same memory space. With pointers, the variables may have different names, but the values will always be the same because they refer to the same place in memory. ColdFusion stores all structures as pointers.

Although ColdFusion's structure storage has no effect with most ColdFusion templates, it has prodigious consequences when structures are copied because it is not actually a copy that is made but a new way to point to the same values.

For example, `stFlightInfo` is copied into a new structure called `stNewFlight`, as shown in the following code. Now that you have a copy, you should be able to alter its values without a problem. But because the second copy is not a new structure at all, but rather a pointer to the original, changing data in one changes the data in both. After all, there is no second structure per se; there are simply two variables pointing to the same structure in memory.

```
<CFSET stFlightInfo = StructNew()>
<CFSET stFlightInfo.destination = "Burlington, VT">
<!--- copy the structure --->
<CFSET stNewFlight = stFlightInfo>
<CFSET stNewFlight.destination = "Hyannis, MA">
<!--- if you think this will print "Burlington" you are wrong! --->
<CFOUTPUT>#stFlightInfo.destination#</CFOUTPUT>
```

TIP

To create an entirely new structure based on the original, use the `StructCopy()` function.

TIP

Because the `SESSION` and `APPLICATION` scopes are cached variables, declaring nested structures within these scopes is advantageous. When you do so, structures persist across page requests.

To declare structures this way, you use a simple `session.varName = StructNew()` statement.

Referring to Queries Using Structure and Array Syntax

ColdFusion query recordsets are complex data types. Although they are neither structures nor arrays, they have been compared to structures of arrays by the ColdFusion community because of the syntactical similarities between the two. You can refer to a query using the standard `QUERYNAME.COLUMNAME` syntax much like a structure. Yet because there are multiple records within a query, you also can refer to a query as `QUERYNAME.COLUMNAME[RECORDNUMBER]`. Consider the following example:

```
<CFQUERY NAME="qGetFlightData" DATASOURCE="FlightInfoDB">
SELECT flightNumber, Destination from flights
ORDER BY destination
</CFQUERY>

<!--- instead of using CFOUTPUT,  use a CFLOOP and array syntax--->
<CFLOOP FROM="1" TO="#qGetFlightData.RecordCount#" INDEX="i">
     <CFOUTPUT>
          Flight Number: #qGetFlightData.flightNumber[i]#
```

```
        destination: #qGetFlightData.flightNumber[i]#
    </CFOUTPUT><BR>
</CFLOOP>
```

Again, queries are neither structures nor arrays; they are queries. Using array functions on a query would throw an error. Yet this array syntax can be useful when you don't need to show every record or multiple nested loops are causing problems.

Summary

Structures are a strong foundation of ColdFusion's architecture. Because much of ColdFusion's internal data is exposed through structures, mastering these complex data types is essential. Structures can store properties and value pairs or associated values. Structures are unordered, and the keys for structures are automatically uppercase when printed. The syntax used for structures is called *array syntax* or *dot notation*. The decision to use one or the other syntax is based on your preference and situational flexibility. Structures can contain other complex data types such as arrays, queries, or other structures.

Sample Questions

1. Choose the output of the following code.

   ```
   <CFSET a = structNew()>
   <CFSET b = a>
   <CFSET a.myVar = 1>
   <CFSET b.myVar = 2>
   <CFSET c = a.myVar + b.myVar>
   <CFSET c = c * b.myVar>
   <CFOUTPUT>#C#</CFOUTPUT>
   ```

   A. 4
   B. 8
   C. 16
   D. 36

2. Choose the correct syntax for looping over a structure.
   A. `<CFLOOP COLLECTION="stStruct" ITEM="i">`
   B. `<CFLOOP COLLECTION="#stStruct#" ITEM="s">`
   C. `<CFLOOP FROM="#stStruct#" TO="#structLen(stStruct)#" INDEX="i">`
   D. `<CFLOOP COLLECTION="#stStruct#" INDEX="i">`

3. Choose all the legal ways of setting values in a structure.
   A. `<CFSET structUpdate(stStruct,"3","hello")>`
   B. `<CFSET structInsert(stStruct,"3","hello")>`
   C. `<CFSET stStruct.3="hello">`
   D. `<CFSET stStruct[3]="hello">`

4. Choose all the statements that are true.
   A. Structure keys are ordered in the order they were set.
   B. Structure keys print in uppercase.
   C. Structure keys always need quotation marks when you use array syntax unless a key is a number or variable.
   D. Structure keys can be dynamic.

5. How can all `APPLICATION` variables be flushed from memory?
   A. `<CFSET structDelete(application,"all")>`
   B. `<CFSET tmp=StructDelete(application,"all")>`
   C. `<CFSET structClear(application)>`
   D. None of the above

PART 4

ADVANCED COLDFUSION

CHAPTER 16

Scripting

<CFSCRIPT>

Although ColdFusion Markup Language (CFML) is a complete language for building ColdFusion templates, you can use an alternative lexicon known as ColdFusion Script. A ColdFusion Script block is surrounded with an open and close <CFSCRIPT> tag as follows:

```
<CFSCRIPT>
// scripting will go here (note the different comment
syntax)
</CFSCRIPT>
```

Benefits of <CFSCRIPT>

Scripting offers a few advantages over using CFML tags. First, scripting is more concise. A <CFSCRIPT> block begins and ends with a CFML tag, but no tags are needed within the block itself. Second, scripting resembles JavaScript and could be easier for developers familiar with traditional development languages to relate to. Finally, scripting provides an easy way to work with the parameters and methods of external COM, CORBA, or EJB objects.

Drawbacks of <CFSCRIPT>

Although scripting is well suited for many tasks, it does not include all of ColdFusion's functionality. Some of ColdFusion's strongest features, such as query services, HTTP, FTP, email, and LDAP are not available within a <CFSCRIPT> block. In fact, only four features are available to the ColdFusion script writer:

1. Variable assignment
2. Looping

3. Conditional statements
4. Object invocation

Going beyond these four realms requires the use of ColdFusion's tag-based syntax.

> **NOTE**
>
> Although many of ColdFusion's services are not available through scripting, you can work with the data returned from these services. For example, a query may return 10 rows of data. Although the query could not be launched through scripting, the 10 rows of data are exposed with no contingencies.

Variable Assignment

In CFML, you assign variables by using the `<CFSET>` tag. In a `<CFSCRIPT>` block, you use a simple assignment statement followed by a semicolon, as follows:

```
<CFSCRIPT>
    // simple variable assignments
    x=1;
    y=2;
</CFSCRIPT>
```

> **NOTE**
>
> As with CFML tags, `<CFSCRIPT>` code is not case sensitive. Every statement in a script block is followed by a semicolon, much like Java or JavaScript. Comments in a script block are preceded by `//`.

As with the `<CFSET>` tag, temporary variables are not needed in a ColdFusion script block. For example, you can use a structure or array function without the need for an equal sign:

```
<CFSCRIPT>
    stMyStruct = StructNew();
    StructInsert(stMyStruct,"new key","new value");
    // the second statement needs no equals sign or temporary variable
</CFSCRIPT>
```

There has never been any need for temporary variables or equal signs in ColdFusion script blocks. Temporary variables were required, however, in `<CFSET>` statements before version 4.5.

Conditional Processing

Conditional processing with `<CFSCRIPT>` is similar to both Java and JavaScript. Much like CFML syntax, a conditional statement can be constructed in two ways: using either `IF` or `SWITCH/CASE`.

IF Examples

A sample IF statement appears as follows:

```
<CFSCRIPT>
     x = 1;
     if(x is 1)
     WriteOutput("In Spanish, the number one is 'uno'<BR>");
     //this line above will run if x is 1
     WriteOutput("<BR>thanks for using our Spanish number converter<BR>");
     // this line will ALWAYS run whether x is 1 or not
</CFSCRIPT>
```

The preceding statement evaluates x in the IF statement and prints "uno" to the browser. Note that no semicolon follows the IF statement. There is also no such thing as an END IF statement. All conditional processing statements run the next line if the expression is true. Therefore, the line that sends Spanish to the browser runs only if x is 1. The second printed statement, however, always runs.

To add statements to the conditional so that more than one line relies on x equaling 1, you must use curly braces like this:

```
<CFSCRIPT>
     x = 1;
     if(x IS 1) { //note the curly braces start here
     WriteOutput("In Spanish, the number one is 'uno'<br>");
     WriteOutput("Uno happens to be 'one' in Italian as well<br>");
     //both of these lines will run if x is 1
     } // the curly braces end
     WriteOutput("<BR>thanks for using our Spanish number converter");
     // this line will ALWAYS run whether x is 1 or not
</CFSCRIPT>
```

ELSE and ELSE IF statements are predictably similar to the preceding example, as you can see in the following code. Using curly braces is recommended to keep things in order, but they are not required.

```
<CFSCRIPT>
     x = 1;
     if(x IS 1)
     {
     WriteOutput("In Spanish, the number one is 'uno'<BR>");
     WriteOutput("Uno happens to be 'one' in Italian as well<BR>");
     }
     else if (x IS 2)
     WriteOutput("In Spanish, the number two is 'dos'<BR>");
     //no curly braces needed, but consider them to organize your code better
     else
     // this line below only runs if x is 2;
     WriteOutput("I don't know what that number is in Spanish<BR>");
     // this line below ALWAYS runs whether x is 1, 2 or something else
     WriteOutput("<BR>thanks for using our Spanish number converter");
</CFSCRIPT>
```

NOTE

You should notice a few things about the script blocks used so far. First, all conditional statements use the same operators as CFML. It is illegal to use = or < but legal to use the operators IS or LT.

Second, <CFSCRIPT> cannot have a <CFOUTPUT> block inside it and is therefore incapable of printing to the browser. To accomplish this task, you can use the WriteOutput() function.

Finally, although <CFOUTPUT> is not allowed within a script block, it is completely legal outside a block, as is any other CFML tag. By nesting a <CFSCRIPT> tag inside a <CFOUTPUT> or <CFLOOP> tag, you can loop over the script statement.

→ Conditional operators were covered in Chapter 3, "Conditional Processing." <CFLOOP> was covered in Chapter 4, "Looping," and <CFOUTPUT> looping techniques were discussed in Chapter 7, "Using Databases."

SWITCH/CASE Examples

A switch case in ColdFusion script is accomplished a bit differently than in CFML. Again, because you cannot use any tags in a <CFSCRIPT> block, you can turn to the following example in lieu of <CFSWITCH>:

```
<CFSCRIPT>
     x = 1;
     SWITCH(x) {
 CASE 1: {
WriteOutput("In Spanish, the number one is 'uno'");
WriteOutput("Uno happens to be 'one' in Italian as well");
BREAK;
}
CASE 2: {
WriteOutput("In Spanish the number two is 'dos');
BREAK;
}
DEFAULT: { WriteOutput("I don't know that number");}
}
</CFSCRIPT>
```

TIP

An important difference between the preceding example and the normal use of a <CFSWITCH> tag involves the BREAK statements needed within each CASE. If you do not place the BREAK statements in each CASE block, the default always runs in addition to the true CASE expression. You can use a missing break tag to your advantage if more than one case tag is to be observed. For instance, within the CASE 1 statement you could set x = 2. If CASE 1 doesn't have any break statements, the new value of x would lead to both CASE 1 and CASE 2 running.

Because ColdFusion runs from top to bottom, having a CASE 2 with x set back to 1 would not cause CASE 1 to run over again.

Looping

A loop construct usually consists of the same three elements. First, an expression takes place when the loop begins. Second, a condition is tested for each iteration and signals when the loop will conclude. Finally, an expression takes place when the loop ends. You create these three elements in various ways using the `<CFLOOP>` tag depending on the type of loop you require. In a `<CFSCRIPT>` block, the loop elements also vary depending on type. The different types of loops available to `<CFSCRIPT>` are described in the following sections.

FOR Loop

A `FOR` loop is one of the most common loop constructs. In a `FOR` loop, as shown in the following code, the loop iterates while the condition remains true:

```
<CFSCRIPT>
// the first loop element (index=1) runs BEFORE the loop
// the element (index LT 10) is the condition
// the last element (index = index+1) will run AFTER each iteration
FOR(index=1; index LT 10; index = index + 1)
// note there is no semi-colon after the loop declaration above
{
// curly braces encircle the code that will loop
     WriteOutput(index);
}
     WriteOutput("loop is done!");
// the above will print after the loop is finished.
</CFSCRIPT>
```

The preceding code prints the numbers 1 through 9. The condition in the loop (`index LT 10`) must be true while the loop iterates. As soon as `index` is 10, the loop terminates.

WHILE Loop

`WHILE` loops do not carry instance variables such as `index` in the `FOR` loop example. Rather, they simply break out of the loop when the condition is met, as shown in this example:

```
<CFSCRIPT>
a = 1;

WHILE (a LT 10)
{
    WriteOutputWriteOutput  ;
    a = a +1;
}
</CFSCRIPT>
```

DO-WHILE Loop

The difference between a `WHILE` loop and a `DO-WHILE` loop is that the condition is tested after each iteration instead of before.

```
<CFSCRIPT>

a=1;
DO
{
    WriteOutputWriteOutput  ;
    a = a +1;
}
WHILE (a LT 10);
</CFSCRIPT>
```

FOR-IN Statement

A `FOR-IN` statement deals exclusively with structures. The expression tested in a `FOR-IN` loop checks to see whether a specific key is inside a structure. Note that it does not actually loop but is used in lieu of a `CFIF`, as shown here:

```
<CFSCRIPT>
myStruct = structNew();
x=1;
mystruct[x]=0;
// x must be a variable fr the 'FOR' statement to work FOR (x IN myStruct)
{
WriteOutput;("this will run because x is 1 and 1 is a key of myStruct")
}
</CFSCRIPT>
```

NOTE

In both conditional and loop constructs, the `break` and `continue` statements serve important roles. The `break` statement exits the entire loop or conditional statement. The `continue` statement, to be used in loops only, iterates the loop from the beginning and runs any post-loop expressions, as in this example:

```
FOR (index=1; index LT 10; index = index + 1)
      {IF(index IS 5) continue;
      WriteOutput(index);
      }
//this will count from 1 to 9 but SKIP 5!
```

Invoking Objects

In ColdFusion 4.5, a new function called `CreateObject()` was added to the language. `CreateObject()` is a new way to call CORBA, COM Java Classes, and Enterprise Java Beans (EJB) from ColdFusion and is well suited for ColdFusion's scripting environment.

→ The alternative mechanism for calling objects from CFML is through the <CFOBJECT> tag. This tag will be covered in Chapter 24, "COM, CORBA, CFX, and Java."

Let's take Java into consideration as our example. An object in Java is created when the `CreateObject()` function is called and the first argument is passed as `"JAVA"` with a second argument as the class name. This loads the class into memory but does not call the constructor methods of the class. A constructor method is the section of Java that registers an instance of the object and appropriates memory for all its properties and methods. Because you can have more than one constructor method, you either must call the default constructor or initialize one directly. You call a specific constructor by referencing the object name and calling a special method known as `init`.

The following example calls a Java object called `BankAccount`. Note that the directory and file path of the `BankAccount.class` file needs to be set up in the ColdFusion Administrator under the JAVA section. A specific constructor is called by using the `init` method. JAVA cannot have more than one constructor that takes the same number of arguments, so the Java Virtual Machine runs the constructor that takes three arguments:

```
<CFSCRIPT>
// load the object into memory
BankAcc =  CreateObject("java","BankAccount");

// now initialize (call the constructor) of BankAccount
BankAcc.init("John Doe","Checking Account Deposit","$50");

// now call some other method of the object
BankAcc.SendMailer("Welcome New Customer Mailer");

// Set properties of the bank Account
if (customerCode is "no risk")
BankAcc.overdraftProtection = "True";
</CFSCRIPT>
```

Based on the preceding code, the Java class is called and invoked from a ColdFusion script block. Parameters and methods of the object can be accessed using the Object name returned by the `CreateObject()` function.

Summary

ColdFusion scripting is an alternative to using CFML and offers a subset of CFML's functionality. Some developers see advantages to using ColdFusion script because it is more concise and tends to run faster in certain circumstances as of the ColdFusion 4.5 release. You cannot use ColdFusion scripting, however, to run queries or speak with external processes other than Java, COM, or CORBA objects. Primarily, you use the scripting language for variable assignments, looping, and conditional statements.

Sample Questions

1. Which of the following cannot be achieved in a `<CFSCRIPT>` block? (Choose all that apply.)
   A. Variable assignments
   B. Looping
   C. HTTP requests
   D. CORBA object invocation

2. Choose all the statements that are true.
   A. There are more operators (such as ++ and `&&`) in scripting than in CFML.
   B. Scripting is capable of doing everything CFML does.
   C. `SWITCH` and `CASE` are available only in `<CFSCRIPT>` blocks.
   D. Scripting allows for `DO-WHILE` looping.

3. What is the output of the following code?

```
<CFSCRIPT>
x=1;
SWITCH(x){
      CASE 1: {x=2; WriteOutput("-World-");}
      CASE 2: {x=1; WriteOutput("-Hello-");}
}
</CFSCRIPT>
```

   A. `"Hello World"`
   B. `"World Hello World"`
   C. `"World"`
   D. `"World Hello"`

CHAPTER 17

Dynamic Functions

Using Dynamic Functions

ColdFusion features three dynamic functions that are all designed to facilitate the run-time creation and evaluation of expressions (and thus *dynamic*). Using a dynamic expression to access or assign variables, it is possible to replace multiple lines of `<CFIF>` and `<CFSET>` statements with a single line of code. The dynamic functions are `IIf()`, `DE()`, and `Evaluate()`. All these functions will be covered in the next few pages.

> **NOTE**
> The ColdFusion documentation lists one additional dynamic function. The one we do not cover in this chapter is the `SetVariable()` function. The reason for this is that this function is not very powerful now that ColdFusion can set variables within other expressions. The `SetVariable()` had more benefits in previous versions of ColdFusion.

→ One of these techniques, dynamic variable assignments, is covered in Chapter 22, "Custom Tags."

> **CAUTION**
> Dynamic functions take longer to parse and optimize than other functions. Be aware that your performance will suffer from using these functions.

IIf()

The name of the `IIf()` function is derived from the programming concept "Immediate IF." The function is used as a powerful replacement of an IF/ELSE statement. The syntax of the `IIf()` function is as follows:

```
IIf(condition, string expression1, string expression2)
```

All three of these arguments are comprised of ColdFusion expressions. The condition is the expression that will be tested. If the condition is `TRUE`, `string expression1` will be returned; if it is `FALSE`, `string expression2` is returned. Because `IIf()` returns something based on a Boolean (`TRUE` or `FALSE`), it is to be used in place of a simple IF/ELSE statement. Yet, because an `IIf()` occupies one line of code, it is much more concise than an IF/ELSE statement. Take the following examples:

Example 1: IF/ELSE

```
<CFIF DayOfWeek(now()) IS 1>
    <!--- we are closed on Sunday --->
    <CFSET bClosed=1>
<CFELSE>
    <!--- we are open all other days --->
    <CFSET bClosed=0>
</CFIF>
```

Example 2: `IIf()`

```
<CFSET IIf(DayOfWeek(Now()) IS 1,"bClosed=1","bClosed=0")>
<!--- this does the same thing as example 1 but on 1 line! --->
```

> **TIP**
>
> Although example 2 is a true expression, there are times when a developer might want to return something printable. To return the string without evaluating it as an expression, single quotes can be used as follows:
>
> ```
> <CFSET IIf(DayOfWeek(Now()) IS 1,"bClosed=1","bClosed=0")>
> <CFOUTPUT>
>     #IIf(bClosed,"'We are closed!'","'We are open'")#
> </CFOUTPUT>
> <!--- The expressions will be returned without being evaluated --->
> ```
>
> Note that the `DE()` function could also be used instead of the single quote method. The `DE()` function will be explained in the next subsection.

It is important to understand that `IIf()` returns the result of the expression it has evaluated. Example 2's first use of `IIf()` might not appear to return anything at all, but it does. Setting a variable in ColdFusion returns the value of the variable itself. Therefore, the code in example 2 will return the number `1` if it is Sunday and the number `0` if it is not.

It is also important to understand how ColdFusion processes multiple expressions and what is returned after evaluating each one. ColdFusion evaluates multiple expressions from left to right and will return the rightmost expression. Therefore, using scripting syntax, we could place a number of expressions inside of the `IIf()` function and return the last one evaluated:

```
<CFSET bOpen=IIf(bClosed,"txt = 'closed';0","txt = 'open';1")>
<!--- there are TWO expressions (separated by semicolon) per condition --->
<!--- if bClosed is 1, then txt equals "closed" AND bOpen equals "0" --->
<!--- if bClosed is 0, then txt equals "open" AND bOpen equals "1" --->
<CFOUTPUT>
#txt# <!--- this wills print "open" or "closed" based on the IIf()--->
</CFOUTPUT>
```

> **CAUTION**
>
> There are two problems to take note of when using `IIf()`. The first point is that sometimes what is returned is not the actual value, but the return code `YES`, as is always the case when using functions such as `StructInsert()` and `StructUpdate()`. This will not necessarily cause errors, but must be taken into account.

➔ Structure functions and their return codes were covered in Chapter 15, "Structures."

> **CAUTION**
>
> The second and more hazardous problem is that as of ColdFusion 4.5, pound signs may not be used in an `IIf()` statement. Escaping pound signs by using two pound signs next to one another in a string is also not possible.

DE()

The `DE()` function (it stands for "Delay Evaluation") is mostly used within other dynamic functions such as `IIf()`. As you saw in the last subsection, there are times when control is needed over expression evaluation. If a certain function takes an expression as an argument, it will return the result of the expression after ColdFusion has processed it. If, however, the developer intends to return the expression itself, without evaluation, the `DE()` function will prevent ColdFusion from conducting this evaluation. There is a handful of reasons why this is useful, the most obvious one being the printing of a certain string within an `IIf()`.

```
<CFSET IIf(DayOfWeek(Now()) IS 1,"bClosed=1","bClosed=0")>
<CFOUTPUT>
    #IIf(bClosed,DE("we are closed"),DE("we are open"))#
</CFOUTPUT>
```

This example shows that `DE()` can be used just as the single quotes were used in the previous subsection: to escape evaluation and return the string. But the `DE()` function does more than return literals. Imagine if an expression were contained within a variable. A hypothetical example of this might be a text box in which a user could type an expression such as "2+2." The developer could check to make sure that the expression did not divide by zero and then return a result. To better understand this example, look at the following code:

```
<CFSET FORM.expression="2/0">
<!--- pretend that the user typed the above in and submitted the form--->
<CFOUTPUT>
#IIf(FORM.expression CONTAINS "/0",DE(FORM.expression),FORM.expression)#
</CFOUTPUT>
<!--- the above will print "2/0" as output. But if
FORM.expression was something that did not divide by zero
(which is illegal) the output would be the result of the
expression.  For instance 2+2 would result in 4. --->
```

Evaluate()

The `Evaluate()` function is used to return the result of an expression. Here is a simple example of the `Evaluate()` function:

```
<CFSET FORM.expression="2+2">
<CFSET result=Evaluate(FORM.expression)>
<CFOUTPUT>
    #FORM.expression# equals #result#
</CFOUTPUT>
<!--- this will print "2+2 equals 4" --->
```

Multiple expressions can be passed to the `Evaluate()` function as arguments. Remember that when ColdFusion processes multiple expressions, it always returns the rightmost one. In the two examples that follow, the rightmost expression is the one that is returned.

Example 1: Passing Multiple Expressions in One Argument

```
<CFSET FORM.expression="2+2">
<CFPARAM NAME="bCompleted" DEFAULT="0">
<CFSET result=Evaluate("bCompleted = 1; Evaluate(FORM.expression)")>
<!--- only 1 argument was passed to the evaluate function --->
<!--- there are 2 expressions in this 1 argument --->
<!--- the two expressions are separated with a semi-colon --->
<!--- without the second evaluate function we would return '2+2' not '4' --->
<CFOUTPUT>
#FORM.expression# equals #result# <BR>
#IIf(bCompleted,"'expression evaluated!'","'not evaluated'")#
</CFOUTPUT>
<!--- this will print "2+2 equals 4 expression evaluated!" --->
<!--- note that 2 expressions were passed --->
```

In this first example, the `Evaluate()` function has one argument with two expressions. The first expression sets the variable `bCompleted` equal to `"1"` and the second evaluates the expression `"2+2"` (which returns `"4"`). Because the rightmost expression is returned, `RESULT` equals `"4"` . The nested `Evaluate()` function is necessary to return the result (`"4"`) instead of the literal expression (`"2+2"`).

Example 2: Passing Multiple Expressions as Separate Arguments

```
<!--- we will add 2 to whatever number the user types in --->
<CFSET FORM.expression="2">
<CFPARAM NAME="bCompleted" DEFAULT="0">
<CFSET result=Evaluate("bCompleted = 1;x=2","FORM.expression + x")>
<CFOUTPUT>
#FORM.expression# plus 2 equals #result# <BR>
#IIf(bCompleted,"'expression evaluated!'","'not evaluated'")#
</CFOUTPUT>
<!--- this will print "2+2 equals 4 expression evaluated!" --->
<!--- note that 3 expressions were passed. --->
<!--- the big difference here is that one of the expressions set --->
<!--- a variable 'x' which was used in the latter expression --->
```

The only important difference between example 1 and example 2 is that example 2 can use the results of prior expressions in later ones because the arguments are fully evaluated from left to right. In example 1, setting a variable and using it in a later expression would cause an error because the expressions are in the same argument.

> **TIP**
>
> An interesting way of using the `Evaluate()` function is to piece expressions together through concatenation. For example, you could allow users to create ColdFusion variables on their own and decide if they were to be structures or arrays. This could be done by piecing together the correct function names and keys/indexes based on what the user selected in a form. Look at the following example:
>
> ```
> <CFPARAM NAME="FORM.createArray" DEFAULT="1">
> <CFPARAM NAME="FORM.createStructure" DEFAULT="0">
> <CFPARAM NAME="FORM.variableName" DEFAULT="myVar">
> <CFSET function1="ArrayNew">
> <CFSET function2="StructNew">
> <!--- did the user want to create an array? --->
> <CFIF FORM.CreateArray IS 1>
>  <CFSET Evaluate("FORM.variableName = " & function1 & "(1)")>
> <CFELSEIF FORM.CreateStructure IS 1>
>  <CFSET Evaluate("FORM.variableName = " & function2 & "()")>
> </CFIF>
> ```
>
> This logic actually creates a new array or structure by piecing together the correct combination of characters. If the user wants to create an array, we need to do an `ArrayNew(1)` and, if we need to create a structure, we need to issue a `StructNew()`. These are accomplished by using string expressions and concatenation within the evaluate argument.

Summary

Using the dynamic functions (`IIf()`, `DE()`, and `Evaluate()`) makes it possible to write powerful and highly reusable code in small and easy to manage code blocks.

Sample Questions

1. Choose all the statements that are true.
   A. The `DE()` function is always used to display output.
   B. The `DE()` function stops CF from processing expressions.
   C. `DE()` and `IIf()` can be used together.
   D. The letters in `DE()` stand for "DO EVALUATION."

2. What will the output of the following code be?
   ```
   <CFOUTPUT>#IIF(1 is 1,"1;2;3","'Hello'")#</CFOUTPUT>
   ```
   A. 1
   B. 2
   C. 3
   D. Hello

3. What does the following code do?
   ```
   <CFSET x="Array">
   <CFSET Evaluate("p = " & x & "New(1)")>
   ```
   A. Creates an array named "x."
   B. Creates an array named "p."
   C. The code will not work.
   D. None of the above.

4. What does z equal?
   ```
   <CFSET x="y">
   <CFSET y="x">
   <CFSET z = IIf(x is y,DE(x),x)>
   ```
   A. x
   B. y
   C. null
   D. None of the above

CHAPTER 18

Stored Procedures

Using Stored Procedures

Stored procedures are sequences of precompiled SQL statements stored in a database. These SQL statements are later referenced by name and executed at runtime. Because stored procedures are precompiled, they run considerably faster than SQL, which is sent from a client application such as those written in ColdFusion. They are sent via a <CFQUERY>.

In addition to being faster, stored procedures are also more secure than normal SQL statements. Stored procedures can perform SQL on a table that a user does not have access to, and a database administrator can create procedures that hide certain columns of data or do calculations before data is returned.

Stored procedures can be built to both accept and return parameters to a ColdFusion template. This means that a query can be dynamic. A stored procedure can also return recordsets back to ColdFusion in the form of an array or a query.

To issue a stored procedure against a database, you use the <CFSTOREDPROC> or <CFQUERY> tags.

> **NOTE**
>
> Most of the major database vendors offer stored procedure support with different advantages and disadvantages. Stored procedure syntax is different in each type of database, with many similarities between Microsoft SQL Server and Sybase because they were initially the same product. The following stored procedure code would run in either Sybase or Microsoft SQL Server:

```
Create Procedure spCheckInventory @status varchar(50)
As
declare @ret int
```

```
SELECT @ret = ProductRequestedID,productName
FROM Inventory
WHERE Status = @status
return (isNull(@ret,0))
```

The preceding statement needs to be executed once only. From that point on, the stored procedure will be called through the following SQL statement:

```
EXECUTE spCheckInventory 'in stock'
```

→ A full explanation of how ColdFusion integrates stored procedures is given in Chapter 35, "Advanced Database Features."

<CFQUERY> Versus <CFSTOREDPROC>

To execute a stored procedure, you can use either the <CFQUERY> or <CFSTOREDPROC> tags. However, if a native driver is not available and ODBC is used, the <CFSTOREDPROC> tag is your only option for executing a stored procedure. The reason for this is that <CFQUERY> will pass only ODBC-compliant SQL to an ODBC driver. Stored procedure execution code is not standard ODBC because it varies with each database engine.

You'll discover other advantages to using the <CFSTOREDPROC> tag besides its support within an ODBC environment. Stored procedures can return recordsets to the ColdFusion template more efficiently through the <CFSTOREDPROC> tag. This tag also provides support for multiple recordsets returned from a stored procedure, meaning that you can create more than one recordset from the same procedure. Finally, some variables, such as the status-code that is created when the tag is called, are not available through a <CFQUERY>.

The standard SQL for running a stored procedure is by referencing the stored procedure's name after the EXEC statement followed by parameters. The following example shows how ColdFusion would execute a stored procedure through the use of the <CFQUERY> tag:

```
<CFQUERY NAME="qCheckInventory" DATASOURCE="mySqlServer">
     EXEC spCheckInventory
     @Status = 'in stock'
</CFQUERY>
<!--- see what the status is and tell the user --->
<CFIF qCheckInventory.ret>That item is in inventory!</CFIF>
```

Again, this method of calling stored procedures is perfectly reasonable, yet the <CFSTOREDPROC> tag has a few advantages, which will be discussed in the next section.

Using <CFSTOREDPROC>

After you create a stored procedure, you use a <CFSTOREDPROC> tag to execute the query. This tag has two child tags that are used to pass parameters into the stored procedure and to receive data back. Parameters are sent to the stored procedure by the <CFPROCPARAM>

tag and can be received by either the <CFPROCPARAM> or <CFPROCRESULT> tags. The most efficient way to receive recordsets back from a stored procedure is to use the <CFPROCRESULT> tag because it returns data as a recordset.

> **NOTE**
>
> Older versions of ColdFusion did not support the <CFPROCRESULT> tag on Oracle and were therefore limited to using the <CFPROCPARAM> tag to both send and receive data to the stored procedure.

<CFPROCPARAM>

Most stored procedures depend on parameters that are sent from the client application. For each parameter, a <CFPROCPARAM> tag is used. You must know each parameter's data type as it was declared in the stored procedure. This data type is passed as the required attribute CFSQLTYPE of the <CFPROCPARAM> tag.

Another required attribute of <CFPROCPARAM> is the TYPE attribute. It has three different values, as shown in Table 18.1, that affect other attributes in various ways.

Table 18.1 Options for the *TYPE* Attribute of *<CFPROCPARAM>*

Value	Description
IN	The parameter is expected by the stored procedure, and you are passing the parameter.
OUT	A result is expected from the stored procedure, and the <CFPROCPARAM> tag will be used to create a variable of a specific name to accept this returned data.
INOUT	Sending and receiving a parameter of the exact same name. If they were not named the same, you would have used a <CFPROCPARAM> for the IN parameter and a second <CFPROCPARAM> for the OUT parameter.

The <CFPROCPARAM> tag's VALUE attribute works only when it is sending parameters into the stored procedure using IN. This process is pretty intuitive. Alternatively, the VARIABLE attribute works only when it's getting parameters out of a stored procedure using OUT and represents the ColdFusion variable name holding the returned data. Finally, the DBVARNAME attribute passes the correct name of the stored procedure's variable, such as @RET in the stored procedure example at the beginning of this chapter.

> **TIP**
>
> At first glance, the <CFPROCPARAM> tag appears to the best way to get data in and out of a stored procedure. In reality, it is rarely used to get data out of a stored procedure. The tag was once the only solution available for Oracle developers because the <CFPROCRESULT> tag was not available to them. Because it now works with Oracle, using the <CFPROCRESULT> tag to attack most requirements is more efficient. This tag is covered in the next section.

> **NOTE**
> When more than one record is sent back from a <CFPROCRESULT> tag, it is exposed as an array.

<CFPROCRESULT>

The <CFPROCRESULT> tag is the final piece of the stored procedure puzzle. After a parameter is sent and the stored procedure is executed, a recordset can be returned to the ColdFusion server through this tag. The only required attribute of the tag is NAME, which creates the recordset variable in ColdFusion. The following example shows the tag in action:

```
<CFSTOREDPROC PROCEDURE="spCheckInventory" DATASOURCE="mySqlServer">
<!--- sent the parameter --->
<CFPROCPARAM TYPE="IN" CFSQLTYPE="CF_SQL_CHAR"
VALUE="in stock" DBVARNAME="@param1">
<!--- get the result back from the stored procedure --->
<CFPROCRESULT NAME = "qItemsInStock">
<!--- Note that CFSTOREDPROC has an END tag! --->
</CFSTOREDPROC>
<!--- here is what is in inventory --->
<CFOUTPUT QUERY="qItemsInStock">
    #productName#<BR>
</CFOUTPUT>
```

Multiple Recordsets

A very useful feature of stored procedures is their capability to return multiple recordsets to the client. ColdFusion supports this capability by giving different numbers to the <CFPROCRESULT> tag to identify each given recordset.

For this purpose, the RESULTSET attribute is available. The resultsets must be addressed specifically by their number, or they will not be exposed. If, for example, a stored procedure returns 10 recordsets and the RESULTSET attribute is not set, only the first recordset is returned. To take the example further, if the RESULTSET attribute is set to "10", only the last recordset is returned. Now consider the following example:

```
<!---  checkInventory returns multiple recordsets --->
<CFSTOREDPROC PROCEDURE="spCheckInventory" DATASOURCE="mySqlServer">
<!--- send the parameter --->
<CFPROCPARAM TYPE="IN" CFSQLTYPE="CF_SQL_CHAR"
VALUE="in stock" DBVARNAME="@param1">
<!--- get the FIRST result back from the stored procedure --->
<CFPROCRESULT NAME = "qMoreThan100InStock">
<!--- get the SECOND result back from the stored procedure --->
<CFPROCRESULT NAME = "qLessThan100InStock" RESULTSET = "2">
</CFSTOREDPROC>
<!--- here is what is in inventory --->
<CFOUTPUT QUERY="qMoreThan100InStock">
```

```
    #productName#<BR>
</CFOUTPUT>
<CFOUTPUT QUERY="qLessThan100InStock">
    #productName#<BR>
</CFOUTPUT>
```

> **NOTE**
> Another optional attribute of the <CFPROCRESULT> tag is MAXROWS. This attribute limits the number of rows that come back from the stored procedure.

Summary

Stored procedures are precompiled SQL statements that are stored in a database and executed at runtime. Each database has its own stored procedure syntax that can be sent from ColdFusion using native drivers and a <CFQUERY>. A more efficient mechanism for calling stored procedures is the <CFSTOREDPROC> tag. This tag has an end tag and takes two possible nested tags: <CFPROCPARAM> and <CFPROCRESULT>. <CFPROCPARAM> can send and receive parameters, whereas <CFPROCRESULT> was built to take resultsets and expose them as ColdFusion recordsets.

Sample Questions

1. When are stored procedures better than views or queries? (Choose all that apply.)
   A. They execute faster.
   B. They are more secure.
   C. They are easier to create.
   D. They are standard through ODBC.

2. When should the TYPE attribute of the <CFPROCPARAM> tag be set to INOUT? (Choose one.)
   A. When a parameter needs to be sent back from a stored procedure only
   B. When a parameter is sent to a stored procedure and a different parameter is returned
   C. When a parameter of the same name is sent and received from the stored procedure
   D. When a stored procedure optionally accepts parameters

3. <CFPROCRESULT> returns what type of data?
   A. Structure of arrays
   B. Queries
   C. Arrays
   D. Simple Data

CHAPTER 19

Transactions

Using Transactions

Relational databases are used by millions of people every day. Many of these people are actually using the same databases simultaneously. Doing so would pose a problem if relational databases did not support transactions. Transactions prevent multiple users from editing the same data at the same time. They also allow a series of queries to succeed in bulk or not at all. If transactions were not possible, databases would be useless in multiuser environments.

Say that a college student runs out of money and asks his mother for a wire transfer. His mother goes to the bank, fills out the correct transfer forms, and hands them to the teller. The teller withdraws $100 from her account and in the same transaction deposits it into her son's account at his local bank a few hundred miles away. Because these two actions take place within a single database transaction, the withdrawal will be cancelled if the deposit fails. Therefore, even though the withdrawal is immediate, it is not "committed" to the database until the deposit succeeds a few minutes later at the remote bank. This idea of binding all actions in one transaction means that no money would be withdrawn from the mother's account unless the son's bank successfully took the deposit. Second, a transaction will "lock" the mother's bank account until it is finished. This prevents the woman from going to another teller to withdraw more money than her eventual balance would reflect.

Two concepts are critical to understanding transactions and can be translated into database features offered by the major database vendors. These two concepts are *locking* and *isolation*.

Locking

Locking is a simple idea that is exposed through complex algorithms in each database engine. Fortunately, for our purposes as ColdFusion developers, we need only concern ourselves with the simple ideas of exclusive or shared locking.

In the wire transfer example, the bank's database system might give exclusive privileges to the transaction so that no other reads could take place. If the woman conducting the wire transfer went to another teller to ask for her current balance, the second teller would inform her that her balance could not be calculated because a pending transaction was in process. This means that the wire transfer placed an exclusive lock on the information being changed. If, on the other hand, the teller told her that her balance was $300, this would mean that a shared lock had been placed on her account. A shared lock would allow her to see the balance but make no updates to it.

> **NOTE**
> Although an explanation of shared and exclusive locks is important, it does not mean that ColdFusion can declare locks on the database. Usually, locking is handled by the database on its own. In addition, databases can escalate a lock from record to table to database, depending on how much data is being modified. ColdFusion has no bearing on these affairs. Yet ColdFusion does have the capability to change isolation levels, which affects the lock type. Isolation levels are covered next.

Isolation

Isolation levels are the only way that ColdFusion can recommend lock types to the relational database. Isolation levels were created to increase performance by giving the database a "plan" for locking records before the transaction executes.

Four isolation levels are supported by relational databases, and all are subsequently supported by ColdFusion's transaction tags. These four isolation levels are covered in the following four sections.

> **NOTE**
> The isolation levels described next affect performance. They are listed from the worst performing (`SERIALIZABLE`) to the best (`READ COMMITTED`).

→ Other performance considerations related to the ColdFusion server are explored in Chapter 38, "Server Performance Tuning."

SERIALIZABLE

`SERIALIZABLE` is the highest isolation level provided by a database and is also the default. `SERIALIZABLE` isolation is equivalent to an exclusive lock. No data can be read by other transactions until the transaction that owns the lock is finished.

REPEATABLE READ

REPEATABLE READ is the second highest isolation level. A repeatable read is similar to the SERIALIZABLE level except that other SQL statements can insert data during the transaction and potentially change the results of a transaction if the transaction repeats a query that yields the newly inserted data. If you know ahead of time that inserted data will not affect the transaction, using REPEATABLE READ is preferred to using a SERIALIZABLE isolation level for performance reasons.

READ COMMITTED

The third highest level of isolation, READ COMMITTED, means that locks will be shared for both inserts and updates across transactions. So a transaction could read some data once and, before finishing, read the data that had changed since the original read a second time. Note that the other transactions (the ones updating) must be finished for the read to be different. A successfully finished transaction is said to have been *committed.*

READ UNCOMMITTED

The final level of isolation and the best performing of the four is READ UNCOMMITTED. This isolation level is the most dangerous to use because dirty reads are very likely. A *dirty read* occurs when a certain transaction reads data that has not been committed. If this isolation level were employed for the wire transfer example, the woman could be the victim of some erroneous accounting. Say that the bank were to run its interest rate calculations on her account after her withdrawal of $100. Now imagine if her son's bank went offline and was not able to accept the deposit. Because the entire transaction would fail, her interest rates would be calculated incorrectly. In this way, a READ UNCOMMITTED isolation level allows inserts and updates to be read whether or not a transaction has finished.

<CFTRANSACTION>

Transactions and isolation levels are handled through the <CFTRANSACTION> tag. This tag takes an end tag and encircles all ColdFusion queries and logic pertinent to a given transaction. If no isolation levels are sent, the default would be SERIALIZABLE.

The following example demonstrates the wire transfer example. Notice that this example uses the custom tag <CFX_SENDWIRE> to send information to the son's bank. This tag does not really exist but is used to demonstrate the concept. This nonexistent tag returns the variable wireResult equal to 1 or 0 based on successful wire transfers.

```
<CFTRANSACTION>
     <!--- remove $100 from the woman's account --->
     <CFQUERY DATASOURCE="AccountDB">
     Update Account
     Set Balance =  Balance - 100
     Where AccountID = 4334044033
     </CFQUERY>
```

```
    <!--- enter the woman's name in the wire transfer log --->
    <CFQUERY DATASOURCE="TransferLog">
    Insert into transferLog
    (accountID,Time,BankID,wiredAmount,recipientAccountID)
    Values (4334044033,getDate(),3344212,100,4403343402)
    </CFQUERY>

    <!--- call C++ wire transfer library to send data to other bank --->
    <CFX_SENDWIRE BANKID="3344212" AMOUNT="100" ACCOUNTID ="4403343402">
    <CFIF wireResult is 0><CFABORT></CFIF>
    <!--- if aborted transaction won't finish--updates/inserts cancel --->
</CFTRANSACTION>
```

> **NOTE**
> <CFTRANSACTION> has no required attributes. The ISOLATION attribute can be set to READ_UNCOMMITTED, READ_COMMITTED, REPEATABLE_READ, and SERIALIZABLE. The default ISOLATION is SERIALIZABLE.

Controlling Commits

So far, we have looked at an example in which <CFTRANSACTION> took no attributes. We briefly explained isolation levels in the note following this example. The only other attribute for <CFTRANSACTION> is ACTION, which controls what is committed to a database and what is not.

COMMIT

When a transaction is finished and the close tag of <CFTRANSACTION> is found by the ColdFusion server, all the updates made to the database are subsequently committed. This means that the status of the updates changed from questionable to certain, and the locks are released.

If, however, a commit makes sense within a given transaction before the transaction's completion, a nested <CFTRANSACTION> tag can be used with an ACTION of COMMIT. Turning back to the wire transfer example, say that the woman decided to give wire transfers to all her children instead of just one. In this new situation, the bank considers this a single transaction and thus locks the table once. But each successful deposit can force a COMMIT to the database and allow other transactions to read more accurate balance information. The new example looks like this:

```
<CFTRANSACTION>
    <!--- here is a list of all her children's bank IDs ---->
    <CFSET bankIDList = "234234234,2345234,6456456456,34534345">
    <!--- here is a list of all her children's account numbers --->
    <CFSET AccountIDList = "34234234,234562345,6123563,635789345">

    <!--- 4 accounts... loop four times --->
<CFLOOP FROM = 1 TO= 4 INDEX="i">
    <!--- remove $100 from the woman's account --->
```

```
    <CFQUERY DATASOURCE="AccountDB">
    Update Account
    Set Balance =  Balance - 100
    Where AccountID = 4334044033
    </CFQUERY>

    <!--- call the wire transfer tag (sends data to bank #2 --->
    <CFX_SENDWIRE BNKID="#listGetAt(bankIDList,i)#"
       AMOUNT="100" ACCOUNTID ="#listGetAt(AccountIDList,i)#">
    <CFIF wireResult is 0><CFABORT></CFIF>
    <CFTRANSACTION ACTION="COMMIT"/>
       <!--- commit each deposit when it completes --->
</CFLOOP>

    <!--- enter the woman's name in the wire transfer log --->
    <CFQUERY DATASOURCE="TransferLog">
    Insert into transferLog
    (accountID,Time,BankIDList,wiredAmount,recipientAccountIDList)
    Values (4334044033,getDate(),'#bankIDList#',100,'#accountIDList#')
    </CFQUERY>

</CFTRANSACTION>
```

NOTE

The statement `<CFTRANSACTION ACTION="COMMIT"/>` may look strange because of the forward slash at the end of it. This slash is known as *XML syntax* and is required by ColdFusion for tags that always take end tags. Because this specific example of `<CFTRANSACTION>` doesn't have an end tag, you must signify the end tag with the forward slash. The alternative would be to specify `<CFTRANSACTION ACTION="COMMIT"><CFTRANSACTION/>` (with nothing in between the two tags), which is both legal and supported.

ROLLBACK

Another `ACTION` type in addition to `COMMIT` is `ROLLBACK`. Rolling back is a way of telling the transaction to purposely fail. In database vernacular, these two are the only options for any transaction. Either a transaction commits the new changes, or it rolls back to the original state of the database.

Using `ROLLBACK` is a better solution for the example than using `<CFABORT>`. If you look at the sample code so far, it will abort based on a deposit failure at one of the children's banks. This is not the best scenario because each deposit is contingent on the success of the previous one. Instead of using `<CFABORT>`, you can use `<CFTRANSACTION ACTION="ROLLBACK"/>` (note the XML syntax as explained in the preceding note).

```
<CFTRANSACTION>
    <!--- here is a list of all her children's bank IDs --->
    <CFSET bankIDList = "234234234,2345234,6456456456,34534345">
```

```
    <!--- here is a list of all her children's account numbers --->
    <CFSET AccountIDList = "34234234,234562345,6123563,635789345">

    <!--- 4 accounts... loop four times --->
<CFLOOP FROM = "1" TO= "4" INDEX="i">
    <!--- remove $100 from the woman's account --->
    <CFQUERY DATASOURCE="AccountDB">
    Update Account
    Set Balance =  Balance - 100
    Where AccountID = 4334044033
    </CFQUERY>

    <!--- call the C++ wire transfer  tagsends data to the other bank --->
    <CFX_SENDWIRE BNKID="#listGetAt(bankIDList,i)#" AMOUNT="100"
       ACCOUNTID ="#listGetAt(AccountIDList,i)#">
    <CFIF wireResult is 0>
         <CFTRANSACTION ACTION="ROLLBACK"/>
       <!--- rollback on failures --->
    <CFELSE>
         <CFTRANSACTION ACTION="COMMIT"/>
       <!--- commit each deposit when it completes --->
    </CFIF>
</CFLOOP>

    <!--- enter the woman's name in the wire transfer log --->
    `<CFQUERY DATASOURCE="TransferLog">
    Insert into transferLog
    (accountID,Time,BankIDList,wiredAmount,recipientAccountIDList)
    Values (4334044033,getDate(),'#bankIDList#',100,'#accountIDList#')
    </CFQUERY>

</CFTRANSACTION>
```

NOTE

The third and last option for the `ACTION` attribute is `BEGIN`. It indicates that a transaction is starting and is the default value.

NOTE

Within many client/server systems, you need to start a transaction in a window and continue it through other windows until it is committed or rolled back. Unfortunately, ColdFusion has a template-based architecture and, as such, does not support this type of transaction. All transactions must be started and ended on the same page.

> **TIP**
>
> A popular technique for database administrators is to build transactions into stored procedures instead of using the <CFTRANSACTION> tags. As was discussed in Chapter 18, stored procedures are precompiled and run faster than passing SQL from ColdFusion. In addition, multiple transactions can be placed within a single stored procedure, allowing transactions to complete regardless of the ColdFusion server's availability. Finally, some databases, such as Microsoft's SQL Server, offer robust features wherein a transaction can spawn remote procedures on other databases.

➔ Calling stored procedures via CFML was covered in Chapter 18, "Stored Procedures." Stored procedure syntax will be discussed in Chapter 35, "Advanced Database Features."

Summary

Transactions are an integral part of any relational database. You control these transactions through a ColdFusion application by using the <CFTRANSACTION> tag. This tag has no required attributes but controls isolation levels through the ISOLATION attribute and can conditionally commit or roll back parts of a transaction through the ACTION attribute. The <CFTRANSACTION> tag uses XML syntax when the ACTION attribute is set to COMMIT or ROLLBACK. Transactions cannot be spanned across pages.

Sample Questions

1. Choose all the statements that are true.
   A. The <CFTRANSACTION> tag can control isolation levels.
   B. Isolation levels affect performance.
   C. Isolation levels affect locking.
   D. ColdFusion enforces isolation when a database does not.

2. What is the primary purpose of <CFTRANSACTION>? (Choose one.)
   A. To commit all inserts to the database
   B. To make sure dirty reads do not take place
   C. To support COMMIT and ROLLBACK features of a relational database system
   D. To supplement the <CFLOCK> tag in locking database records

3. What is wrong with the following code?

```
<CFTRANSACTION>
     <CFQUERY DATASOURCE....>
     <CFTRANSACTION ACTION="commit">
</CFTRANSACTION>
```

   A. Commits must be done in a <CFIF> block.
   B. No forward slash appears at the end of the COMMIT tag.
   C. Transaction tags can't be nested.
   D. Queries must be done after commits are executed.

4. Which isolation level is least efficient?
   A. `SERIALIZABLE`
   B. `REPEATABLE READ`
   C. `READ UNCOMMITTED`
   D. `READ COMMITTED`

CHAPTER 20

Debugging

Debugging Overview

Development tools such as ColdFusion offer a number of helpful utilities that help to solve and avert problems. These problems, or "bugs," are systematically isolated in a process known as "debugging." Debugging tools are glimpses into an application's circuitry. If a template fails or takes an inordinate amount of time to execute, the developer needs to look under the hood and see what is misfiring.

Error messages alone will not yield enough information to solve a problem. Error messages are normally used as starting points for a debugging strategy.

> **TIP**
>
> As a rule, solve problems as soon as they occur. No matter how mundane an issue might seem, the ramifications and complexities will grow exponentially if a problem is not solved immediately after it is discovered.

Although debugging utilities provide information about performance and inconsistent behavior, they are most critical in isolating exceptions. Exceptions are events that stop ColdFusion from processing any template. The most common exceptions include dividing by zero and placing an equal sign in a `<CFIF>` clause instead of an `IS` or `EQ`.

➔ Exceptions that usually cause errors can be handled in other ways. This is known as "exception handling" and is covered in Chapter 21, "Error Handling."

Exposed Information

Every time a ColdFusion template runs, information is made available to the developer. Most of this information is exposed by toggling certain debug settings in the ColdFusion Administrator. The debug settings provide a list of categories. Each category represents a type of debugging that can be performed. The manner in which debugging information is exposed varies depending on its category. Next, we will cover each category of information and how it is exposed.

> **NOTE**
>
> The next series of subsections detail all the debugging information that can be exposed through the ColdFusion Administrator. To turn any of these options on, open the browser-based Administrator at
>
> `http://{hostname}/cfide/administrator/index.cfm`
>
> and after logging in click on "debugging."

Performance Monitoring

Performance monitoring is a helpful tool in tracking the efficiency of a ColdFusion application under load. This can be helpful in deciding whether additional hardware should be used or whether processing logic should be moved into a stored procedure or a fully compiled language such as C++.

After performance monitoring has been selected in the ColdFusion Administrator, there are two ways to look at the performance of the server on Windows NT or Windows 2000. The first technique is to open the Windows performance monitor in Administrative Tools and from the monitor open the file `C:\cfusion\bin\ColdFusionServer.pmc`. This will yield a graphical view of server performance data. The standard features for the Windows performance monitor are supported such as changing colors, display types, and styles.

> **TIP**
>
> On a UNIX system, performance monitoring is handled through a command-line interface. An executable in the ColdFusion directory named `cfstat` is run from a shell prompt, and will expose the information as text. The specific information will be detailed in a moment.

On any operating system, performance monitoring can be done in real time through the use of the ColdFusion function `GetMetricData()`. This function takes one argument, which is the name of the performance monitor system used by the OS. On Windows, the argument is `"PERF MONITOR"` and on UNIX, it is `"cfstat"`. The function returns a structure with a number of keys. The keys of this structure match the data that is exposed through the visual and textual performance monitoring features.

```
<CFSET stDebug = GetMetricData("PERF MONITOR")>
<CFLOOP COLLECTION = "#stDebug#" ITEM="i">
    <CFOUTPUT>the debug info for #i# is #stDebug[i]#</CFOUTPUT><BR>
</CFLOOP>
<!--- the above will print debug info on a Windows system --->
```

The data exposed through performance monitoring, including the key names returned through `GetMetricData()` are shown in Table 20.1.

Table 20.1 Data Returned Through ColdFusion Performance Monitoring

Key Name	Description
`avgDBTime`	Average database transaction time
`avgQueueTime`	Average queue time
`avgReqTime`	Average request time
`bytesIn`	Bytes incoming per second
`bytesOut`	Bytes outgoing per second
`cachePops`	Cache pops per second
`dbHits`	Database hits per second
`InstanceName`	The instance name of the ColdFusion Service
`pageHits`	Page hits per second
`reqQueued`	Number of queued requests
`reqRunning`	Number of running requests
`reqTimedOut`	Number of timed requests

Stack Trace

Turning on the Stack Trace option is useful only if error handling is utilized because a stack trace involves tags that must be nested in an error handling statement. Essentially, a stack trace indicates the line number and tag names of the tags around the exception. The stack trace information is exposed through an array of structures in the `CFCATCH` collection.

> **CAUTION**
>
> Turning on the stack trace could significantly decrease the performance of a large application.

> **NOTE**
>
> As stated, the stack trace is exposed programmatically as an array of structures. Although this variable might not make sense without reading the error handling chapter, the basic format for the variable is as follows:

```
#CFCATCH.TAGCONTEXT[i].line#
<!--- i is the line number of the error--->
<!--- i+1 is the line number of the first tag after the error--->
#CFCATCH.TAGCONTEXT[i].column#
<!--- i is the column number of the error--->
<!---  i+1 is the column number of the next tag after the error--->
#CFCATCH.TAGCONTEXT[i].template#
<!--- the path of the template that threw the error occurred --->
```

➔ The CFCATCH collection is covered in Chapter 21, "Error Handling."

Show Variables

By turning on this debug option, a list of variables will be printed at the bottom of every requested ColdFusion page. The variables shown are limited to certain types and scopes, forcing the developer to manually print the variables that are not output to the page. Manual debugging will be discussed later in this chapter.

The types of variables that are output to the page through the show variables option are

- `CGI`
- `FORM`
- `URL`
- Local variables

> **TIP**
>
> At the bottom of the debug settings screen in the ColdFusion Administrator is a text box and add button where IP addresses can be entered. By entering IP addresses, the debug output will be viewable by only those users whose IP addresses match the ones in the list. If no addresses are entered, all users will see exposed debug information.

Show Processing Time

This simple debug option will be printed at the bottom of each ColdFusion template just like the Show Variables option. The information consists of the processing time to execute the template requested.

Detail View

Whereas the Show Processing Time option displays the sum of all templates that were executed through a single request, the Detail View option yields a template-by-template list of processing times. Therefore, if a ColdFusion template is calling some custom tags and including pages, using the Show Processing Time option makes it easier to witness what page contains potential bottlenecks.

> **NOTE**
>
> The Detail View option will not work until it has been turned on and the ColdFusion server has been restarted. This is the only piece of debug information where ColdFusion must be cycled in order to initiate the feature.

Show SQL and Datasource Name

To print the SQL and datasource information to a page, this option must be toggled. Although it might seem that the datasource would be obvious to the developer, it is highly recommended that this be stored in a variable and declared on the `Application.cfm` page. Using the request scope for datasources is also practical because it will be available to all pages and custom tags.

Because SQL statements can be dynamic in a ColdFusion page, it is very useful to see the resulting SQL that was passed to the database. The Show SQL option will display each query as it was sent to the database driver, not as it appears in the source code.

Show Query Information

When ColdFusion performs a query, it creates the recordset object no matter whether records were returned or not. A `<CFOUTPUT>` tag that loops through a query will not fail on an empty result set; it will simply not loop. Because Web browsers are very touchy when it comes to HTML tables, it can be impossible to tell whether a query returned no records or if the table was formatted incorrectly.

The Show Query Information option solves this problem by automatically printing the record count to the bottom of the page. This information also includes the processing time of the query and can give the developer an indication of how efficient the SQL code is. Frequently, a very slow query should be moved into a stored procedure to help with performance.

> **TIP**
>
> The ColdFusion Administrator does not need to be utilized in order to show query information on a page. ColdFusion supports an alternative method that involves placing the word `DEBUG` inside of a `<CFQUERY>` tag as follows:
>
> ```
> <CFQUERY NAME="qWhatever" DATASOURCE="mySQLServer" DEBUG>
> ```
>
> By placing this toggle inside the `<CFQUERY>` tag, debug information will automatically be printed to the page regardless of the Administrator debug settings.

Display Template Path

When custom tags and `<CFMODULE>` are used, it is hard to tell which version of a given template is running during a given request. By turning on this option, the full path of each page is given when an exception occurs.

Manual Debugging

Manual debugging is the process of using CFML tags to expose information to trace errors or strange behavior. When considering our list of variables displayed in debug mode, we are limited to `CGI`, simple local variables, and `URL` and `FORM` variables. If the need arises to print something in the `SESSION` scope, for example, there is no way to do it without outputting the variable directly to the page using a `<CFOUTPUT>` tag.

Another consideration for manual debugging is that the debug output provided by ColdFusion will expose values only after the entire page has been executed. Sure, the page might have experienced an exception and halted, but the developer has no control over how much of the page will run and which "stage" of a certain variable should be printed in the debug output. The manual debug method is one of the only ways to provide this information. By using the `<CFABORT>` tag after printing a variable's value, a glimpse of time is frozen and the chosen stage of a variable is exposed.

The first thing to do before placing these tags in a ColdFusion template is to critically read the error messages returned in a browser. This will tell you where the problem occurred (line number) and on which template. Sometimes, syntax errors can cause ColdFusion to return line numbers that are incorrect, but usually the problem is somewhere nearby, perhaps a few lines off.

The following represents a manual debug page:

```
<CFSET X="1,2,3,4,5,a,7">
<CFLOOP LIST="#X#" INDEX="i">
    <!--- manually debug for i --->
    <CFIF NOT isNumeric(i)>
          <CFOUTPUT>i equals: #i# at loop num:#ListFind(X,i)#</CFOUTPUT>
          <CFABORT>
       </CFIF>
    <CFSET Y = i + 3>
    <!--- I keep getting an error above that 'i' is not numeric --->
</CFLOOP>
```

The preceding code above shows how you could use a combination of <CFOUTPUT>, functions, and a <CFABORT> to figure out why a problem was occurring.

> **TIP**
>
> Another useful debugging technique is to use the `GetTickCount()` function to ascertain how long a template or code block is taking to execute. `GetTickCount()` must be called twice, with the first result subtracted from the second. This will calculate the total number of milliseconds that has elapsed.
>
> ```
> <CFSET start = GetTickCount()>
> <CFLOOP FROM ="1" TO="30000" INDEX="i">
>     <!--- I wonder how long this will take? --->
> </CFLOOP>
> <CFSET end = GetTickCount()>
>     <CFOUTPUT>
>     <!--- here is how long this took: --->
>     Total Milliseconds elapsed: #evaluate(end - start)#
>     </CFOUTPUT>
> ```

ColdFusion Studio Debugger

Manual debugging seems to be the most effective way to debug a page, but the ColdFusion Studio debugging features have much to offer. Because the ColdFusion Developer Certification exam is completely text based, it is hard to imagine many questions about this feature beyond its sheer capabilities and architecture.

ColdFusion Studio communicates with the ColdFusion server through a special protocol named RDS or "Remote Development Service." RDS is unique to Allaire's platform and is the mechanism through which ColdFusion Studio can login to a ColdFusion Server to modify and browse `.CFM` files over the Internet.

There are two steps in setting up ColdFusion Studio to communicate through RDS. First, a new RDS server must be created from the resource window by selecting local files, dropping the select box at the top of the window to choose Allaire FTP and RDS, and right-clicking on the atlas icon. Next, ColdFusion Studio's development mapping must be coordinated to work with this server. Development mappings can be found a number of ways, but the most direct is by pressing Alt+M.

After RDS is set up, ColdFusion's debugger can be used to debug a page. The first thing to do when debugging a page is to set stop points in the templates based on the errors you are attempting to trap. Stop points will halt the ColdFusion server from running the template, present you with a list of variables and their values, and enable you to continue stepping through your code.

Stop points can be placed in a page by clicking to the left of the line numbers in ColdFusion Studio's edit window. A red Stop sign will appear indicating that the server will halt when it comes to this spot. Clicking the same spot a second time will bookmark the spot and a third will remove all demarcations.

Stop points will work only if ColdFusion Studio is in debug mode. This mode is spawned by the ColdFusion debug toolbar, which can be added to the quickbar but usually appears at the bottom of Studio's screen. After debug mode has started and a stop point is reached, a little window will appear showing information about the current state of the template. The following information is obtainable through the debug window:

- Most variables of various scopes (`SESSION`, `CLIENT`, and so on)
- HTML output so far (up to the last stop point)
- Queries including records returned and SQL sent
- Specific variables being "watched" (defined by developer)
- Tag stack (indents nested tags and included pages and custom tags)

Log Files

The final topic of discussion for debugging an application is log files. Log files give a developer an audit of events. If a fatal exception occurs, it will be written to the ColdFusion log file when the error is returned to the user. As well as the error itself, other information will be stored, such as the user's browser type and the IP address from which the user originated.

In addition to ColdFusion error logs, other types of log files are available to the developer. All ColdFusion's log files are stored in either the `CFUSION\log` directory (Windows) or the `opt/coldfusion/log` directory (UNIX).

The log files are named and described in Table 20.2.

Table 20.2 ColdFusion Log Files

Log File Name	Description
`exec.log`	Problems with the ColdFusion service
`rdsservice.log`	Problems with the RDS service
`application.log`	Problems reported to the user
`webserver.log`	Problems occurring between the Web service and the ColdFusion stub
`schedule.log`	Logs scheduled events and problems with them
`server.log`	Similar to `webserver.log` but with less intelligible diagnostic information that is intended for the Allaire Technical Support team
`customtag.log`	Problems with custom tags
`remote.log`	This is for distributed ColdFusion applications where the Web server is split from the application server
`error.log`	Errors related to sending mail from the ColdFusion server; (`cfusion\mail\log` [Windows] or [UNIX])

Summary

Debugging is a primary component to any application development process. ColdFusion offers a variety of utilities to debug an application including exposure of variables, visual debug tools, and programmatic functions and tags. Manual debugging offers the most flexibility and control, and certain features, such as performance monitoring, can allow for greater insight into a ColdFusion environment's overall strengths and weaknesses. Allaire offers a multitude of log information stored in specific directories and accessible with any text editor.

Sample Questions

1. What types of variables are not exposed through server-side debug options?
   A. `CGI`
   B. `FORM`
   C. `SESSION`
   D. `URL`

2. To use the `GetTickCount()` function correctly:
   A. Use it twice and take the second reading from the first
   B. Call it once after a complicated code block
   C. Loop over it to keep it synchronized with the system clock
   D. Pass one argument to it the with name of the count variable

3. The ColdFusion Studio debug window shows (choose all that apply):
   A. Error codes
   B. Tag stack
   C. HTML output
   D. Watched variables

CHAPTER 21

Error Handling

Understanding ColdFusion Error Handling

By default, when an error occurs, ColdFusion displays diagnostic information to the user, and an entry is made in one of the ColdFusion logs. Not only does this make for a poor user experience, but it also means that the error was not trapped and dealt with in a better manner.

Several ColdFusion tools are available to handle errors in a better way. We'll discuss <CFERROR> first and then <CFTRY>. After we cover exceptions, we'll take a second look at <CFERROR>.

<CFERROR TYPE="Request">

When an error occurs, diagnostic information is displayed using a default page that looks nothing like the rest of the application. Using <CFERROR> allows you to decide the following:

- What parts, if any, of the error message are shown to the user
- The look and feel of the page

The <CFERROR> tag has the attributes listed in Table 21.1.

Table 21.1 <CFERROR> Tag Attributes

Attribute	Description
TYPE	The type of error to catch. For now, consider Request and Validation.
TEMPLATE	The template to be displayed instead of the default error diagnostic page.
EXCEPTION	To be discussed later in the chapter.
MAILTO	An optional attribute that sends an email address to the template specified.

The first type of error we'll cover is Request. It traps any error unless it is a server-side validation error. The ideal location for a <CFERROR> tag is in the Application.cfm file. If you do not place the <CFERROR> tag in the Application.cfm you would have to place the tag on every page in your application.

➔ You can find further information about server-side validation errors in Chapter 9, "FORM Variables."

➔ You can find further information about the Application.cfm file in Chapter 6, "The Application Framework."

Consider the following <CFERROR> tag placed in an Application.cfm file:

```
<CFERROR TYPE="Request" TEMPLATE="ErrorTemplate.cfm">
```

Any errors that occur on a ColdFusion template call for ErrorTemplate.cfm to be processed. This includes both ColdFusion syntax errors, which cause parsing errors, as well as errors that occur during template execution. For instance, a <CFQUERY> tag without a DATASOURCE attribute causes the error template to be called because that is a syntax error. By the same token, a <CFQUERY> tag with a DATASOURCE attribute that points to a nonexistent data source also calls the error template.

What should be on the error template? That is your decision. Most likely, you will want to have it look like the rest of your site. You may also choose to have some information about the error, and error variables can help you do that.

The error variables available are listed in Table 21.2.

Table 21.2 Error Variables for Type Request

Variable	Description
Error.Diagnostics	Detailed error diagnostics from the ColdFusion server.
Error.MailTo	Email address of the administrator who should be notified (corresponds to the value set in the MAILTO attribute of <CFERROR>).
Error.DateTime	Date and time when the error occurred.
Error.Browser	Browser that was running when the error occurred.
Error.GeneratedContent	The failed request's generated content.
Error.RemoteAddress	IP address of the remote client.
Error.HTTPReferer	Page from which the client accessed the link to the page where the error occurred. It is equal to the empty string if there is not a referrer.
Error.Template	Page being executed when the error occurred.
Error.QueryString	URL query string of the client's request. It is equal to the empty string if there is not a referrer.

> **TIP**
>
> You don't have to remember all these variable names. In ColdFusion Studio, they are available for selection in the Tools, Expression Builder, Variables, CFERROR Request Variables menu.

You can use these variables only on the error template page. They act like regular ColdFusion variables in the sense that they must have # signs around them. But unlike other ColdFusion variables, they do *not* have to be surrounded with a `<CFOUTPUT>` block. In fact, when the type is `Request` or `Validation`, no ColdFusion tags on the page specified in the `TEMPLATE` attribute are executed.

> **NOTE**
>
> There is a very good reason that no ColdFusion tags can be used on the error template when the type is `Request` or `Validation`. Consider what would happen if the error template itself had a syntax error. It would call the error template again, which would have an error and call the error template again, which would have an error, and so on.
>
> To avoid the chance of having an infinite loop, you cannot use ColdFusion tags on the error template when the type is `Request` or `Validation`. Even if you use some ColdFusion tags on the page, they are ignored.

<CFERROR TYPE="Validation">

As you learned earlier, when the type is `Request`, it traps all errors except when server-side validation errors occur. Server-side validation errors are trapped when the type is `Validation`.

On a form, you can use two `<INPUT>` tags as follows:

```
<INPUT TYPE="text" NAME="TheNumber">
<INPUT TYPE="hidden" NAME="TheNumber_integer"
➥VALUE="This is my error message">
```

You can use a `<CFERROR>` tag in the `Application.cfm` like this:

```
<CFERROR TYPE="VALIDATION" TEMPLATE="DisplayErrorValidation.cfm">
```

When you use the tags shown here, if the user fills the text box with a string, an error of type `Validation` will occur and the `DisplayErrorValidation.cfm` template will be called. The same rules apply to building this error template as apply to building the Request template, except that the `CFERROR` variables you can use on a validation error template are different. They are listed in Table 21.3.

Table 21.3 Error Variables for Type Validation

Variable	Description
`Error.ValidationHeader`	Text for the header of a validation message
`Error.InvalidFields`	Unordered list of validation errors that occurred
`Error.ValidationFooter`	Text for the footer of a validation message

> **NOTE**
>
> `Error.ValidationHeader` is the following text: "Form Entries Incomplete or Invalid. One or more problems exist with the data you have entered."
>
> `Error.ValidationFooter` is the following text: "Use the *Back* button on your web browser to return to the previous page and correct the listed problems."
>
> `Error.InvalidFields` is a bulleted list of the default error messages, or the message in the `VALUE` attribute of the hidden form tag, if used.

Exception Handling

<CFERROR> traps both parsing and runtime errors. Errors that occur when the template is executed are also called *exceptions*. Exceptions include any event that disrupts the normal flow of instructions in a ColdFusion page when it is being executed. Exceptions can be more intelligently handled than what you've seen so far using <CFERROR>.

<CFTRY>/<CFCATCH>

When you use the <CFTRY>/<CFCATCH> tag set, exceptions can be caught and then acted upon programmatically. For instance, instead of throwing an error when ColdFusion attempts to write a duplicate indexed value to a database, the error can be caught and the user can be informed of the problem and asked to change the offending data.

The general format of catching an exception in ColdFusion is as follows:

```
<CFTRY>
    Possible error producing code
<CFCATCH TYPE="ExceptionType">
    Code to run if error caught
</CFCATCH>
additional <CFCATCH></CFCATCH> blocks
</CFTRY>
```

> **CAUTION**
>
> It is important to understand that <CFTRY>/<CFCATCH> does *not* catch syntax errors like <CFERROR> does. For instance, using a <CFTRY> block around a <CFQUERY> tag without a `DATASOURCE` attribute does nothing because the syntax of the <CFQUERY> is not correct and the page cannot be parsed correctly. If, on the other hand, the `DATASOURCE` attribute is there, but the listed data source does not exist, the <CFTRY> block catches that exception.

The following is a simple <CFTRY>/<CFCATCH> example. It assumes that a personalized header is included. If, for some reason, the personalized header is not available, a standard header is displayed.

```
<CFTRY>
     <CFINCLUDE TEMPLATE="#Personalized#.cfm">
<CFCATCH TYPE="MissingInclude">
     <CFINCLUDE TEMPLATE="StandardHeader.cfm">
</CFCATCH>
</CFTRY>
```

The TYPE attribute in the <CFCATCH> tag is the exception type. Table 21.4 lists the possible exception types and the situations in which they are used.

Table 21.4 Exception Types

Exception Type	Description
Application	Custom exception types using <CFTHROW> without specifying a custom type.
Database	Database operations fail.
Expression	Expression evaluation fails.
Lock	Locking operations fail.
MissingInclude	Included files cannot be found.
Object	Code using <CFOBJECT> fails.
Template	General application page errors.
Security	Code using ColdFusion security fails.
Custom Type	Custom exception types by using <CFTHROW> and specifying a custom type.
Any	All exceptions caught.

TIP

If you use multiple <CFCATCH> blocks and one of them is the catchall type Any, be sure that it is the last one in the set. Only one of the <CFCATCH> blocks will be executed, and if TYPE="Any" happens to be the first, it and only it will ever be processed.

<CFCATCH> Variables

When an error is caught, you should attempt to "fix" it in the <CFCATCH> block—that is, programmatically supply a solution to the problem. This task is made easier by variables that are available in the scope of the <CFCATCH> block. A set of variables is defined for all exception types. Other variables exist only for certain exception types. Those variables defined for all exception types are listed in Table 21.5.

Table 21.5 Variables Defined for All Exception Types

Variable	Description
`Type`	The exception type as specified in `<CFCATCH>`.
`Message`	The exceptions message.
`Detail`	A message from the CFML interpreter. Here, you can see which tag threw the exception.

Table 21.6 summarizes the other `<CFCATCH>` variables and which exception types they are used with. The table shows the exception type, the variable name, and an explanation of the variable.

Table 21.6 Variables Defined for Specific Exception Types

Exception Type	Variable Name	Description
`Database`	`NativeErrorCode`	The error code that has meaning when you use native drivers or OLE DB drivers.
`Database`	`SQLState`	The error code that has meaning when you use ODBC drivers.
`Expression`	`ErrNumber`	An internal expression error number.
`Lock`	`LockName`	The name of the lock. The value is `Anonymous` if the lock is not named in the `<CFLOCK>` tag.
`Lock`	`LockOperation`	The operation that failed.
`MissingInclude`	`MissingFileName`	The name of the file that could not be included.
`Custom`	`ErrorCode`	Values you set when using custom exception types.
`Custom`	`ExtendedInfo`	Values you set when using custom exception types.

CAUTION

Both `NativeErrorCode` and `SQLState` have values when an exception of type `Database` is caught. Only one of them is meaningful, as described in the text. For example, if you're using an ODBC driver, `NativeErrorCode` has a value, but it is meaningless.

<CFTHROW>

In some cases, centralizing exception handling is advantageous. For instance, you might have a page that calls a number of custom tags. Rather than deal with exceptions in detail on every custom tag, you could simply throw the error back to the calling page in all cases and deal with the exceptions in detail there.

To do so, you can use the <CFTHROW> tag, which is a useful tool. The attributes available when using <CFTHROW> are listed in Table 21.7.

Table 21.7 <CFTHROW> Tag Attributes

Attribute	Description
TYPE	The custom exception type you name. This attribute is optional.
MESSAGE	A message you select.
DETAIL	Detailed information you select.
ERRORCODE	An error code you select.
EXTENDEDINFO	Extended information you select.

For an example of <CFTHROW>, consider a custom tag that checks inventory against the number ordered, as shown in the following code. If the inventory is less than the number ordered, an exception is raised.

```
<CFIF Ordered GTE Inventory>
     <CFTHROW> TYPE="Reorder" MESSAGE="Reorder product #ProdName#"
      ➥EXTENDEDINFO="#Now()#"
</CFIF>
```

This code uses a custom exception type named `Reorder`. You also can see that the `MESSAGE` and `EXTENDEDINFO` attributes pass back to the calling page the name of the product to reorder and the time stamp indicating when the exception was thrown.

If the name of the custom tag with this code were called `PlaceOrder.cfm`, you could call it in a <CFTRY> block as follows:

```
<CFTRY>
     <CF_PlaceOrder>
<CFCATCH TYPE="Reorder">
     <CFOUTPUT>#CFCATCH.Message#.  The alert occurred at
                ➥#CFCATCH.ExtendedInfo#.</CFOUTPUT>
</CFCATCH>
</CFTRY>
```

> **NOTE**
>
> If the `TYPE` attribute were not used in <CFTHROW>, you could have caught the exception by using `TYPE="Application"` in <CFCATCH>. The purpose of the `Application` type is to catch exceptions from <CFTHROW> when a type is not specified.

<CFRETHROW>

In some cases, you might want to throw the exact error that occurred. For instance, a database error occurs on a custom tag, and you want to throw that exact error to the calling page and deal with it in that location. The <CFRETHROW> tag does this job.

Using this tag saves you from having to build a custom type and supply the appropriate values for the MESSAGE, DETAIL, ERRORCODE, and EXTENDEDINFO attributes. Assume the following code is in a custom tag called MyInsert.cfm:

```
<CFTRY>
     Some database action performed here, for example an insert
<CFCATCH TYPE="Database">
     <CFRETHROW>
</CFCATCH>
</CFTRY>
```

You then can handle the call to the custom tag like this:

```
<CFTRY>
     <CF_MyInsert>
<CFCATCH TYPE="Database">
     Database error occurred!
     <CFOUTPUT>The error code is #CFCATCH.SQLState#</CFOUTPUT>
</CFCATCH>
</CFTRY>
```

This code shows that the exact error that was originally thrown on the custom tag (in this example of type Database) can be caught on the calling page.

<CFERROR> and Exceptions

Earlier in the chapter, you learned about <CFERROR> with the TYPE attribute equal to Request and Validation. Now that you've learned about exceptions, you can extend the use of <CFERROR>.

> **NOTE**
>
> Before ColdFusion 4.5x, you could not use exceptions with <CFERROR>. This was very frustrating at times because, as you've seen with the type equal to Request or Validation, you cannot use any ColdFusion tags on the error template. This meant that you could not use <CFMAIL> to email that an error occurred or write the errors to a database using <CFQUERY>. That issue is now resolved.

<CFERROR TYPE="Exception">

The <CFERROR> tag directs program execution to a designated error template when the type is Request or Validation. The information from the error template is displayed and program processing ends. The same is true when the type is Exception, except that on the error template, you have access to the full set of ColdFusion tags, as well as the <CFERROR> variables to use as needed.

If you do not specify an exception type using the EXCEPTION attribute, the default is Any, so any exception that occurs is directed to the error template. You can also use multiple <CFERROR> tags in Application.cfm as follows:

```
<CFERROR TYPE="Exception" TEMPLATE="ExpressoinTemplate.cfm"
➥EXCEPTION="Expression">
```

```
<CFERROR TYPE="Exception" TEMPLATE="DatabaseTemplate.cfm"
➥EXCEPTION="Database">
```

This code directs exceptions of type `Expression` to one template and of type `Database` to another.

> **TIP**
>
> You might think that you don't need `<CFERROR>` with type `Request` if you are using type `Exception`. This is not true. The Request template is used if an exception occurs on the template specified with the type equal to `Exception`.

<CFERROR TYPE="Monitor">

If you use a `<CFTRY>`/`<CFCATCH>` block to trap exceptions, nowhere is it recorded that an error has occurred. The error is not shown to the user, nor is it entered in the ColdFusion logs. This situation may not be optimal. It is possible that you would like the error to be caught and programmatically compensated for, but still know that the error has occurred. You can implement this situation by using `<CFERROR>` and setting the type to `Monitor`.

When the type is set to `Monitor`, the behavior of program processing is similar to when the type is `Exception`—with one huge difference. When the type is `Monitor` and an exception occurs, processing is redirected to the error template; then processing returns to the page where the exception occurred.

It makes little sense to monitor the exception and then return to the place where the exception happened and have the error diagnostic information displayed to the user. But when you couple `<CFERROR>` with a `<CFTRY>`/`<CFCATCH>` block, you have the best of both worlds. On the error template specified in `<CFERROR TYPE="Monitor">`, you can send email or write to a database where the exception is documented. Then processing returns to the place where the exception was raised, and that exception is programmatically compensated for so that the user does not know the exception occurred.

<CFERROR> and <CFTRY> Together

If you use a `<CFTRY>`/`<CFCATCH>` block to catch an exception, the `<CFERROR>` tag does *not* do its job and redirect processing to the error template. The `<CFTRY>`/`<CFCATCH>` block makes it seem that an exception did not occur. In essence, the `<CFTRY>` "overrides" the `<CFERROR>`.

Sitewide Error Handler

In the Settings area of the ColdFusion Administrator, you can find an option to provide a path for the sitewide error handler. This is a global way to specify `<CFERROR TYPE="Exception">`. The template specified in the ColdFusion Administrator becomes the template where processing is directed if an exception occurs.

> **NOTE**
>
> On the template specified as the sitewide error handler, you can use ColdFusion tags. You also have access to the `<CFERROR>` variables.
>
> If a `<CFERROR>` is specified in `Application.cfm` or on an actual page, it overrides the setting from the ColdFusion Administrator.

Missing Template Handler

One error we have not dealt with so far is a missing ColdFusion template. In Web server software, you can specify a template to display `404 Not Found` errors, but this does not work if the missing page has a `.cfm` extension. The request for the page would be handed off to ColdFusion, and a standard `404` error page would be displayed. If you want to make this template have the look of your site, you can specify its location in the Settings option of the ColdFusion Administrator.

Summary

ColdFusion has a rich environment to catch syntax errors and exceptions that occur when a template is being parsed or processed. `<CFERROR>` with the `TYPE` attribute set equal to `Request` or `Validation` redirects processing to a template where you cannot use other ColdFusion tags. If you use the type set to `Exception`, processing is redirected to a template where you can use ColdFusion tags. If you want to have an error template processed and then return to the page where the exception occurred, set the type to `Monitor`.

Rather than redirect processing to an error template, you might want to catch the error and deal with it programmatically. You can do so by using the `<CFTRY>`/`<CFCATCH>` tag set.

Sample Questions

1. Which of the following `<CFERROR>` types is used to check form input?
   - A. `Monitor`
   - B. `Validation`
   - C. `Exception`
   - D. `Error`
2. A `<CFTHROW>` is used with no `TYPE` attribute. What type of exception should you use to catch it?
   - A. `Expression`
   - B. `Any`
   - C. `Database`
   - D. `Application`
3. Which value for the `TYPE` attribute in `<CFERROR>` should you use to have the error template processed and then return to the place where the exception occurred?
   - A. `Monitor`
   - B. `Validation`
   - C. `Exception`
   - D. `Request`

PART 5

EXTENDING COLDFUSION

CHAPTER 22

Custom Tags

What Is a Custom Tag?

ColdFusion comes with a great number of useful tags and functions. Using these tags and functions in combination enables you to create powerful Web applications. ColdFusion custom tags take your productivity even further by enabling you to create your own reusable, modular, and maintainable tags.

➔ Functions are introduced in Chapter 2, "Working with Variables and Expressions."

At their simplest, custom tags are just regular ColdFusion templates that act like little self-contained programs that perform tasks. You can think of them as extensions of the regular ColdFusion tags and functions, except that you get to code them to do whatever you want!

➔ More advanced forms of custom functionality are discussed in Chapter 23, "Advanced Custom Tags," and Chapter 24, "COM, EJB, CFX, and Java."

Why Use Custom Tags?

The three main reasons for using custom tags are

- The benefits of creating reusable and modular code
- Maintainability
- Hiding complex code

These three reasons are related, and the latter two are byproducts of the first.

Two of the most important tags that you learn as a beginning ColdFusion developer are `<CFQUERY>` and `<CFOUTPUT>`.

➔ `<CFQUERY>` is introduced in Chapter 7, "Using Databases," and `<CFOUTPUT>` is introduced in Chapter 2, "Working with Variables and Expressions."

The following example shows how these two tags might be used together to query the database for information and then to display the results in an HTML table.

```
<!--- first query the database --->
<CFQUERY NAME="GetEmployees" DATASOURCE="HR">
SELECT FirstName, LastName, Phone, Email
FROM Employees
</CFQUERY>
<!--- second display the table caption --->
<H1>All Company Employees</H1>
<!--- then display the query results in a table --->
<TABLE BORDER="1">
<TR>
    <TH>First Name</TH>
    <TH>Last Name</TH>
    <TH>Phone Number</TH>
    <TH>Email Address</TH>
</TR>
<CFOUTPUT QUERY="GetEmployees">
<TR>
    <TD>#FirstName#</TD>
    <TD>#LastName#</TD>
    <TD>#Phone#</TD>
    <TD>#Email#</TD>
</TR>
</CFOUTPUT>
</TABLE>
```

You have probably used similar code a thousand times in your ColdFusion applications, which makes it a good candidate for a custom tag. Instead of typing all that code every time, you could just call this functionality by just typing one tag:

```
<CF_QUERYPRINTTABLE DATASOURCE="HR" TABLENAME="Employees"
➥COLUMNNAMES="FirstName, LastName, Phone, Email"
➥COLUMNHEADERS="First Name, Last Name, Phone Number, Email Address"
➥CAPTION="All Company Employees">
```

This custom tag will use the attributes passed to it to generate the same results as the preceding example, but this tag is more flexible because you can reuse the code by merely passing it different values through the attributes each time you need the functionality.

NOTE

Developers who have programmed in other languages might have encountered the ability to create reusable functionality by developing custom functions. ColdFusion comes with a set number of functions and the language does not give developers the ability to create their own functions. Reusable, modularized code is created in the form of custom tags.

Every programmer has looked at code that he or she built a year previously and cringes. As you develop your skills you find better, more efficient ways of coding, and you will want to return to your old code and improve it. If you do not use custom tags, you will have to hunt through all your code to find and update the multiple places where you embedded code for one piece of functionality. That could take weeks or even months, depending on the complexity of your application. However, if you used custom tags, you can open the one template with the functionality code, update it, and all the applications that use it will immediately benefit from the change.

NOTE

Using many custom tags in your applications can have an impact on performance because ColdFusion takes time to initialize them into memory the first time they are loaded. However, despite this drawback, it is still recommended that you use custom tags anytime you feel that your code is redundant. First, the drain on resources isn't that great. Second, you will find that the time and resources that you save yourself from maintaining multiple instances of the same code far outweigh the cost of buying more hardware to support the use of custom tags.

If you work within a team of developers, custom tags can have an additional benefit. Teams often consist of people with different skill sets and a varying a degree of proficiency even within the same skill set. In a situation like this, it is often beneficial to have senior developers create custom tags that junior developers can then use to perform common functions.

A senior developer can even encrypt the custom tag template so that a junior developer does not become confused by the complexity of the code.

➔ Template encryption is discussed in Chapter 1, "Web Technology and Terminology."

Simple Custom Tags

In our earlier example, the custom tag we discussed used attributes. We'll discuss attributes in more detail in the next section. However, the simplest form of custom tag takes no attributes at all. Such tags simply perform one task.

Despite their one-track nature, simple custom tags can be quite powerful. Consider the custom tag `<CF_EmbedFields>`, created by Ben Forta. This tag takes no attributes, but is indispensable when working with multiple form pages.

TIP

`<CF_EmbedFields>`, along with the other custom tags mentioned in this chapter, can be found on the Allaire Developer's Exchange at `http://devex.allaire.com/developer/gallery/`. You should make it a habit to visit this site often. A good rule of thumb is to always search the site for custom tags before you build one yourself.

URL and FORM variables enable developers to pass information from one page to another, but if information must persist across multiple pages, most developers use APPLICATION, SERVER, SESSION, COOKIE, or CLIENT variables.

→ FORM and ACTION pages are discussed in Chapter 9, "FORM Variables." SESSION, COOKIE, and CLIENT variables are introduced in Chapter 11, "Session State Management."

The complexities of persistent variables, however, are sometimes overkill for simple problems. For instance, if you have a wizard that takes users through multiple forms, you don't necessarily want to maintain that information in SESSION variables.

The custom tag <CF_EmbedFields> forces FORM variables to be passed from form page to form page by embedding the results of one form submission in the next form as hidden form fields.

The following code makes up the functionality of <CF_EmbedFields>:

```
<!--- Check that fieldnames exists --->
<CFIF IsDefined("FORM.fieldnames")>
 <!--- Create empty list of processed variables --->
 <CFSET fieldnames_processed="">
 <!--- Loop through fieldnames --->
 <CFLOOP INDEX="form_element" LIST="#FORM.fieldnames#">
  <!--- Try to find current element in list --->
  <CFIF ListFind(fieldnames_processed, form_element) IS 0>
   <!--- Make fully qualified copy of it (to prevent accessing
        ➥the wrong field type) --->
   <CFSET form_element_qualified="FORM." & form_element>
   <!--- Output it as a hidden field --->
   <CFOUTPUT>
   <INPUT TYPE="hidden" NAME="#form_element#"
             ➥VALUE="#Evaluate(FORM_element_qualified)#">
   </CFOUTPUT>
   <!--- And add it to the processed list --->
   <CFSET fieldnames_processed=
         ➥ListAppend(fieldnames_processed, form_element)>
  </CFIF>
 </CFLOOP>
</CFIF>
```

This code evaluates the special FORM variable FORM.FieldNames, which is a list of all the names of the FORM variables being passed from a FORM.

→ FORM variables and, specifically, the special variable FORM.FieldNames, are discussed in Chapter 9, "FORM Variables." Lists are discussed in Chapter 13, "Lists."

As the code loops over the FORM.FieldNames list, it generates one HTML hidden form field for each field that was passed from the previous form. Using this custom tag, you can easily continue to pass information from page to page, essentially maintaining state, without worrying about the complexities of using a database or session state variables.

Calling Custom Tags

Creating a custom tag is the easy part. Like any other ColdFusion template, a simple custom tag is merely a bunch of CFML code saved into a file with a `.cfm` file extension.

Custom tags are really defined by how they are accessed. Most ColdFusion pages are run when the Web server passes them to the ColdFusion application server. Custom tags are run when they are called from within another ColdFusion template.

> **NOTE**
>
> In Chapter 5, "Redirects and Reuse," you were introduced to the `<CFINCLUDE>` tag. This tag calls another page to be run. However, it should not be confused with a custom tag.
>
> Consider this analogy. If you're typing up a word processing document in Microsoft Word and you need to grab text from another document and insert it into your current document, you just do a cut and paste command. That is like using `<CFINCLUDE>`—just pulling data into the current page. This data becomes part of the page; it is no different than any other text in the document. However, when you need to print the document, this actually calls up a separate but related program. This separate program is the custom tag in our analogy. It is associated and dependent on the main program, but runs in its own space. The variables in the space are *protected*, which means that they cannot be accessed or overwritten by the calling page.

Simple Syntax (CF_)

After you've created a file that you will use as a custom tag, you need a way of calling that page to run. There are a number of ways to do this.

The easiest method is to use simple syntax. If you have a custom tag template that you have named `customtag.cfm`, you can simply call it by typing `<CF_CUSTOMTAG>`. Notice that the filename is prefixed with `<CF_` and the `.cfm` extension is dropped from the name.

When using simple syntax, ColdFusion automatically looks for the custom tag in the same directory as the calling template. If it can't find the custom tag there, it searches in a special directory that is created by ColdFusion upon installation, usually called `C:\Cfusion\CustomTags`.

> **TIP**
>
> It is possible to change the system Registry to have it automatically look in other directories for custom tags. This can be done by modifying this key:
> `HKEY_LOCAL_MACHINE\SOFTWARE\ALLAIRE\COLDFUSION\CURRENTVERSION\CUSTOMTAGS`.
> Modify Registry settings with care!

<CFMODULE>

You can also call a custom tag using the built-in ColdFusion tag <CFMODULE>. <CFMODULE> enables you to use two separate methods to call the custom tag.

The first method only works if the custom tag is in the special directory C:\Cfusion\CustomTags. The syntax is as follows:

```
<CFMODULE NAME="Developers.Emily.Header">
```

The value Developers.Emily.Header calls the header.cfm custom tag in a directory called Emily, which is in a directory called Developers. Developers is a subdirectory of C:\Cfusion\CustomTags.

> **TIP**
>
> If you're in a hosted environment, your ISP might allow you to have access to your own directory inside C:\Cfusion\CustomTags. The ColdFusion application server recursively searches through the CustomTags directory, and all its subdirectories, until it locates the custom tag in question. This can be a problem if two people being hosted on the same server have named their custom tags identically. For instance, header.cfm is a common name for a custom tag. If one person has her custom tag template in C:\Cfusion\CustomTags\Developers\Emily\header.cfm and another person has his custom tag template in C:\Cfusion\CustomTags\Developers\Matt\header.cfm, there will be a problem when calling this custom tag using simple syntax like <CF_Header>. When Matt calls <CF_Header> from within his own application, he will always run the header.cfm custom tag in the Emily directory because that will be the first file by that name that ColdFusion encounters as it recursively searches alphabetically through the subdirectories of C:\Cfusion\CustomTags. Using <CFMODULE> with the NAME attribute enables you to specify explicitly which custom tag in C:\Cfusion\CustomTags will run.

<CFMODULE> gives us an even more flexible means of calling a custom tag. So far, we have been restricted to putting our custom tags in the same directory as the calling page, or in the C:\Cfusion\CustomTags directory. Using the TEMPLATE attribute of <CFMODULE>, you can place a custom tag anywhere and call it using either a relative path or a ColdFusion mapping.

```
<!--- using a relative path --->
<CFMODULE TEMPLATE="../customtags/header.cfm">
<!--- using a ColdFusion mapping --->
<CFMODULE TEMPLATE="/customtags/header.cfm">
```

→ ColdFusion mappings were introduced in Chapter 5, "Redirects and Reuse."

Attributes

Custom tags should be built with flexibility. This essentially means that the more attributes one takes, the better!

Earlier in the chapter, we discussed the sample custom tag used to query the database and output the data in an HTML table:

```
<CF_QUERYPRINTTABLE DATASOURCE="HR" TABLENAME="Employees"
➥COLUMNNAMES="FirstName, LastName, Phone, Email"
➥COLUMNHEADERS="First Name, Last Name, Phone Number, Email Address"
➥CAPTION="All Company Employees">
```

The attributes we list here could be considered the absolute minimum to make the custom tag run properly. However, we could easily enhance the custom tag by adding more attributes for formatting issues:

```
<CF_QUERYPRINTTABLE DATASOURCE="HR" TABLENAME="Employees"
➥COLUMNNAMES="FirstName, LastName, Phone, Email"
➥COLUMNHEADERS="First Name, Last Name, Phone Number, Email Address"
➥CAPTION="All Company Employees" WIDTH="80%" CELLPADDING="3"
➥CELLSPACING="0" BORDER="0" HEADERBGCOLOR="blue" DATABGCOLOR="yellow">
```

To make the query in the custom tag recognize the attributes, do the following:

```
<CFQUERY NAME="MyQueryName" DATASOURCE="#ATTRIBUTES.DATASOURCE#">
SELECT #ATTRIBUTES.ColumnNames#
FROM #ATTRIBUTES.Tablename#
</CFQUERY>
```

> **CAUTION**
>
> The `ATTRIBUTES.` prefix is required when referencing values passed into a custom tag using attributes.

Notice that the only value that is hardcoded in the preceding query is the name of the query itself. Because the query name is being used only to output the values within the custom tag itself, it is not necessary for us to change it. Similarly, the rest of the code to display the caption and the HTML table will also reference these attributes.

For this custom tag to work at all, we have to make sure that certain attributes are passed. `DATASOURCE`, `TABLENAME`, `COLUMNNAMES`, `COLUMNHEADERS`, and `CAPTION` are all required for the custom tag to function even on the most limited basis. You don't want the code to break when one of the attributes is not assigned, so you should implement some validation at the beginning of your custom tag to display error messages if a required attribute is missing. Such code might look like this:

```
<CFIF NOT IsDefined("ATTRIBUTES.DATASOURCE")>
    The DATASOURCE attribute is required.
    <CFABORT>
</CFIF>
```

➔ To perform validation, review Chapter 3, "Conditional Processing" and the discussion in Chapter 9, "FORM Variables," about custom validation.

NOTE

The code uses <CFABORT>, which will stop ColdFusion dead in its tracks. As soon as ColdFusion encounters this tag, it immediately stops whatever it was doing. There might be instances where this immediate halt is too abrupt and unnecessary. In these instances, consider using <CFEXIT> instead. This tag will stop the processing of the custom tag, but will not hinder ColdFusion from finishing the processing of the calling page. Used outside of a custom tag, <CFEXIT> acts just like <CFABORT>.

Now, after we've validated that all the required tags are passed, we need to address the issue of the optional attributes. CELLPADDING, CELLSPACING, BORDER, HEADERBGCOLOR, and DATABGCOLOR are all optional attributes that affect only the display of the HTML table. If they are used, the table should take on the declared physical characteristics. However, if they are not used, the custom tag should revert to default values for these attributes.

To set default values, you use the <CFPARAM> tag as follows:

```
<CFPARAM NAME="ATTRIBUTES.BORDER" DEFAULT="0">
```

➔ <CFPARAM> was introduced in Chapter 2, "Working with Variables and Expressions."

Notice that the value of the NAME attribute is ATTRIBUTES.BORDER—with the ATTRIBUTES. scope prefix. This simply states that you are creating a default value specifically for the BORDER attribute.

Caller Scope

The relationship between a regular template file and a custom tag can often be one-sided, meaning that the template passes information to the custom tag, but not vice versa. There are instances, however, when the custom tag should pass data back to the calling template.

A login script for security can be wrapped into a custom tag. This script will take the username and password passed into it, along with attributes that declare which data-source and table to authenticate against, and pass back a flag that declares whether the user has logged in successfully.

Most often in scenarios like this, the name of the flag being returned to the calling page is determined by the person who created the login custom tag. If you're working in a team environment, this is not always ideal because, most likely, your team has created coding standards for the naming of variables. Therefore, it would be better if you could tell the custom tag what you would like to name the variable being returned, as in the following custom tag call:

```
<CF_LoginScript USERNAME="#FORM.UserName#" PSSWD="#FORM.PSSWD#"
➥DATASOURCE="HR" TABLENAME="Users" LOGINFLAG="rLoginFlag">
```

The preceding code declares that the `USERNAME` and `PASSWORD` are being passed from a form submission and that the `LOGINFLAG` that is returned should be named `rLoginFlag`, where the team has decided that all variables returned from custom tags should be prefixed with the letter `r`.

To create a local variable from within a custom tag, you simply type the following code, just as you would for any local variable:

```
<CFSET rLoginFlag="1">
```

→ Local variables are introduced in Chapter 2, "Working with Variables and Expressions."

Now, to force this local variable to be passed back into the calling page, you must prefix it with `CALLER.`:

```
<CFSET CALLER.rLoginFlag="1">
```

`CALLER.` tells ColdFusion to allow this variable to escape the protection of the custom tag and make it available to the calling page.

To dynamically name and create the variable, type:

```
<CFSET "Caller.#Attributes.LoginFlag#"="1">
```

Because we declared that `ATTRIBUTES.LoginFlag` will have a value of `rLoginFlag`, the variable is ultimately named `Caller.rLoginFlag`, and because of the `Caller.` prefix, it will be exposed to the calling page.

Using these techniques you can not only pass variables back into the calling page, but name them uniquely, as well.

> **TIP**
>
> These techniques are also applied to prevent naming conflicts. Because the person creating the custom tag might not be aware of your naming conventions, he might inadvertently give a name to the variable being returned to the calling page that is the same name as a variable in your application. Because the variable being exposed back to the calling page in the `Caller.` scope essentially becomes a local variable in the calling page, it can inadvertently overwrite the other variable. By explicitly naming the variable being returned, you can avoid this conflict.

Summary

Custom tags enable you and your development team to create modular code with an incredible degree of maintainability. In this chapter, we reviewed how even simple, everyday code can be converted into a reusable custom tag.

Custom tags can be written with or without attributes, and can be invoked in a number of ways. Within the custom tag, you should perform validation on the attributes and set default values for them as necessary. Additionally, we reviewed one of the more novel ways of making a custom tag more effective by enabling the developer to dynamically name any variables being returned to the calling page.

In the next chapter, "Advanced Custom Tags," you will review how to create custom tags that have even more functionality than those we have discussed in this chapter.

Sample Questions

1. Which code would you use to create a variable in a custom tag that could be passed back into the calling page?
   A. <CFSET FirstName="Emily">
   B. <CFSET Caller.FirstName="Emily">
   C. <CFSET SetVariable(FirstName, "Emily")>
   D. <CFSET ExposeVariable(FirstName, "Emily")>

2. Which of the following does not implicitly declare the directory in which ColdFusion should look for the custom tag called mycustomtag.cfm?
   A. <CF_MyCustomTag>
   B. <CFMODULE TEMPLATE="/files/mycustomtag.cfm">
   C. Modifying the Registry key HKEY_LOCAL_MACHINE\SOFTWARE\ALLAIRE\OLDFUSION\CURRENTVERSION\CUSTOMTAGS
   D. mycustomtag.cfm

3. What is the best way to set default values for optional custom tag attributes?
   A. <CFPARAM NAME="MyAttribute" DEFAULT="MyValue">
   B. <CFSET MyAttribute="MyValue">
   C. <INPUT TYPE="hidden" NAME="MyAttribute" VALUE="MyValue">
   D. <CF_MYCUSTOMTAG MYATTRIBUTE="MyValue">

CHAPTER 23

Advanced Custom Tags

What Are Advanced Custom Tags?

In the last chapter, you learned how creating and using custom tags can improve the maintainability of your code and increase your overall productivity. All that will remain true during our discussion of advanced custom tags in this chapter.

The main reason to implement advanced custom tags is increased functionality. The main programmatic difference between regular custom tags and advanced ones is that the latter utilizes the ability to nest custom tags within each other. The nested custom tag architecture actually increases the power of custom tags because it allows them to interact with each other to better perform tasks.

To find good reasons for using nested custom tags, you do not have to look any further than the ColdFusion language itself. `<CFHTTP>`, `<CFQUERY>`, and `<CFMAIL>` all use nested tags called `<CFHTTPPARAM>`, `<CFQUERYPARAM>`, and `<CFMAILPARAM>`, respectively.

➔ <CFHTTP> and <CFHTTPPARAM> are discussed in Chapter 31, "Other Internet Protocols." <CFQUERY> is discussed in Chapter 7, "Using Databases," and <CFQUERYPARAM> is discussed in Chapter 35, "Database-Specific Features." <CFMAIL> and <CFMAILPARAM> are both introduced in Chapter 29, "Email Integration."

In each of these cases, the *base* or *parent* tag is completely functional on its own, but by adding the use of the *subtag* or the *child* tag, the tag becomes even more powerful.

For instance, alone, <CFHTTP> enables you to create an HTTP call inside your ColdFusion template. By adding <CFHTTPPARAM>, however, you can now not only grab another Web page, but you can also post variables to it.

Alone, <CFQUERY> connects you to a datasource. By adding <CFQUERYPARAM>, you can perform data validation on the variables being passed into the SQL statement and declare the variable's data type.

<CFMAIL> also has increased functionality when using its child tags. By itself, <CFMAIL> sends plain text or HTML mail through an SMTP server. However, when you use <CFMAILPARAM> in conjunction with <CFMAIL>, you can send one or more attachments with the email message.

Tag Pairs

Let's say that you have a custom tag called <CF_PrintDate> that only contains the following code:

```
<CFOUTPUT>
Today's Date: #DateFormat(Now(), "mm/dd/yyyy")#
</CFOUTPUT>
```

When you run this custom tag, you will find that it simply prints out a formatted date. Now evaluate this call:

```
<CF_PrintDate>
</CF_PrintDate>
```

The preceding code actually calls the custom tag twice—you will see the date printed twice on the screen. This should emphasize to you that, regardless of whether the call to the custom tag references a start or an end tag, it will always run the custom tag.

> **NOTE**
>
> If you use <CFMODULE> to call the custom tag, you can also use it as an end tag, like so: </CFMODULE>.

→ <CFMODULE> was first introduced in the previous chapter, "Custom Tags."

However, it is not useful for us to run the same code when we call the start and the end tags. Typically, when the start tag is run, the custom tag's environment is created—meaning that the necessary default variables and validation are performed here. The actual functionality of the custom tag is usually run when the end tag is accessed.

ThisTag Scope

Nested custom tags have some degree of intelligence about their own state. We will use the ThisTag scope to access the information, or *tag instance data*, that the tags know about themselves.

ThisTag.ExecutionMode

`ThisTag.ExecutionMode` is a variable that tells us whether we're in the start, inactive, or end mode of a tag pair set. Start mode refers to the start tag, end mode refers to the end tag, and inactive mode refers to any code or text that is run between the two tags.

Within our custom tag, we can specify what part of the program we would like to run in start or end mode. We simply evaluate which mode ColdFusion is currently processing, and have the program react accordingly. The following code shows how we determine the value of `ThisTag.ExecutionMode`:

```
<CFSWITCH EXPRESSION="#ThisTag.ExecutionMode#">
<CFCASE VALUE="start">
    <!--- in start mode, initialize variables --->
    <CFPARAM NAME="Attributes.FirstName" VALUE="Emily">
</CFCASE>
<CFCASE VALUE="end">
    <!--- in end mode, perform the processing --->
    <CFOUTPUT>#ATTRIBUTES.FirstName#</CFOUTPUT>
</CFSWITCH>
```

→ <CFSWITCH> and <CFCASE> were introduced in Chapter 3, "Conditional Processing."

When ColdFusion runs the start tag, `ThisTag.ExecutionMode` will evaluate to `start` and only the `<CFPARAM>` tag will be run. When ColdFusion runs the end tag, `ThisTag.ExecutionMode` will evaluate to `end` and the value of `ATTRIBUTES.FirstName` will be evaluated and printed.

ThisTag.HasEndTag

`ThisTag.HasEndTag` is a variable that holds instance data about whether a particular start tag has an associated end tag. This value is used for validation purposes. Some custom tags should not be processed without an end tag present. Analyze the following code:

```
<CFIF NOT ThisTag.HasEndTag>
    This custom tag requires an end tag.
    <CFEXIT>
</CFIF>
```

→ <CFIF> was introduced in Chapter 3, "Conditional Processing." <CFEXIT> was introduced in Chapter 22, "Custom Tags."

Because `ThisTag.HasEndTag` has either a `yes` or a `no` value, it can be directly evaluated to a true or false statement by using the `<CFIF>` tag. In the preceding code, if `ThisTag.HasEndTag` is not true, an error will be printed and the custom tag will be aborted. The usual place for this logic to occur is within the `start` case of the `ThisTag.ExecutionMode` evaluation.

ThisTag.GeneratedContent

Any text that is typed or generated by ColdFusion during the inactive mode of `ThisTag.ExecutionMode` (in other words, between the start and the end custom tags) can be accessed by evaluating the variable `ThisTag.GeneratedContent`.

At first glance, this doesn't seem like that useful a variable. However, if we evaluate the `<CF_StripWhiteSpace>` custom tag created by Nate Weiss, we find that it has a very interesting use. The functionality of this custom tag is created using the following code:

```
<CFIF ThisTag.ExecutionMode is "End">
<!--- Replace multiple whitespace characters with a single space --->
<CFSET ThisTag.GeneratedContent=
      ➥REReplace(ThisTag.GeneratedContent, "[[:space:]]{2,}", "", "ALL")>
</CFIF>
```

To use this custom tag, you place an opening `<CF_StripWhiteSpace>` tag above your code and an ending `</CF_StripWhiteSpace>` below your code. The opening `<CF_StripWhiteSpace>` tag doesn't do anything. ColdFusion will evaluate all the code between the two tags normally. However, when the application server reaches the end `</CF_StripWhiteSpace>` tag, it will access all the resultant ColdFusion output that was created during inactive mode (using `ThisTag.GeneratedContent`) and will strip out all extra white space from the string.

Child Tags

In the earlier example, you see how introducing an end tag can improve the functionality of your custom tags. In this section, the power of custom tags is increased even further by introducing child tags to the scenario.

Almost every Web site has some sort of menu system that helps the visitors navigate through the site. We will use a nested menu system to discuss the use of nested custom tags.

> **TIP**
>
> Custom tags can be nested more than one level deep. You can nest custom tags within custom tags as far as you desire. However, for performance reasons, it is recommended that you do not nest deeper than necessary.

In the following code, we call two custom tags multiple times to create a menu structure:

```
<CF_MENU TEXT="Products" URL="products.cfm" CONTAINSITEMS="yes">
   <CF_MENUITEM TEXT="ColdFusion Studio" URL="productinfo.cfm?prod_ID=4">
   <CF_MENUITEM TEXT="ColdFusion Professional"
       ➥URL="productinfo.cfm?prod_ID=5">
   <CF_MENUITEM TEXT="ColdFusion Enterprise"
       ➥URL="productinfo.cfm?prod_ID=8">
```

```
</CFMENU>
<CF_MENU TEXT="Support" URL="help.cfm" CONTAINSITEMS="yes">
    <CF_MENUITEM TEXT="Knowledge Base" URL="helptools.cfm?tool_ID=1">
    <CF_MENUITEM TEXT="Developer's Exchange" URL="helptools.cfm?tool_ID=2">
</CFMENU>
<CF_MENU TEXT="About Allaire" URL="about.cfm" CONTAINSITEMS="no">
```

The tag `<CF_MENU>` will display the main sections of the Web site, whereas the `<CF_MENUITEM>` tags will display specific pages within the section. Note, however, that `<CF_MENU>` does not have to contain child tags, and can stand alone as a top-level menu item if necessary.

Custom Tag Functions

There are two functions that are used with custom tags to extend the intelligence of instance data and facilitate the transfer of data in a nested custom tag architecture.

GetBaseTagList()

When working with nested custom tags, we need a method of validation that helps us ensure that the tags are properly nested. The function `GetBaseTagList()` will be used for just this purpose. Review the following code:

```
<CFSET ParentTag=GetBaseTagList()>
<CFIF NOT ListFindNoCase(ParentTag, "CF_Menu")>
    This child tag must be embedded within a parent tag called <CF_Menu>
    <CFABORT>
</CFIF>
```

We place this code within the child tag, `<CF_MENUITEM>`. `GetBaseTagList()` returns a list of all the names of tags surrounding, and including, the child tag. After you have that list, you can use the string function `ListFindNoCase()` to check whether the parent tag is one of the tags surrounding the child tag. If the parent tag `<CF_MENU>` does not surround the child tag, the error message will be displayed.

> **CAUTION**
>
> `GetBaseTagList()` can help you validate to ensure that your child tag is, in fact, embedded inside the correct parent tag. However, if you have multiple levels of nesting, you will have to do further parsing and validation to ensure that the tags are nested in the correct order.

GetBaseTagData()

To create the most reusable and flexible custom tags, it is a good idea to make sure that a child tag can react differently to commands within the parent tag. In our example, the parent tag `<CF_MENU>` has an attribute called `CONTAINSITEMS`. If the value of this attribute is set to `yes`, the child tags will be displayed below the parent tag. If the value of this attribute is set to `no`, no child tags will be displayed, even if child tags are listed.

For the child tags to react appropriately, they must know whether the parent tag has declared if CONTAINSITEMS is yes or no. We will use the function GetBaseTagData() within the child tag to grab this data from the parent tag. Evaluate the following code:

```
<CFSET stGetParentTagVars=GetBaseTagData("CF_Menu")>
<CFSET ParentTagContainsItems=stGetParentTagVars.Attributes.ContainsItems>
```

In the first <CFSET> statement, all the variables in the parent tag <CF_MENU> are pulled into the child tag as a structure and placed within a new structure called stGetParentTagVars.

> **CAUTION**
> There is a bug in the function GetBaseTagData() that causes it to act unexpectedly. This function should return all the parent tag variables in a structure. However, if you try to use structure functions to evaluate the data being returned, you will come out with an empty structure. We know that the structure actually exists, however, because the values are present.

➔ Structures are discussed in Chapter 15, "Structures."

In the second <CFSET> statement, we access the CONTAINSITEMS attribute from directly within the stGetParentVars structure. After we have this value, we can easily use it within conditional statements to force different behavior from the child tag.

<CFASSOCIATE>

We have just discussed how to pass variables from the parent tag into the child tag. Now we have to reverse our track and discuss a way to pass child data back into parent data.

We will accomplish this task by using a ColdFusion tag called <CFASSOCIATE>. This tag grabs all attributes passed into a child tag and organizes them as structures. In our previous example, one of the child tags declared was as follows:

```
<CF_MENUITEM TEXT="ColdFusion Studio" URL="productinfo.cfm?prod_ID=4">
```

If we took the attributes of this child tag and converted them into a structure, they might be represented in this manner:

```
Menu item #1
TEXT="ColdFusion Studio"
URL="productinfo.cfm?prod_ID=4"
```

If we took the next two child tags and represented their attributes in the same manner, we would have this:

```
MENU Item #2
TEXT="ColdFusion Professional"
URL="productinfo.cfm?prod_ID=5"
```

and this:

```
Menu Item #3
TEXT="ColdFusion Enterprise"
URL="productinfo.cfm?prod_ID=8"
```

From what you know about structures and arrays, you should be able to see immediately that organizing data in this manner makes it obvious that the data could be stored as an array of structures.

→ Lists, arrays, and structures are discussed in Chapters 13, 14, and 15, respectively.

This is exactly what `<CFASSOCIATE>` does—converts every child tag's attribute set into a structure which is then placed into an array. The syntax for the tag is

```
<CFASSOCIATE BASETAG="CF_Menu" DATACOLLECTION="MenuItemData">
```

The first attribute, `BASETAG`, declares the parent tag to which you will be passing all the child tag data. The `DATACOLLECTION` attribute is what you use to name the array of structures that holds all child tag data.

> **NOTE**
> If you do not explicitly name the array of structures using the `DATACOLLECTION` attribute, by default ColdFusion refers to it as `AssocAttribs`.

Once all the data is passed back into the parent tag, the variable is referred to as part of the `ThisTag` scope. In our example, when back in the parent tag, we would refer to the array of structures as `ThisTag.MenuItemData`. You would use your knowledge of arrays and structures to access the data being held within this variable.

> **NOTE**
> The array of structures is passed back into the `end` mode of the parent tag set.

Summary

The introduction of the nested custom tag architecture has really increased the power of the tasks that you can perform using ColdFusion. Using the ColdFusion language itself as a guide, you have seen how using nested custom tags can increase the functionality of your code.

Although CFML custom tags are extremely powerful, you are still confined to the limitations of the ColdFusion language itself. In the next chapter, "COM, CORBA, CFX, and Java," you will review how utilizing other languages can further enhance the functionality of your ColdFusion applications.

Sample Questions

1. Which variable of the `ThisTag` scope declares if the tag is in start or end mode?
   - A. `ThisTag.GeneratedContent`
   - B. `ThisTag.StartOrEnd`
   - C. `ThisTag.HasEndTag`
   - D. `ThisTag.ExecutionMode`

2. Variables that are available to the parent tag in a nested custom tag architecture can be best made available to the child tags in what way?
   - A. By serializing the variables into a WDDX packet and then passing it to the child tag using `CFHTTP`
   - B. By calling them using the function `GetBaseTagData()`
   - C. By putting them into a memory-resident scope such as `SESSION` or `APPLICATION` variables
   - D. By rescoping them into the request scope

3. The `<CFASSOCIATE>` tag is used with nested custom tags to do what?
   - A. Pass generated content to the custom tag's end mode
   - B. Pass data from the start mode into the end mode
   - C. Pass a child tag's data back to the parent tag
   - D. Pass a parent tag's data into the child tag

CHAPTER 24

COM, CORBA, CFX, and Java

Extending CF with Other Technology

In the last two chapters about custom tags, we discussed how creating your own tags can benefit your applications in terms of quick maintenance and increased flexibility and power.

➔ Custom tags were discussed in Chapters 22, "Custom Tags," and Chapter 23, "Advanced Custom Tags."

ColdFusion is a very useful language because it helps Web developers quickly develop applications that in other languages would take too long to develop. However, there will be times when you will need to implement tasks that are outside the capabilities of ColdFusion.

The Allaire development team has taken this into account and has implemented tags and technology that will enable you to go beyond the boundaries of ColdFusion without losing the advantages of the language.

Working with Components and <CFOBJECT>

`<CFOBJECT>` is the means by which you integrate components into your ColdFusion environment. Through this tag you can execute COM, DCOM, CORBA, and Java objects.

COM objects are available as DLLs or EXEs whereas Java objects are available as class files. CORBA objects are server files that are specific to the language in which they are written.

> **TIP**
>
> If you are an ISP and want to disable the use of <CFOBJECT> in your hosted environment, you can do so by unchecking the Enable CFOBJECT tag check box in the `Basic Security` link of the `Server` section in the ColdFusion Administrator.

COM and DCOM

The *Component Object Model (COM)* is a Microsoft specification that enables you to implement component modules in your program. COM objects can be written in many languages—as long as each language understands COM, it will understand any COM object even if it is written in another language.

The fact that COM objects can be written in many languages gives it an immediate advantage over the CFX custom tags. Whereas CFX custom tags are written specifically for use within the ColdFusion environment, COM objects can be used across many applications.

> **NOTE**
>
> One major disadvantage of COM objects is that they are very Microsoft-centric, which means that they are best used in a Windows environment. Microsoft has also ported COM to other Unix-based platforms such as Solaris, but ColdFusion does not support COM on Unix and will not recognize any COM objects in a distributed environment that involves Unix.

> **TIP**
>
> Before you call a COM object from within your ColdFusion code, you must first register it with the system. Most objects will come with instructions on how to do this.

To call a COM object in ColdFusion, you type the following:

```
<CFOBJECT TYPE="COM" CLASS="Allaire.Comex.1" NAME="objCompany" ACTION="Create">
```

This example, written by Bushan Byragani (ColdFusion Engineering Manager of Allaire), creates a Company object. After that object is created, you can populate it with properties such as the following:

```
<CFSET objCompany.company_name="Allaire">
<CFSET objCompany.for_profit="1">
<CFSET objCompany.revenues="85000323.56">
```

The following code then creates a department and populates it with an array of employees:

```
<CFSET objDoc=objCompany.CreateDepartment('Documentation')>
<CFSET doc_employees=ArrayNew(1)>
<CFSET doc_employees[1]="MetMaker, Baldy">
```

```
<CFSET doc_employees[2]="HealthFood, Donuts">
<CFSET doc_employees[3]="Mellow, Fellow">
<CFSET objDoc.AddEmployees(doc_employees)>
```

➔ Arrays were discussed in Chapter 14, "Arrays."

The information that you have entered into the object can be used within your ColdFusion page as follows:

```
<CFOUTPUT>
    Company Name: #objCompany.company_name#<br>
    For Profit: #objCompany.for_profit#<br>
    Revenues: #objCompany.revenues#<br>
    Departments: #objCompany.department_count#<br>
</cfoutput>

<CFSET Revenue=objCompany.revenue>
<CFSET Revenue.Q1="22124345.83">
<CFSET Revenue.Q2="18536444.02">
```

This code first assigns the `objCompany.revenue` object to the ColdFusion local variable `Revenue`, and then assigns it quarterly earnings.

> **NOTE**
>
> ColdFusion also enables you to use distributed objects through the *Distributed Component Object Model (DCOM)*. DCOM objects can be used over a network and do not need to reside on the same machine as the ColdFusion server.

CORBA

The *Common Object Request Broker Architecture (CORBA)* is another distributed object technology. This technology is spearheaded by the *Object Management Group (OMG)* and is more of a community standard than is COM.

However, unlike many community standards, CORBA is a pretty expensive choice for implementing objects. ColdFusion developers likely will not adopt CORBA as a way to extend ColdFusion. However, for organizations that have already made an investment in CORBA, ColdFusion provides an easy way to extend and interact with that technology.

If you do find a need to use ColdFusion with CORBA, you can interact with the CORBA objects using `<CFOBJECT>` like this:

```
<CFOBJECT ACTION="connect" CLASS="c:\\cfo_account.ior2" NAME="objAccount"
➥TYPE="CORBA" CONTEXT="IOR">
```

This code, again from Bushan Byragani, is a simple banking example. After you have told ColdFusion which CORBA server to access in the previous code and what to name the object to reference in your code, you can set and retrieve attributes:

```
<!--- setting an attribute --->
<cfset objAccount.long_attrib="43453">
<!--- retrieving an attribute --->
<CFSET balance=objAccount.balance()>
```

Because you've written the account balance attribute into a ColdFusion local variable, you can use the results of the CORBA statement in any way that you want.

→ Local variables were introduced in Chapter 2, "Working with Variables and Expressions."

> **NOTE**
> You can use `<CFTRY>` and `<CFCATCH>` for exception handling of `<CFOBJECT>`. When an exception is thrown, the class that threw the error is noted in the `CFCATCH.Message` variable. `<CFTRY>` and `<CFCATCH>` were introduced in Chapter 21, "Error Handling."

Java Objects and EJB

You can also call *Enterprise Java Beans (EJB)* or any Java object using `<CFOBJECT>`.

The following code instantiates the Java object that creates a JPEG image from any text that the programmer feeds into the call:

```
<!--- using the CFOBJECT tag --->
<CFOBJECT TYPE="JAVA" ACTION="Create" NAME="image" CLASS="HelloWorldGraphic">
<CFSET temp=image.createImage("Hello World!")>
<!--- using the CreateObject() function --->
<CFSCRIPT>
image=CreateObject("Java", "HelloWorldGraphic");
image.init();
imglen=image.createImage("Hello World!");
</CFSCRIPT>
```

> **NOTE**
> In the code, we have explicitly initialized the constructor using the code `image.init();`. If you do not explicitly initialize it, ColdFusion will make an implicit call to the default constructor.

The JPEG that is created is placed in a directory as defined in the Java code itself. You can access the JPEG similar to any other file on your system.

Consider wrapping this code into a custom tag to enhance its usability.

CFX

ColdFusion custom tags do not have to be written in CFML. If you're a C++ or Java programmer, you can easily integrate your programs as CFX custom tags into ColdFusion using the ColdFusion Administrator.

For example, Tom Frey of ASDC.net created a CFX custom tag called <CFX_EXCEL> that allows you to query a ColdFusion datasource and write the results of that query directly to a Microsoft Excel spreadsheet.

> **TIP**
>
> You can find Tom's <CFX_EXCEL> tag in the Developer's Exchange at `http://devex.allaire.com/developer/gallery/`

In this case, the custom tag is available as a *dynamic link library (DLL)* because it has been written using the C/C++ API for Microsoft Windows. A Java CFX would be available as a class file, and, on the Solaris platform, the CFX custom tags would be shared objects.

In any case, you must register the CFX with the ColdFusion application server using the `CFX_Tags` link in the `Extensions` section of the CF Administrator interface.

To use the <CFX_EXCEL> custom tag, type the following into your ColdFusion template:

```
<!--- grab all employees from the database --->
<CFQUERY NAME="GetEmployees" DATASOURCE="HR">
SELECT *
FROM Employees
</CFQUERY>
<!--- place the recordset returned into a spreadsheet using CFX_EXCEL --->
<CFX_EXCEL QUERY="GetEmployees" FILE="C:\XLS\OUTPUT.XLS">
```

> **NOTE**
>
> To use the Java option, make sure that you register the Java Virtual Machine in the ColdFusion Administrator. These settings can be found in the `Server` section under the link for `Java`.

> **CAUTION**
>
> Because CFX tags are placed into memory, they can cause server instabilities if they are not accessed correctly. Ideally, the programmer who creates them should make sure that they are thread-safe. However, if they are not thread-safe and you still need to use them, you can use <CFLOCK> to accomplish the same task. <CFLOCK> is discussed in Chapter 12, "Locking."

Java

As discussed in earlier sections of this chapter, you can leverage Java objects and beans using <CFOBJECT> and <CFX>. Now we will review how ColdFusion gives you access to *Java Server Pages (JSP)* and Java servlets.

As you know from your experience with ColdFusion development, ColdFusion applications can be created very quickly. Java applications don't get nearly as quick a start as ColdFusion applications, but, in addition to having reusable components in the form of EJBs and class libraries, their advantages are scalability, portability, and performance.

> **NOTE**
>
> JRun is Allaire's Java application server. It is built to meet the specification of Java 2 Enterprise Edition (J2EE). With JRun you can use Enterprise JavaBeans, Java Transaction API, Java Messaging Service, JavaServer Pages, and Java servlets. There is even a JRun Studio development environment to help with your Java development.

JSP

Java Server Pages is a tag-based scripting language, similar to ColdFusion, that gives developers a simplified interface to Java servlet development. However, unlike ColdFusion, when the JSP pages are run, the Java application server compiles the code into servlets.

Evaluate the following JSP code:

```
<%--- grab the URL variable FNAME and write to a local variable ---%>
<% String FNAME==request.getParameter("FNAME") %>
<%--- grab the URL variable LNAME and write to a local variable ---%>
<% String LNAME==request.getParameter("LNAME") %>
<!--- print out name --->
<%=fname%> <%=lname%>
```

Using the scripting parameters, the previous code grabs URL variables and prints them to the HTML page.

Querying the database in JSP can be much more involved because you would usually have to call straight Java code. However, the JRun engine comes with tag libraries, which are the equivalent of ColdFusion custom tags. These tag libraries allow JSP developers to access the Java code to query the database without having to actually interact with the Java code itself.

```
<%@ page import="allaire.taglib.*,java.sql.*" %>
<%@ taglib uri="jruntags" prefix="jrun"%>
<%--- Execute SQL ---%>
<jrun:sql datasrc="forta.com" id="articles">
SELECT title
FROM articles
</jrun:sql>
<%--- Loop through results ---%>
<jrun:foreach item="i" group="<%= articles %>">
<%= i.title %><BR>
</jrun:foreach>
```

Using JRun tag libraries, a JSP programmer can easily reference Java code without having to get his feet too wet.

<CFSERVLET>

You can bypass JSP entirely if you are a Java programmer by implementing a special form of Web- and HTTP-aware compiled Java code called servlets. Using the <CFSERVLET> tag, you can run these Java servlets on a JRun server.

```
<CFSERVLET CODE="domainLookup" JRUNPROXY="127.0.0.1:51000" TIMEOUT="300"
➥WRITEOUTPUT="yes" DEBUG="Yes">
    <CFSERVLEYPARAM NAME="whois" VALUE="#FORM.domain#">
</CFSERVLET>
```

> **NOTE**
>
> The DEBUG attribute of <CFSERVLET> writes debug output to the JRun logs, not the ColdFusion server logs.

This code, contributed by Hussain Chinoy of Granularity, uses <CFSERVLET> to call a Java servlet on a JRun server. This servlet performs a WHOIS domain lookup using the domain name passed from a FORM field. <CFSERVLET> uses nested tag architecture to allow you to pass multiple parameters into the servlet using the child tag <CFSERVLETPARAM>.

> **CAUTION**
>
> In JRun 3.0, the JRUNPROXY attribute is required when using <CFSERVLET>.

Summary

Although ColdFusion is a great programming language that is optimized for rapid development, there are simply things that it cannot do. When you need to extend the abilities of ColdFusion, you can do so using CFX custom tags, and using <CFOBJECT> to call COM and CORBA objects as well as Java objects. <CFSERVLET> is also useful for incorporating Java servlets into ColdFusion.

Sample Questions

1. In which of the following two languages can CFX custom tags be written?
   A. Java
   B. C++
   C. Pascal
   D. Visual Basic

2. You do not have to know any Java to work with JavaServer Pages.
   A. True
   B. False

3. The *D* in DCOM stands for what?
   A. Distributed
   B. Detailed
   C. Documented
   D. Dynamic

CHAPTER 25

WDDX

XML Overview

To understand Web Dynamic Data Exchange (WDDX), you first need to have a basic understanding of the Extensible Markup Language (XML) and why it was created.

XML is a markup language, like HTML or CFML. However, while the latter are both rigid languages with a finite number of tags (if you exclude custom tags in CFML) that have strictly defined properties, XML was created explicitly for flexibility in data exchange. In other words, with XML you get to make up your own tags to represent your data.

Let's explore how XML differs from HTML by looking at the following HTML code:

```
<TABLE>
<TR>
     <TD>33-2112</TD>
     <TD>10</TD>
     <TD>S</TD>
</TR>
<TR>
     <TD>29-3564</TD>
     <TD>8</TD>
     <TD>M</TD>
</TR>
<TR>
     <TD>21-1153</TD>
     <TD>10</TD>
     <TD>L</TD>
</TR>
</TABLE>
```

This HTML tells the browser to display the data in a nice HTML table. But do you have any idea what that data means? You can't possibly know because the HTML explains only the formatting, not what the data represents.

Now take a look at the following code:

```
<SKU>33-2112</SKU>
<QUANTITY>10</QUANTITY>
<SIZE>S</SIZE>
<SKU>29-3564</SKU>
<QUANTITY>8</QUANTITY>
<SIZE>M</SIZE>
<SKU>21-1153</SKU>
<QUANTITY>10</QUANTITY>
<SIZE>L</SIZE>
```

Here, you can see that the data actually represents some sort of inventory. This information can now be sent from a clothing supplier to a clothing store representative, and it would make sense to each person.

To a browser, the HTML will be interpreted appropriately, because browsers have a built-in interpreter for HTML. Certain browsers may need a little more information to decipher the meaning of those XML tags. Because the names of the tags are all arbitrary, you must have a document that defines what each tag represents. This document is called a *Document Type Definition,* or DTD.

Although, in practice, browsers don't really work this way, ideally, HTML is just XML data. The browser could use HTML DTDs to interpret the HTML that you type on a page. When you type `<TABLE>`, the browser looks in its HTML DTD and knows to start creating a table.

> **NOTE**
>
> To learn more information about XML, check out `http://www.xml.com/pub/a/98/10/guide0.html`. It's a good place to start.
>
> To learn more details about using HTML and XML together, you can look for XHTML on `http://www.w3c.org`.

The major benefit of a system like this is that the data can be sent from one program to another, and if both programs understand the DTD, they can freely pass data back and forth.

XML and WDDX

WDDX is Allaire's contribution to the XML community. It is an open-source XML DTD that defines generic data types such as strings, arrays, structures, and recordsets.

The following example shows a ColdFusion two-dimensional array of the data from the previous code:

```
<CFSCRIPT>
     aProducts=ArrayNew(2);
     aProducts[1][1]="33-2112";
     aProducts[1][2]="10";
     aProducts[1][3]="S";
     aProducts[2][1]="29-3564";
     aProducts[2][2]="8";
     aProducts[2][3]="M";
     aProducts[3][1]="21-1153";
     aProducts[3][2]="10";
     aProducts[3][3]="L";
</CFSCRIPT>
```

If you then take this data and convert it into WDDX, you see the following:

```
<wddxPacket version='1.0'><header></header><data><array length='3'>
➥<array length='3'><string>33-2112</string><string>10</string><string>S
➥</string></array><array length='3'><string>29-3564</string><string>8</string>
➥<string>M</string></array><array length='3'><string>21-1153</string>
➥<string>10</string><string>L</string></array></array></data></wddxPacket>
```

> **NOTE**
>
> Converting data into a WDDX packet is called *serialization,* and converting it from WDDX back to native data is called *deserialization*.

Notice that the packet doesn't give the data a name as in the earlier example (like SKU or Quantity); rather, it defines the data generically as strings and arrays.

If you take this packet and pass it to an ASP program or a Perl script that understands the WDDX DTD, then those programs can convert the data back into variables that are understood by their own systems.

The real power of WDDX is that it allows you to use a simplified implementation of XML without having to worry about learning XML or DTDs. The WDDX DTD is interpreted by either ColdFusion or the other system that understands WDDX. The user never has to get his hands dirty.

➔ To learn more about WDDX, go to http://www.wddx.org.

CFWDDX

To turn the preceding code example into a WDDX packet, you can use a tag called <CFWDDX> like this:

```
<CFWDDX ACTION="CFML2WDDX" INPUT="#variables.aProducts#" OUTPUT="NewPacket">
```

> **CAUTION**
>
> Note the # signs around the value for the INPUT attribute. If you forget them, ColdFusion thinks that you are trying to serialize the literal string Variables.aProducts.

Table 25.1 explains the attributes to the <CFWDDX> tag.

Table 25.1 <CFWDDX> Attributes

Attribute	Description
ACTION	Tells ColdFusion what action to take on the variable.
INPUT	Tells ColdFusion which variable to serialize.
OUTPUT	Names the variable into which ColdFusion will place the packet.
TOPLEVELVARIABLE	If you are using WDDX to create JavaScript, this is the name of the JavaScript variable being created.

Table 25.2 explains the possible values for the ACTION attribute.

Table 25.2 Values for the ACTION Attribute

Value	Description
CFML2WDDX	Serializes ColdFusion data into a WDDX packet
WDDX2CFML	Deserializes the ColdFusion data from a WDDX packet to ColdFusion data
WDDX2JS	Deserializes a WDDX packet into native JavaScript
CFML2JS	Turns ColdFusion data directly into JavaScript data using WDDX as a bridge

➔ JavaScript and ColdFusion are only two of the languages that understand WDDX. Some others are PHP, Perl, ASP, Python, and Java. To learn more details about how to integrate WDDX with these other programming languages, go to http://www.wddx.org.

If you have a query recordset called GetStates and want to serialize it into a WDDX packet, you can type

```
<CFWDDX ACTION="CFML2WDDX" INPUT="#GetStates#">
```

Because the preceding CFWDDX code doesn't have an OUTPUT attribute, rather than the data being put into a variable, it is output directly to the page itself.

> **CAUTION**
>
> WDDX packets do not like special characters such as < or > outside the XML tags themselves. When you're developing applications, you probably have the ColdFusion debugging settings turned on in the ColdFusion Administrator. The debugging is displayed at the bottom of your HTML page using HTML code. This means that when

your WDDX packet is written to the page, it becomes corrupted by the extra HTML debugging information.

To deal with this problem, always place the tag `<CFSETTING SHOWDEBUGOUTPUT="No">` at the top of your page. It suppresses debugging on the page.

➔ The ColdFusion Administrator debugging options were discussed in Chapter 20, "Debugging."

TIP

Two ColdFusion functions that are helpful for creating valid WDDX packets are `XMLFormat()` and `IsWDDX()`. The former converts special characters in data to an acceptable XML format. The latter was introduced in ColdFusion 4.5.1 Service Pack 2 and verifies that the WDDX packet is valid.

Using WDDX with Other Technology

The most important point to remember about serializing and deserializing a WDDX packet is that what you put in is what you get out. So, if your ColdFusion application takes a query recordset and turns it into a WDDX packet and then passes it on to an ASP program, that program ends up with a recordset as well.

WDDX is a powerful tool when used for syndication purposes. When you're sharing data between two Web sites, getting the data in just the right format can be difficult if both sites use different programming languages. Now, with WDDX, if both programs understand the WDDX DTD, they have a translator that allows them to transfer data seamlessly.

➔ Syndication will be discussed in more detail in Chapter 31, "Other Internet Protocols."

Summary

There is a movement afoot to try to make programming languages more universal. XML facilitates data sharing between diverse and disparate applications and services. WDDX provides some of the core benefits of XML without requiring learning and understanding XML itself—and on all major platforms (including ColdFusion).

Sample Questions

1. Which of the following is *not* a valid `ACTION` attribute for the `CFWDDX` tag?
   A. `CFML2ASP`
   B. `CFML2JS`
   C. `WDDX2CFML`
   D. `CFML2WDDX`

2. What do you call the document that declares what XML tags represent?
   A. Code Conversion Document
   B. Tag Declaration Sheet
   C. Document Type Definition
   D. XML Tag Definition

3. Which of the following options would you use to convert a ColdFusion two-dimensional array called `aNames` into a WDDX packet and write the results to the page?

   A. `<CFWDDX ACTION="CFML2WDDX" INPUT="#aNames#">`

   B. `<CFWDDX ACTION="CFML2PAGE" INPUT="#aNames#">`

   C. `<CFWDDX ACTION="CFML2WDDX" INPUT="#aNames#" WRITETOPAGE="Yes">`

   D. `<CFWDDX ACTION="CFML2WDDX" INPUT="#aNames#" OUTPUT="This.Page">`

PART 6

SERVICES AND PROTOCOLS

CHAPTER 26

Full Text Searching

Understanding Full Text Searching

ColdFusion ships with a custom implementation of the Verity97 search engine, commonly abbreviated to Verity. This enables developers to perform full text searches on both database queries and file libraries. Verity generates a read-optimized set of indexes called a collection, and provides search tools to retrieve result sets ranked by relevancy.

→ The company Verity has a range of enterprise-level search and indexing products available. The ColdFusion Verity97 implementation is a customized version of one of its core products.

See `http://www.verity.com/` for more details.

A Verity collection is a group of files and associated metadata optimized for searching. Collections include various word indices, an internal documents table containing document field information, and pointers to the actual files for file and path indexes. ColdFusion provides a variety of Verity functions to create, maintain, and optimize collections. This maintenance can be performed through the ColdFusion administrator or with the `<CFCOLLECTION>` and `<CFINDEX>` tags.

Searching a Verity collection is fast and leverages the search command vocabulary of the Verity engine. Users can perform sophisticated searches using `<CFSEARCH>`, handling Booleans, wildcards, and other advanced search options.

> **NOTE**
> Verity97 can index and search most popular office file types including text, HTML, XML, RTF, Adobe PDF, Microsoft Word, WordPerfect, Excel, and PowerPoint. For a complete listing of all the supported file types, refer to your ColdFusion documentation.

Verity Collections

A Verity collection is a read-optimized, logical database made up of a number of physical files stored on your Web server's hard drive. When a collection is created, the physical files and directories that make up the Verity collection are written to the server. A registry entry is also created under

```
HKEY_LOCAL_MACHINE/SOFTWARE/Allaire/ColdFusion/CurrentVersion/Collections
```

This entry associates the collection's logical name with its physical file structure on disk. The logical name is also used when referring to collections via the `COLLECTION` attribute of both the `<CFINDEX>` and `<CFSEARCH>` tags.

➔ Registry keys and values are discussed in Chapter 27, "System Integration."

Creating and Indexing Collections

A Verity collection can be created in a number of ways: through the ColdFusion Administrator, the `<CFCOLLECTION>` tag, or some other third-party Verity tool. The initialization of the collection effectively sets up the directory structure and records a logical name for the collection in the registry.

```
<CFCOLLECTION ACTION="CREATE"
              COLLECTION="SnailsAndPuppyDogTails"
              PATH="C:\CFUSION\Verity\Collections"
              LANGUAGE="English">
```

The default directory location for all collections is

```
\CFUSION\Verity\Collections\
```

After a collection is created, ColdFusion will reference the name assigned for the collection as well as the name of the collection root directory. Using the earlier example, you should end up with

```
\CFUSION\Verity\Collections\SnailsAndPuppyDogTails\
```

The root directory of each collection contains two subdirectories: `custom` and `file`. The type of index used will dictate which of these folders is populated with index data. Within the active branch, additional directories are created, such as `ASSISTS`, `MORGUE`, `PARTS`, `PDD`, `STYLE`, `TEMP`, `TOPICIDX`, `TRANS`, and `WORK`. These directories store different components of the Verity infrastructure and for all intents and purposes, interaction with these elements is left to ColdFusion.

➔ For more information on the Verity collection file structure, try "Understanding Verity Collections in ColdFusion," by Jeremy Petersen. The article is located at http://www.allaire.com/Handlers/index.cfm?ID=18429

<CFCOLLECTION> can also be used to map an alias to an existing Verity collection that was created by a tool other than ColdFusion. The ACTION, COLLECTION, and PATH attributes are required. The path must point to a valid Verity collection; mapping does not validate the path. Deleting a mapped collection unregisters the alias; the base collection is not deleted.

Maintaining Collections

A collection starts life empty and must be populated using <CFINDEX>. <CFINDEX> can be used to create both file- and query-based indices. The collection simply needs to know where to find the body of words that the engine is to search on and what information will make up the result key to be returned on a successful match. Additional attributes are available for filtering and providing result summaries among other features.

A file library containing a mixture of Microsoft Office document file types could be indexed using the following:

```
<CFINDEX ACTION="UPDATE"
        COLLECTION="SnailsAndPuppyDogTails"
        KEY="c:\filestore\whatboyslike"
        TYPE="PATH"
        EXTENSIONS=".doc, .xls, .ppt, .pdf"
        RECURSE="Yes">
```

The nominated KEY attribute for TYPE="PATH" is a directory on the server. Each record in the index will use the filename as the key value. The EXTENSIONS attribute enables you to restrict the file types to be indexed in the specified directory. RECURSE="YES" instructs ColdFusion to work recursively through all subdirectories in the branch of the nominated root directory.

A database query with large text fields could be indexed efficiently using the following:

```
<CFQUERY NAME="qGirlsLike" DATASOURCE="Lifes_Mysteries">
SELECT *
FROM AllThingsNice
</CFQUERY>

<CFINDEX ACTION="UPDATE"
        COLLECTION="SugarAndSpice"
        KEY="Things_ID"
        TYPE="CUSTOM"
        TITLE="Sugar"
        QUERY="qGirlsLike"
        BODY="Spice"
```

```
        CUSTOM1="AllThings"
        CUSTOM2="">
```

In this example, KEY, TITLE, BODY, and CUSTOM1 are all fields in the collection index that are mapped to a specific column in the query object. KEY is the unique identifier for the record (the primary key in this instance), TITLE is a descriptive name (not unique), BODY refers to the document to be searched, and CUSTOM1 and CUSTOM2 are developer-definable fields that are returned with the search results. In effect, any query object can be used to populate a CUSTOM index including queries generated from <CFPOP>, <CFLDAP>, and <CFQUERY>.

CAUTION

In theory, there is no set limit to the size of Verity collections. However, in practice the amount of information that can be indexed by a single Verity collection depends largely on the type of data (for example, HTML, PDF, or Word) and the production system's resources (such as RAM and processor speed). Testing the limits of your own collections before going to production is worth considering.

In general, Allaire suggests that approximately 100MB of data (that is the size of the files, not the size of the index) is the upper limit for ColdFusion-based Verity collections. If you need to run larger collections, you can index your data into many smaller collections and reference those together as a comma-delimited list in your <CFSEARCH> tag:

```
<CFSEARCH COLLECTION="library1, library2, library3"
          NAME="qResults"
          CRITERIA="bill AND ben">
```

As your application data changes, the Verity collection must be updated in order to synchronize with the information stored in your database or file store. <CFINDEX> with both UPDATE and DELETE actions can be used to update collections one record at a time. This type of action might be coupled with data changes in the application to ensure that the Verity collection is always up to date.

```
<!--- updating a document in a file store index --->
<CFINDEX ACTION="UPDATE"
        COLLECTION="SnailsAndPuppyDogTails"
        KEY="c:\filestore\whatboyslike\escargot.doc"
        TYPE="FILE">
<!--- deleting a single record from query based index --->
<CFINDEX ACTION="DELETE" COLLECTION="SugarAndSpice" KEY="1234">
```

The entire index could be PURGED and ready for repopulation or, alternatively, cleared and repopulated using the REFRESH action. However, these options are not always suitable for regular update procedures and might be very time-consuming on large data stores.

> **CAUTION**
>
> On a high-traffic site, you might need to schedule downtime for the search interface while the collection is maintained. If you choose to maintain the collection after every data change in the application, the collection might not be available for searching during frequent or prolonged update periods.

From time to time, the Verity collection can become corrupted. If this happens, the collection can be repaired using `<CFCOLLECTION>`. In some instances, you might need to delete the collection entirely and reindex.

```
<CFCOLLECTION ACTION="REPAIR" COLLECTION="SugarAndSpice">
```

> **TIP**
>
> You can remove a Verity collection from the server manually. Don't forget to remove the corresponding registry entries, directory structure, and files.

`<CFINDEX>` *must be locked* during `UPDATE`, `DELETE`, `REFRESH`, and `PURGE` operations. In addition, make sure that neither the collection nor any of its files are open while it is being updated because this might cause corruption. Likewise, `<CFCOLLECTION>` *must be locked* during `OPTIMIZE` and `REPAIR` operations.

The application should implement a named, `EXCLUSIVE` lock around operations that involve modifying the collection. A named, `READONLY` lock should be used for searching the collection.

→ Detailed coverage of `<CFLOCK>` is available in Chapter 12, "Locking."

> **NOTE**
>
> The optional International Search Pack enables you to specify a language other than English when creating a new collection. If you have documents in several languages, it can be worthwhile to create a separate collection for each language.
>
> More information about the International Search Pack can be found at `http://www.allaire.com/Handlers/index.cfm?ID=2486`

Optimizing Collections

Verity collections require regular optimization, depending on the frequency of updates to the collection. Verity adds additional files to the collection rather than performing a complete re-index each time the collection is updated. This is a faster update mechanism, but it eventually leads to collection fragmentation. When a search is performed, each file in the collection is checked for a match. The more files or fragmentation in the index, the slower the search. Optimization compacts and aggregates the Verity metadata files, significantly improving the overall performance of the search engine.

Collections can be optimized through the ColdFusion administrator or programmatically using the `<CFCOLLECTION>` tag.

```
<CFCOLLECTION ACTION="OPTIMIZE" COLLECTION="SugarAndSpice">
```

> **TIP**
>
> Every update leads to further fragmentation of the Verity collection. Fragmented collections take up significantly more disk space and can eventually slow the collection to the point of being unsearchable.
>
> One method of minimizing fragmentation is to reduce the number of transactions being performed on the collection. Rather than updating the collection every time you update your data, you should consider periodic updates that bulk all your data changes into a single submission for updating the Verity collection.
>
> In any event, optimize regularly!

Creating a Search Interface

The `<CFSEARCH>` tag is used to query Verity collections. Typically, an application has a form that collects search parameters from the user and this form is submitted to an application page that invokes the `<CFSEARCH>` tag. `<CFSEARCH>` generates a query object containing records from the specified collection that match the keywords of the `CRITERIA` attribute.

```
<CFSEARCH COLLECTION="SnailsAndPuppyDogTails"
          NAME="qSearchResults"
          TYPE="SIMPLE"
          CRITERIA="#FORM.keywords#">
```

There are two search `TYPES`: simple and explicit. The `CRITERIA` attribute of a simple search is commonly just a list of keywords. `CRITERIA` for an explicit search can use any number of Verity operators and modifiers to refine the results, but they must be explicitly invoked.

> **NOTE**
>
> If you search for a string that is all uppercase or all lowercase, the search is not case sensitive:
>
> ```
> CRITERIA="COLDFUSION"
> CRITERIA="coldfusion"
> ```
>
> If you search for a string that is mixed case, the search is case sensitive:
>
> ```
> CRITERIA="ColdFusion"
> ```

A simple query expression is "simple" only in that you, as the developer, do not need to specify any special Verity operators. You can enter multiple words separated by commas, in which case the comma is treated like a logical `OR`. If you omit the commas, the query expression is treated as a phrase. Wildcards can be specified for pattern matching. In addition, the `SIMPLE` search `TYPE` packs a very powerful combination of the Verity engine `STEM` operator and `MANY` modifier.

A STEM search automatically includes those words that are derived from the ones listed in the CRITERIA. For example, a word such as "view" will return records that contain "view," "viewing," "views," and so on.

The MANY modifier ranks search results according to a relevancy score. Relevancy is based on the density of the search term in the searched data. The more often a word appears in a document, the higher the document's score. Furthermore, where a keyword has the same frequency in two documents, the smaller document will have a higher relevancy. For example, a 500-page report that mentions the word "corruption" ten times is less significant than a five-page document that also has ten instances of the search term.

An explicit query expression can include any of the Verity operators and modifiers. However, they all must be explicitly specified. You might consider assembling an explicit search expression programmatically from an advanced search form or simply letting power users submit their own expressions.

➔ Details on how to build Verity query expressions can be found in Chapter 11, "Session State Management" and in "Indexing and Searching Data" of the "Developing Web Applications with ColdFusion" manual that ships with ColdFusion and ColdFusion Studio.

The query object generated by <CFSEARCH> can be processed as usual with <CFOUTPUT> to build a table of results. The available query columns are listed in Table 26.1. All that remains is to provide a drill-down interface to the individual records or documents.

➔ Dynamic URL parameters are covered in Chapter 8, "URL Variables."

Table 26.1 <CFSEARCH> Result Variables

Result	Description
URL	URL indicated in the <CFINDEX> tag used to populate the collection plus the filename for the document matched.
KEY	The full filename of the document in a FILE or PATH collection type or the value of the query column indicated in the KEY attribute of CUSTOM index.
TITLE	Value of the title of HTML, PDF, and Office documents (FILE or PATH), or value of the column indicated in the TITLE attribute (CUSTOM).
SCORE	Relevancy score dynamically calculated by Verity based on the search CRITERIA.
SUMMARY	Contains the automatic summary generated by <CFINDEX>. The default selects the best three matching sentences, up to a maximum of 500 characters.
CUSTOM1	Value of the column indicated in the CUSTOM1 attribute of the <CFINDEX> tag (CUSTOM).
CUSTOM2	Value of column indicated in the CUSTOM2 attribute of the <CFINDEX> tag (CUSTOM).

Table 26.1 continued

Result	Description
RECORDCOUNT	The number of records in the result set.
CURRENTROW	The current row being processed by a loop such as <CFOUTPUT>.
COLUMNLIST	The list of column names for the result set.
RECORDSSEARCHED	Total number of records searched.

For query-based collections, the primary key is ordinarily returned in KEY and can be used in a WHERE clause to return the complete record. File-based collections use a combination of the URL or KEY columns depending on how the collection was originally populated. For example, assuming the URLPATH attribute of <CFINDEX> was used:

```
<!--- query the collection --->
<CFSEARCH COLLECTION="SnailsAndPuppyDogTails"
          NAME="qSearchResults"
          TYPE="SIMPLE"
          CRITERIA="#FORM.keywords#">
<!--- format and output the results --->
<TABLE>
<TR>
        <TD>Score</TD>
        <TD>Document</TD>
</TR>
<CFOUTPUT QUERY="qSearchResults">
<TR>
        <TD>#Score#</TD>
        <TD><A HREF="#URL#">#Title#</A><BR>#Summary#</TD>
</TR>
</CFOUTPUT>
</TABLE>
```

NOTE

External Verity collections (that is, those not created in ColdFusion) can be referenced using the EXTERNAL="YES" attribute of both the <CFINDEX> and <CFSEARCH> tags. The collection name (in the COLLECTION attribute) should be set to the directory path where the collection resides on the hard drive.

The only fields you can reference in an external collection are KEY and SCORE. These are the only fields common to all Verity collections (regardless of the interface through which the collection is created). This means you will not have access to URL, TITLE, SUMMARY, CUSTOM1, or CUSTOM2. Likewise, any custom fields (non-ColdFusion) in external collections cannot be referenced.

> **TIP**
>
> The <CFSEARCH> result set is limited to 64KB. Using broad search terms, coupled with a large enough collection your users might hit the limit, throwing an error. The easiest way to handle the problem is to catch and trap the error and instruct the user to be more specific about his search criteria.

→ Error trapping is discussed in Chapter 21, "Error Handling."

→ Full text searching can also be performed in SQL databases using the `LIKE` operator. SQL searches and pattern matching are covered in Chapter 32, "Basic SQL."

> **CAUTION**
>
> Searching and performing collection maintenance simultaneously can lead to corruption of the collection. Ensure that your search and maintenance code are appropriately locked with named `READONLY` and `EXCLUSIVE` locks, respectively.

Summary

ColdFusion integration of the Verity97 search engine enables developers to implement powerful free-text searching. Collections can be indices of all kinds of document types or, alternatively, can represent the contents of a database query.

`<CFCOLLECTION>` is used for basic collection maintenance from creating to optimizing the data. `<CFINDEX>` is responsible for populating and updating Verity collections. `<CFSEARCH>` enables users to run complex searches across single or multiple collections.

Sample Questions

1. Which Verity features are inherent in a `SIMPLE` query expression?
   A. `STEM` operator
   B. `MANY` modifier
   C. `NEAR` operator
   D. Wildcards

2. Which tag is used to optimize a Verity collection?
   A. `<CFCOLLECTION>`
   B. `<CFINDEX>`
   C. `<CFOPTIMIZE>`
   D. `<CFFILE>`

3. Which Verity collection operations must be exclusively executed?
   A. Updating
   B. Optimization
   C. Repairing
   D. Searching

CHAPTER 27

System Integration

Server File Management

ColdFusion provides comprehensive server-side file and directory management through a series of tags: <CFFILE>, <CFCONTENT>, and <CFDIRECTORY>. <CFILE> is responsible for creating and manipulating files. <CFCONTENT> is primarily used for delivering files of different MIME types from the server to the user. <CFDIRECTORY> handles directory listings and management. Together, they provide a set of tools with which you can build complex file management applications that can be operated through a Web browser.

> **NOTE**
>
> ColdFusion is a server-side technology. It does not allow manipulation of files residing on the client's machine. Client-side file manipulation is very restricted through a Web browser for obvious security reasons. On a standard Web browser, the developer can do little more than ask for the file the user would like to upload.
>
> Client-side file manipulations can only be done through client-side Java applets, ActiveX controls, or similar embedded executables within the Web browser itself. These programs must be authorized by the user to allow additional privileges on their machine.

Working with Files

<CFFILE> is a very flexible tag with features to upload, read, write, append, copy, move, and delete files on the ColdFusion server. The syntax of <CFFILE> is very intuitive and straightforward, but several attributes and their uses deserve some explanation.

For example, to copy a file from one location to another on the server, you would use the following syntax:

```
<CFFILE ACTION="COPY"
        SOURCE="C:\x\sweet.txt"
        DESTINATION="C:\temp\supersweet.txt"
        ATTRIBUTES="ReadOnly,Archive"
        MODE="755">
```

The `ATTRIBUTES` attribute is a comma-separated list of file settings such as `ReadOnly` and `Archived`. Not specifying `ATTRIBUTES` leaves the file with the original settings.

`MODE` is a UNIX-only setting that defines permissions for a file. Valid entries correspond to the octal values (not symbolic) of the UNIX `chmod` command. Permissions are assigned for owner, group, and other, respectively. For example, `MODE="755"` gives `rwx-rw-rw` permissions (owner=read/write/execute, group=read/write, other=read/write). `MODE` is ignored by the Windows OS.

> **CAUTION**
>
> You should carefully implement access to `<CFFILE>` in your application. There are obvious security ramifications for allowing users to perform file management operations on the server. The ColdFusion Administrator application can specifically lock down `<CFFILE>` so that the tag cannot be used on the server at all.

A file can be read into memory as a variable using `<CFFILE>` with the `READ` action. This variable can be processed as per any other variable. The newline character (ASCII 10) is frequently used as a delimiter for each line of the file. It is referenced in ColdFusion using `Chr(10)`, as shown here:

```
<!--- read the file into a variable --->
<CFFILE ACTION="READ"
        FILE="c:\files\daemonite.txt"
        VARIABLE="FileText">
<!-- converting file into a more manageable array format -->
<CFSET aFile=ArrayNew(1)>
<CFLOOP LIST="#FileText#" INDEX="i" DELIMITERS="#Chr(10)#">
    <CFSET tmp=ArrayAppend(aFile, i)>
</CFLOOP>
```

The act of writing and appending to files is essential for generating static HTML content, log files, and other text files on the server. `<CFFILE>` with `ACTION="Write"` creates a file and populates it with the contents of the `OUTPUT` attribute. Appending additional lines of information is easy when you use `ACTION="Append"`. The `ADDNEWLINE` attribute, as shown in the following example, even provides a new line, making it ideal for logging:

```
<CFFILE ACTION="WRITE"
        FILE="helloboys.txt"
```

```
OUTPUT="hello cruel world!"
ADDNEWLINE="Yes">
```

TIP

<CFILE> is fairly cumbersome in its approach to writing when the OUTPUT string value is multilined or contains characters that are text delimiters. A clever approach to this problem is to use a custom tag to capture a long, complex text string as a variable. You might do so by using #thistag.generatedcontent# and a dynamically assigned CALLER.variable. You then can use the CALLER.variable to populate the OUTPUT attribute:

```
<!--- custom tag to capture long string --->
<CF_TEXT2VAR RC="myTextString">
  Where ever there is a "Crazy Date"
  Or a "Dutch Wink" or three
  You are bound to find plenty of haught
  And a battered-sav to see!
</CF_TEXT2VAR>
<CFFILE ACTION="WRITE"
        FILE="helloboys.txt"
        OUTPUT="#myTextString#"
        ADDNEWLINE="Yes">
```

➔ Tag pairs and the THISTAG scope were covered in Chapter 23, "Advanced Custom Tags."

TIP

ColdFusion offers a variety of useful functions for working with the server file system. You often have to work with absolute paths, and several functions are specifically designed to help you determine the appropriate pathnames. Some useful functions include the following:

```
FileExists()
ExpandPath()
GetCurrentTemplatePath()
GetTemplatePath()
```

<CFFILE> can read binary files, such as an image or executable, into a binary object variable in memory like this:

```
<CFFILE ACTION="ReadBinary"
       FILE="c:\cfusion\bin\cfserver.exe "
       VARIABLE="aBinaryObj">
```

The returned variable can be used anywhere in your code like a normal variable. Typically, it is used in conjunction with one of the Web protocols, such as HTTP (using <CFHTTP>) or SMTP (using <CFMAIL>), or writing to a database (using <CFQUERY>). The variable is converted to ASCII using Base 64 (with the ToBase64() function) and can be handled like any other string variable.

→ HTTP and FTP protocols will be covered in Chapter 31, "Other Internet Protocols." SMTP and <CFMAIL> will be discussed in Chapter 29, "Email Integration."

NOTE

You can achieve binary file syndication by using WDDX and Base 64. <CFWDDX> automatically converts a binary variable into Base 64 and serializes the data into an XML packet for transport.

Base 64 provides 6 bit encoding of 8-bit ASCII characters. High ASCII values and binary objects are unsuitable for transport over the web with HTTP or via email using SMTP. The functions `ToBase64()` and its opposite `ToBinary()` can be used to safely convert between ASCII and binary data.

→ WDDX was covered in Chapter 25, "WDDX."

Uploading Files to the Server

File uploading through a Web browser is a part of the HTTP protocol. The HTML interface and form post have nothing to do with ColdFusion per se. However, ColdFusion and <CFFILE> kick in when the form POST reaches the Web server and the uploaded file needs to be saved to the server file system.

CAUTION

Different Web browsers have varying degrees of support for the HTTP protocol. Be sure to check that your application's target audience is using a browser that fully supports file upload.

The standard HTML form needs an additional attribute and input field for file uploads to work, as in this example:

```
<FORM ACTION="upload.cfm"
      METHOD="post"
      ENCTYPE="multipart/form-data">
File to upload:<BR>
<INPUT TYPE="file" NAME="uploadfile" SIZE="30"><BR>
<INPUT TYPE="submit" VALUE="Upload that file!">
</FORM>
```

The `ENCTYPE` attribute specifies the media type used to encode the form data. The default `ENCTYPE` is the MIME type `"application/x-www-form-urlencoded"`, and it's such a mouthful that nobody bothers to specify it in a standard form. However, for a file upload, the media type is different, so you must nominate the appropriate MIME type `"multipart/form-data"` in the `ENCTYPE` attribute so that the upload will work.

The `INPUT TYPE="file"` form field is used exclusively for uploading files. It provides a Browse button that activates an operating system–specific dialog box for selecting a single file. You can upload multiple files at once, but each file must have its own form field of `TYPE="file"`, and each form field requires a unique name.

The action page for the upload form contains a `<CFFILE>` tag with `ACTION="Upload"`. The `FILEFIELD` attribute corresponds to the specific form field name in the form POST for the file you are saving to the server. If multiple files are being uploaded in a single form POST, you need a separate `<CFILE>` for each uploaded file, as shown here:

```
<!--- sample upload.cfm file --->
<CFFILE ACTION="UPLOAD"
        FILEFIELD="UploadFile"
        DESTINATION="c:\temp\"
        NAMECONFLICT="OVERWRITE"
        ACCEPT="image/gif, image/jpg"
 >
```

CAUTION

The trailing backslash for the directory name in the `DESTINATION` attribute of `<CFFILE>` is essential.

If the file upload is successful, ColdFusion writes the file to the server and generates a structure of the file's details. The structure is stored in the `FILE` scope and can be accessed using `FILE.`*`variablename`*.

You can use the `NAMECONFLICT` attribute to nominate how clashing filenames will be handled. The default is `Error`, but you can make more interesting choices:

- `Error` (Default)—The file is not saved, and ColdFusion aborts and returns a runtime error.
- `Skip`—The file is not saved, and no error is thrown. This value is designed for custom error handling based on the values in file upload status parameters.
- `Overwrite`—This value replaces an existing file of the same name in the `<CFFILE>` destination.
- `MakeUnique`—If a name conflict occurs in the destination directory, a unique filename is automatically generated for the uploaded file. This name is available in the `FILE.ServerFile` variable.

When you are managing a file library, you often might want to restrict the files being uploaded to a specific set of MIME types. For example, if you are managing an image library, you may want to restrict uploaded files to those of type GIF or JPG. The `ACCEPT` attribute takes a comma-separated list of valid MIME types as a value and prevents nonconforming MIME types from being uploaded.

TIP

Don't wait for the file to upload before telling your users that they have accidentally (or otherwise) uploaded a restricted MIME type file. You can warn them straight away with some client-side scripting.

Using the document object model of your Web browser and JavaScript, you can examine the string that contains the path and filename that a user is trying to upload (look for something like `document.formName.uploadFieldName.value`). Simply parse this string to make sure the file extension matches a predetermined list of valid file extensions.

Although, the file extension doesn't actually confirm the file MIME type, it's likely to catch nearly all your problems. More often than not, the file extension corresponds to a specific MIME type for that file.

You can use `FILE.FileSize` to reject a file if it is over a predetermined size. Unfortunately, with HTML and CFML, you cannot determine the file size prior to uploading. If a user uploads a file that exceeds your file size restriction, he will have to wait until the whole file is uploaded before you give him the bad news.

TIP

File size is listed in bytes. To format the value as the more familiar kilobytes, use the following:

```
#Numberformat(Evaluate(File.FileSize/1024))# KB.
```

TIP

When a file is uploading via HTTP through a Web browser form post, no feedback is provided on progress. In other words, the user has no idea how long the file upload has left to go.

You should always explain in detail to the user that the file may take some time to upload. Give an estimate of upload time based on file size and common connection speeds. If you have a file size restriction, *always* inform the user before he uploads his file!

Delivering Files from the Server

To deliver a file in a simple Web application, you need only a correctly qualified URL to initiate a download using HTTP. Here's an example:

```
<A HREF="http://www.daemon.com.au/files/leads.xls">Download Leads</A>
```

In more sophisticated applications, you might need to dynamically deliver a file based on a reference in a database. This problem is further complicated by the need to deliver files from an area of the directory tree that is not mapped by the Web server. In other words, the files may not be directly accessible using a URL in the Web browser. This is an absolute requirement for a secure file store where the application needs to authenticate a user before granting access to the file store.

You can choose from three strategies for delivering files securely:

- Deliver an existing file from the file system.
- Create a file on-the-fly and deliver.
- Create a temporary file, deliver, and clean up by deleting the temporary file.

The <CFCONTENT> tag specifies a MIME type header to be sent to the browser so that the file will be interpreted as something other than a normal Web page. For example, you may be delivering a comma-separated value (CSV) file or Word document. The output can be generated on-the-fly, or you can specify an existing file to be delivered from anywhere on the file system of the server. <CFCONTENT> also provides the option of deleting the file being delivered, which is perfect for cleaning up temporary files:

```
<!--- for example, delivering a Word document --->
<CFCONTENT TYPE="application/msword"
          FILE="C:\FileStore\CALENDAR.DOC"
          DELETEFILE="No">
```

The strategy that you choose for file delivery will largely depend on the type of application you are building. However, all three methods run afoul of the same problem: specifying the filename of the delivered file.

Imagine that you have access to a Human Resources database (HR). You need to extract a listing of employees for a specific department and deliver it as a CSV file for use in a spreadsheet program. You can build a code template called employee_list.cfm that queries the database using a URL parameter called URL.DID and generates the appropriate CSV file:

```
<!--- employee_list.cfm --->
<CFQUERY NAME="GetEmp" DATASOURCE="HR">
     SELECT      *
     FROM        Employees
     WHERE       Department_ID = #Val(URL.DID)#
</CFQUERY>

<CFCONTENT TYPE="application/unknown">"ID","LName","FName","Email"
<CFOUTPUT QUERY="GetEmp">#EmpID#,"#LastName#","#FirstName#","#Email#"
</CFOUTPUT>
```

> **TIP**
>
> By specifying a MIME type of "unknown", you guarantee that the Web browser will attempt to save the file to disk rather than spawn an application the Web browser believes is appropriate.

The Web browser calls a URL that ends with the filename employee_list.cfm, as you can see in this example:

```
http://daemon.com.au/hr/employee_list.cfm?did=123
```

The Web browser attempts to save a file called employee_list.cfm. If you want to save a file as something like emplist.csv, you have to trick the Web browser into seeing a different filename like this:

```
http://daemon.com.au/hr/employee_list.cfm/emplist.csv?did=123
```

Note that you specify the URL parameter as usual at the end of the URL itself. The Web browser picks up the last filename specified and uses it as the filename to save as.

Alternatively, you could try using the "Content-Disposition" HTTP header as follows to specify the filename for the user:

```
<CFHEADER NAME="Content-Disposition" VALUE="inline; filename=emplist.csv">
<CFCONTENT TYPE="application/unknown">"ID","LName","FName","Email"
<CFOUTPUT QUERY="GetEmp">#EmpID#,"#LastName#","#FirstName#","#Email#"
</CFOUTPUT>
```

→ <CFHEADER> and <CFCONTENT> were discussed in Chapter 5, "Redirects and Reuse."

CAUTION

<CFCONTENT> can deliver any file from the server via the Web browser. Furthermore, you can program the tag to delete any file on the server. For these reasons, you must carefully consider the use of <CFCONTENT>. The tag can be locked down on the ColdFusion Administrator to prevent any use at all by developers.

Working with Directories

The <CFDIRECTORY> LIST action returns a query object of files and directories from the specified DIRECTORY attribute. The remaining actions of <CFDIRECTORY> can be used to create, delete, and rename directories on the server. These actions, as shown in the following example, are straightforward in their implementation and combined can build quite elegant systems for managing directories on the server:

```
<CFDIRECTORY ACTION="LIST"
             DIRECTORY="C:\Inetpub\wwwroot\cftrain"
             NAME="qDir"
             SORT="DESC">
```

NOTE

The query object generated for a <CFDIRECTORY> listing contains files (type FILE) and subdirectories (type DIR). Each directory contains two special relative directory records:

```
'.' the current directory
'..' the parent directory
```

TIP

The following ColdFusion functions are useful for working with directories:

```
DirectoryExists()
GetDirectoryFromPath()
```

TIP

Universal Naming Convention (UNC) pathing on Windows OS and Novell Netware is possible in ColdFusion but requires a few extra steps. When you install ColdFusion, the application server services, by default, start under the standard `system` account. This account does not normally have any network privileges, so network resources are unavailable to ColdFusion. If you modify the service to start under a specific named account, such as `cfuser`, it is possible to grant specific network privileges for that account and thereby grant ColdFusion access to network resources.

The following code snippets use functions on the UNC path for the computer "elfsbane", the file share "cdrive", and the directory "files":

```
#DirectoryExists("\\elfsbane\cdrive\files")#

#FileExists("\\elfsbane\cdrive\files\test.txt")#
```

CAUTION

`<CFDIRECTORY>` gives developers access to the entire directory structure of the server. This potential security risk can be prevented by blocking the use of the tag through the ColdFusion Administrator.

Registry Integration

Windows uses a database called the Registry to maintain system information about users, hardware, and installed software. The various flavors of UNIX supported by ColdFusion run the `windu_registryd40` process to emulate the Windows Registry database.

The Registry stores information through a hierarchy of keys and values:

- Keys can contain either values or other keys.
- A key and any keys/values below it are known as a *Registry branch*.
- Values are split into two components: value name and value data.

TIP

Windows and UNIX users can use `RegEdit` to view and modify Registry settings through a graphical user interface.

The default location for the UNIX registry is:

```
/opt/coldfusion/registry/cf.registry
```

CAUTION

The Registry contains system-critical information. Incorrectly editing the Registry may severely damage your system. At the very least, you should back up the Registry data on the server before tinkering. For obvious reasons, you can restrict developer access to `<CFREGISTRY>` through the ColdFusion Administrator.

You can use <CFREGISTRY> to query the Registry; it returns a standard query object of keys and values. Use the ACTION attribute with GET to retrieve one entry or with GETALL, as shown here, to retrieve multiple keys and values from the Registry:

```
<!--- Grabbing Verity Collections from the Registry --->
<CFREGISTRY
    ACTION="GetAll"
    BRANCH="HKEY_LOCAL_MACHINE\Software\Allaire\
➥ColdFusion\CurrentVersion\Collections"
    TYPE="Any"
    NAME="qReg">

<TABLE BORDER="1">
<TR>
     <TH>Entry</TH>
     <TH>Type</TH>
     <TH>Value</TH>
</TR>
<CFOUTPUT QUERY="qReg">
<TR>
     <TD>#qReg.Entry#</TD>
     <TD>#qReg.Type#</TD>
     <TD>#qReg.Value#</TD>
</TR>
</CFOUTPUT>
</TABLE>
```

TIP

In the <CFREGISTRY> resultset, if #Type# is a key, then #Value# is an empty string. When you specify TYPE="Any", GetAll returns any binary Registry values. However, the binary values #Type# variable contains UNSUPPORTED and #Value# is blank.

The <CFREGISTRY> tag allows you to add, edit, and delete Registry values. You can use the SET action to add or update Registry keys and value data. <CFREGISTRY> simply creates the key or value if it does not already exist. You need to specify attributes for BRANCH, the ENTRY to set, the value's TYPE of data, and the value data itself. You can also use <CFREGISTRY> with the DELETE action to delete Registry keys and values.

For example, the following code snippet turns off basic security in the ColdFusion Administrator by setting the UseAdminPassword ENTRY to zero:

```
<CFREGISTRY
   ACTION="SET"
   BRANCH="HKEY_LOCAL_MACHINE\SOFTWARE\Allaire\ColdFusion\CurrentVersion\Server\"
   ENTRY="UseAdminPassword"
   TYPE="String"
   VALUE="0">
```

> **CAUTION**
>
> If you delete a key, <CFREGISTRY> also deletes all values and subkeys defined beneath the key. Be very careful when using the DELETE action.

> **CAUTION**
>
> The Windows Registry has a defined size (see System under the Control Panel) and does not expand automatically. If you exceed the allocated Registry storage, your Windows system may crash. Generally, the Registry is not a great place to store significant volumes of information. However, it is the default storage database for ColdFusion client variables.

➔ Client variables were discussed in Chapter 11, "Session State Management."

Executing from the Command Line

<CFEXECUTE> enables you to execute any process on the server machine. The process is effectively invoked from the command line, spawning a separate thread. This powerful tag brings a wealth of system applications such as Perl and shell scripts to Windows executables into the domain of the humble ColdFusion template.

You can pass <CFEXECUTE> a series of command-line ARGUMENTS as either a string or an array:

```
<CFEXECUTE NAME="c:\perl\bin\perl.exe "
           ARGUMENTS='-e print "hello world!";'
           TIMEOUT="20">
</CFEXECUTE>
```

> **NOTE**
>
> In Perl, -e allows a line of code to be executed from the command line. You can find information about the Perl language for both UNIX and Windows at http://www.perl.com/ or http://www.perl.org/.

> **NOTE**
>
> On Windows systems, you must specify the extension—for example, .exe—as part of the application's name. The application's full pathname is also required.

The output of the external program is directed to the specified OUTPUTFILE, as shown in the following example. Alternatively, if no file is nominated, the output is written back to the page from which it was called.

```
<CFSCRIPT>
   aArgs=ArrayNew(1);
   aArgs[1]="/all";
</CFSCRIPT>
```

```
<CFEXECUTE NAME="C:\WinNT\System32\ipconfig.exe "
          ARGUMENTS="#aargs[1]#"
          OUTPUTFILE="c:\x\ipsettings.txt"
          TIMEOUT="500"></CFEXECUTE>
```

The TIMEOUT indicates how long in seconds the ColdFusion executing thread will wait for the spawned process to finish. Using the default timeout of 0 forces the ColdFusion thread to spawn a process and immediately return without waiting for the process to terminate. The file is effectively executed asynchronously from the ongoing processing of the calling application page.

> **NOTE**
> The effective user of the ColdFusion executing thread must have permissions to execute the program on the server. If not, a security exception is thrown.

Summary

ColdFusion provides comprehensive server-side file management using <CFFILE>, <CFCONTENT>, and <CFDIRECTORY>. Standard file operations such as move, copy, and delete can be performed using <CFFILE>. <CFFILE> can create or write new files and append to existing files. The <CFFILE> tag reads string and binary files into ColdFusion variables. <CFILE> is required to write uploaded files to disk at the end of an HTTP post. <CFCONTENT> can deliver files of different MIME types from the server to the user's Web browser. <CFDIRECTORY> manipulates and reads directory listings on the server.

<CFREGISTRY> gives you complete access to the Registry system information repository. <CFEXECUTE> enables programmers to spawn processes from the command line of the server.

Sample Questions

1. Access to which of the following tags can be restricted in the ColdFusion Administrator?
   A. <CFFILE>
   B. <CFCONTENT>
   C. <CFDIRECTORY>
   D. <CFREGISTRY>

2. Which of the following tags would you use to effectively write and append to log files?
   A. <CFLOG>
   B. <CFCONTENT>
   C. <CFSCHEDULE>
   D. <CFFILE>

3. Which value of the `ENCTYPE` attribute of `<FORM>` is required to enable file uploads from the browser?

   A. `ENCTYPE="text/plain"`
   B. `ENCTYPE="multipart/form-data"`
   C. `ENCTYPE="application/x-www-form-urlencoded"`
   D. `ENCTYPE` is *not* a required attribute.

CHAPTER 28

Scheduling and Event Execution

Scheduling Events in ColdFusion

The ColdFusion server maintains a list of events or tasks that can be scheduled to run periodically. Scheduling events in ColdFusion is similar to using the UNIX operating system's `cron` table or the `AT` command in the Windows OS. Each event corresponds to a ColdFusion template file that gets executed according to the parameters set in the schedule.

The execution mechanism in ColdFusion is restricted to HTTP calls. A `<CFHTTP>` agent calls the scheduled template and runs the file at the designated time. Any template that can be run by a Web browser can be executed using the scheduler, thereby covering just about everything you might want ColdFusion to achieve.

➔ `<CFHTTP>` and HTTP agents will be covered in Chapter 31, "Other Internet Protocols."

> **NOTE**
>
> Persistent information about individual scheduled tasks is stored in the Windows Registry or the UNIX `windu_registryd40`. The `windu_registryd40` process provides an emulation of the Windows Registry database on UNIX systems.

➔ The Registry was covered in Chapter 27, "System Integration."

Scheduling a Task

You can schedule individual tasks by using the Web-based ColdFusion Administrator application, programmatically by using the <CFSCHEDULE> tag, or by manipulating the Registry. Schedule information is stored in the Registry, which is polled at a set "scheduler refresh interval," and loaded into the ColdFusion server memory. The active schedule list is also reloaded when the ColdFusion service is cycled.

The ColdFusion Administrator provides an easy-to-use interface for maintaining, creating, and deleting schedules through a Web browser. All the features of scheduling are available through a series of form inputs, including a very convenient list of currently active schedules. However, you need access to the administrator application to view these options. Access may not be available in many hosting environments, especially those maintained by ISPs and commercial ColdFusion hosting partners.

<CFSCHEDULE> provides you with access to all the features of the ColdFusion Administrator. You can update, run, or delete individual schedules according to the chosen ACTION. The tag attributes are intuitive and correspond directly to the form fields in the Administrator. However, you cannot display a listing of currently active schedules by using <CFSCHEDULE>.

For example, the Crazy Date schedule that follows should run for three years, firing off every day and running the ../tasks/partydate.cfm application page with a timeout of 300 seconds:

```
<!--- Set up the Crazy Date schedule --->
<CFSCHEDULE ACTION="UPDATE"
            TASK="crazy date"
            OPERATION="HTTPRequest"
            URL="http://127.0.0.1/tasks/partydate.cfm"
            STARTDATE="12/12/00"
            STARTTIME="03:45 AM"
            ENDDATE="12/12/03"
            INTERVAL="Daily"
            REQUESTTIMEOUT="300">
```

You can add or modify schedule information directly through the Registry. Using the Registry is not recommended as best practice, however. If you're familiar with the Registry environment, you will know that playing with the Registry is not for the faint-hearted. However, it is the only place a programmer can get hold of the active schedule list without viewing it through the ColdFusion Administrator, as shown in the following example:

```
<!--- Grab active schedule events from the registry --->
<CFREGISTRY
    ACTION="GETALL"
    NAME="Task_List"
    TYPE="KEY"
    BRANCH="HKEY_LOCAL_MACHINE\SOFTWARE\Allaire\ColdFusion\CurrentVersion\
          ➥Schedule">
```

➔ The Registry was covered in Chapter 27, "System Integration."

The scheduler refresh interval defaults to 15 minutes and can be modified through the ColdFusion Administrator. This interval determines how often the scheduler checks the saved scheduled task list in the Registry for new tasks. On refresh, the scheduler updates the active task list as required. The active task list gets inspected every minute to determine what tasks are ready to be run.

CAUTION

Scheduled events correspond to an application page that must necessarily reside on a mapped area of the Web server. The schedule <CFHTTP> agent executes the task page on the Web server just like any other page in the Web application.

The agent is not sophisticated enough to log in to an application with session management, so the application page is essentially exposed to anyone with a Web browser. Depending on the type of task that you are scheduling, it may not be appropriate for anybody to be able to execute the event page using a Web browser.

Good practice is to secure a nominated "tasks" directory to allow only the local ColdFusion server access to run pages. Using the Web server security for virtual directories, you can restrict access to the Web server's own IP address or `127.0.0.1` for the tasks directory. Alternatively, you can include code like the following at the beginning of the event application page to check the HTTP agent for appropriate CGI variables:

```
<CFIF CGI.remote_host NEQ "127.0.0.1">
      <CFABORT SHOWERROR="Go away, bad person!">
</CFIF>
```

Publishing to Static Pages

You can use scheduled events to publish static Web pages. Normally, scheduled events are executed, perform some task, and don't bother about output to the screen because no one is there to see them work. However, `<CFSCHEDULE>` can be instructed save the results of the event page output and write them to the file system as follows:

```
<!--- Publish static HTML for the wind section --->
<CFSCHEDULE ACTION="UPDATE"
    TASK="Orchestral"
    OPERATION="HTTPRequest"
    URL="http://127.0.0.1/tasks/flautist.cfm"
    STARTDATE="8/7/99"
    STARTTIME="01:30 AM"
    INTERVAL="3600"
    RESOLVEURL="Yes"
    PUBLISH="Yes"
    FILE="theflute.htm"
    PATH="c:\inetpub\wwwroot\windup"
    REQUESTTIMEOUT="600">
```

Setting `PUBLISH="Yes"`, with appropriate directory `PATH` and `FILE` attributes, directs the scheduled event to save the resulting output of its application template to disk.

RESOLVEURL behaves similarly to the attribute in <CFHTTP>. For example, publishing using a scheduled task is ideal for building long-running reports that can be executed during quiet server periods. In addition, dynamic content that is updated infrequently can be published periodically using <CFSCHEDULE> to save hits on the database.

➔ <CFHTTP> and HTTP agents will be covered in Chapter 31, "Other Internet Protocols."

Logging Scheduled Events

The scheduled event's task name, time stamp, and its success or failure status are written to the \cfusion\log\schedule.log (Windows) or /opt/coldfusion/log/schedule.log (UNIX) file.

For example, a log entry for the Orchestral task mentioned earlier might reveal the following:

```
"Information","TID=960","12/04/00","03:30:00","Scheduled action Orchestral,
➥ template http://127.0.0.1/tasks/flautist.cfm submitted successfully."
```

Unfortunately, the log is not terribly informative above telling you whether the event was successfully executed. If a task failed and generated a ColdFusion runtime error, you would expect to see the details of the error indicated in the ColdFusion application.log.

Alternative Scheduling Options

Most operating systems have mechanisms for scheduling the periodic execution of tasks. ColdFusion can be executed from the command line by calling the server executable and passing the location of the template to be executed. For example, in Windows:

```
c:\cfusion\bin\cfml.exe c:\inetpub\wwwroot\rpt\status.cfm
```

By scheduling the command-line execution of a ColdFusion template, you can utilize the operating system's own scheduling service to execute ColdFusion code periodically.

Windows NT and Windows 2000 operating systems use the at command. at can be used to list existing commands in the schedule or to schedule commands and programs to run on a computer at a specified time and date. The Windows Schedule service must be running to use the at command. The following code snippet could be used to schedule a ColdFusion template to run every Monday and Tuesday at 11.00 p.m.:

```
at 23:00 /every:M,T "c:\cfusion\bin\cfml.exe c:\inetpub\wwwroot\rpt\
➥status.cfm"
```

Parameters can be passed to the ColdFusion template by setting environment variables. For example, a Windows batch file could be written to set a URL parameter and execute ColdFusion code:

```
@echo off
set "QUERY_STRING=department=1234"
set "CF_TEMPLATE_PATH=c:\inetpub\wwwroot\rpt\status.cfm"
c:\cfusion\bin\cfml.exe
```

The UNIX operating systems uses a handy little utility called Cron. Cron is controlled by a set of files called "crontabs." A master file is stored in the /etc/crontab directory, along with crontab files for individual users in /var/spool/cron/.

crontab *filename* will install the file you specified as a new crontab. The crontab command has some other switches that list, edit, and remove crontabs, but the basic syntax is all you need. If you want to edit the crontab, you simply reinstall the file with a new crontab command. A sample crontab file follows:

```
#m h dom mon dow user command
 5 0  *   *   *  root /opt/coldfusion/bin/cfml /wwwroot/rpt/status.cfm
# run five minutes after midnight daily
```

→ For more information, run man cron and man crontab for your particular flavor of UNIX.

NOTE

It is a little easier for the sysadmin to set up cron jobs in Red Hat Linux. The /etc/crontab file automatically executes items in several subdirectories at regular periods. Those subdirectories are

/etc/cron.hourly

/etc/cron.daily

/etc/cron.weekly

/etc/cron.monthly

All the sysadmin must do is drop a shell script or executable link in one of the directories and it will automatically be run at the appropriate time.

ColdFusion supports the Red Hat Linux distribution. More information can be found at http://www.redhat.com/.

Summary

The schedule event subsystem of ColdFusion is ideal for periodic, asynchronous execution of CFML templates. You can schedule tasks via the Web by using the ColdFusion Administrator, programmatically by using the <CFSCHEDULE> tag, or by modifying the Registry. You also can direct scheduled tasks to publish their output to files such as static Web pages. Event execution timings are managed by the ColdFusion server and have their own log file for recording success or failure.

Sample Questions

1. How does the ColdFusion scheduler execute code in a specified template?
   - A. Using an HTTP call
   - B. Using cron or AT processes, depending on the operating system
   - C. Using command-line arguments
   - D. None of the above

2. Where is scheduled event information stored?
   A. `cfexec.ini` file
   B. Registry
   C. Any nominated ODBC data source
   D. All of the above

3. What do you use to modify scheduled event information?
   A. The ColdFusion Administrator
   B. `<CFSCHEDULE>`
   C. `<CFREGISTRY>`
   D. `<CFEVENTEDIT>`

CHAPTER 29

Email Integration

Sending Mail with ColdFusion

ColdFusion provides out-of-the-box support for sending email through Simple Mail Transfer Protocol (SMTP) mail servers with the <CFMAIL> tag and receiving mail from Post Office Protocol (POP) servers using the <CFPOP> tag.

The ColdFusion Application Server does not ship with its own built-in SMTP or POP mail server. To provide messaging services for your application, you must have access to a separate SMTP server and/or POP email account.

Sending Simple Text Email

<CFMAIL> behaves similarly to <CFOUTPUT>. Whereas <CFOUTPUT> outputs information back to the Web browser, <CFMAIL> outputs the same information to an email message. The additional attributes of <CFMAIL> correspond to those fields you require to correctly format an email message.

<CMAIL> can contain CFML, and it resolves variables just like <CFOUTPUT>. However, although <CFMAIL> does accept a QUERY attribute, its behavior depends on how the query is used. This issue is discussed in detail later in this chapter.

You can specify multiple recipients by providing a comma-separated list of qualified email addresses as follows:

```
<CFMAIL TO="john@doe.com,jane@doe.com"
        FROM="pal@yourfriend.com"
        SUBJECT="Hope you're feeling better!"
        CC="buddy@myfriend.com"
        BCC="agent@watchingyou.com">
<CFIF recipient is "alive">
This is a get well soon... hope I'm not too late.
</CFIF>
This message was sent #DateFormat(Now())#.
</CFMAIL>
```

→ Lists were covered in Chapter 13, "Lists."

You can specify a default SMTP mail server in the ColdFusion Administrator. Alternatively, you can specify SMTP settings in the `<CFMAIL>` tag itself, which will override the default settings. If no SMTP server is specified at all, a standard ColdFusion runtime error occurs.

TIP

Text inside an email message is not like a Web page. Whitespace can be very important, and every space, tab, or return affects the formatting of the email message. So you need to be careful how you format your ColdFusion code within the `<CFMAIL>` tag.

Long lines of text without line breaks may cause some email clients to display the message improperly. It is good practice to force text wrapping in your message by putting in a new line at the end of every 65 characters or so. Several third-party Custom Tags are available to help implement text wrapping.

CAUTION

If you accidentally place a single full stop (`'.'`) in the body of an email, some SMTP servers see it as a command to end the message and may truncate your text at that point.

Sending HTML Email

You can make `<CFMAIL>` send HTML mail by setting the appropriate attribute, as shown in the following example:

```
<CFMAIL FROM="newsletter@funstuff.com"
        TO="geoff@hottermail.com"
        SUBJECT="This month in Fun Stuff!"
        TYPE="HTML">
<H1>November Fun Stuff</H1>
<P>Jump for joy fun stuff brings you <b>plenty</b> of
things to keep you <font color="red">amused</font> for hours</P>
</CFMAIL>
```

The `TYPE` attribute sets headers for the receiving email client instructing that the email message has embedded HTML to be rendered. Images in the HTML are typically referenced with absolute URLs to servers online and are not included in the HTML message itself.

CAUTION

Not all email clients can handle HTML mail. Indeed, even those clients that can may have users who set their preferences to view email as text rather than HTML. HTML mail in a text email client is difficult to read.

If you reference images in your message, the recipient must be online to be able to see the images. Otherwise, all she'll see are series of broken images.

Query-Driven Email

Just like <CFOUTPUT>, <CFMAIL> can loop over a query object, as shown here, resolving each record in the query into an individual and personalized email:

```
<CFMAIL QUERY="GetCustomers"
    FROM="service@goatherders.com"
    TO="#GetCustomers.EMail#"
    SUBJECT="Registration Verification">
Dear #GetCustomers.FirstName# -
We'd like to verify.. blah.. blah..
</CFMAIL>
```

You can use the GROUP attribute in a similar fashion to GROUP in <CFOUTPUT>. You also can group sets of records to send a series of individual email messages, each with the records of a particular group category.

Using a nested set of <CFOUTPUT> tags has a slightly different effect than you might normally expect. The code behaves as though you are using GROUP but where all the records belong to a single group category. The text within the nested <CFOUTPUT> tag is repeated for every row in the nominated query, as shown in the following example, while the text surrounding it serves as the header and footer for a single email message:

```
<CFMAIL QUERY="ProductRequests"
    FROM="webmaster@mega.com"
    TO="marketing@mega.com"
    SUBJECT="MegaDeveloper Status Report">
Here is a list of people who have inquired about
MegaDeveloper over the last seven days:
<CFOUTPUT>
#ProductRequests.FirstName# #ProductRequests.LastName#
(#ProductRequests.Company#) - #ProductRequests.EMailAddress#
</CFOUTPUT>
Regards,
The WebMaster
webmaster@mega.com
</CFMAIL>
```

Sending File Attachments

<CFMAILPARAM> is a sub-tag of <CFMAIL>. You can use it as follows to send MIME-encoded file attachments:

```
<CFMAIL FROM="athos@musketeer.fr"
    TO="richelieu@cardinal.fr"
    SUBJECT="Monthly Reports"
    >
Dear Cardinal,
Here is a copy of the monthly dueling reports.
Regards,
Athos
```

```
<CFMAILPARAM FILE="c:\reports\foes_vanquished.xls">
<CFMAILPARAM FILE="c:\reports\foes_nomore.xls">
</CFMAIL>
```

The FILE attribute must specify an absolute path on the ColdFusion server to the file being attached. You can specify multiple files by using multiple <CFMAILPARAM> tags.

A common misconception is that users can combine an email form and file attachment at the same time in their Web applications. The file must be on the ColdFusion server, not the client's workstation, in order for the mail attachment to work. Web-based mail clients operate via a two-step process for attachments: uploading the file(s) to the server and then sending and attaching the files to the email.

➔ Chapter 27, "System Integration," discussed uploading files to the server.

> **NOTE**
>
> In earlier versions of ColdFusion, the MIMEATTACH attribute was used to specify a single file attachment only. This attribute has been superceded by the <CFMAILPARAM> tag, but the server continues to be backward compatible.

Additional Mail Headers

You can set additional mail headers—beyond those that you can specify directly from the <CFMAIL> attributes—for your email by using <CFMAILPARAM> as follows:

```
<CFMAIL FROM="bates@seadog.com"
        TO="pugwash@oldsalt.com"
        SUBJECT="Shipment by sea!">
    <CFMAILPARAM NAME="Reply-To" VALUE="stains@seadog.com">
    What's up land lubbers where's me cargo?
</CFMAIL>
```

Retrieving POP Mail

Post Office Protocol (POP) is a very common store-and-forward mail standard used by Internet service providers and corporate administrators alike for the provision of email.

<CFPOP> contacts a qualified POP email account and retrieves the message file as a ColdFusion query object for use in your application. In effect, <CFPOP> behaves similarly to <CFQUERY>, except that it retrieves information from a POP server rather than a SQL database.

ColdFusion does not ship with a built-in POP server. You must have a valid POP account on an external POP server. The <CFPOP> tag, shown here, requires the server and user account details specified for each retrieval:

```
<CFPOP ACTION="GETHEADERONLY"
       NAME="qGetHeaders"
       SERVER="mail.daemon.com.au"
       USERNAME="modius"
       PASSWORD="secret">
```

<CFPOP> can perform a variety of actions on the POP server; these actions are specifically designed to leverage the POP mail standard:

- GETHEADERONLY—Retrieves message headers only
- GETALL—Retrieves an entire message body
- GETALL—Retrieves file attachments when ATTACHMENTPATH is specified
- DELETE—Deletes messages on the server

The two retrieve actions, GETHEADERONLY and GETALL, are provided to maximize performance. Header information is generally small in size and quick to retrieve. The size of the full message including the body and any attached files is impossible to predict because the information is not available in the GETHEADERONLY query, so the message body and files are generally retrieved one at a time.

NOTE

Building a Web-based POP interface is relatively straightforward. The application involves retrieving the message headers from the server, providing a drill-down to individual messages with the option to retrieve files and the capability to delete unwanted messages from the server. ColdFusion can also use a POP account as a drop box for collecting email messages and processing their contents autonomously. For example, you could schedule a process to poll the POP account periodically, collect the mail, and update a database.

POP Dates

The date field in the <CFPOP> query object is in a specific POP date format and needs to be processed before it can be manipulated like a standard date. The ParseDateTime() function accepts an argument for converting POP date/time objects into Greenwich mean time (GMT):

```
#ParseDateTime(queryname.date, "POP")#
```

File Attachments

File attachments are returned with the GETALL action only if the ATTACHMENTPATH attribute is set to a valid directory path on the ColdFusion server as follows:

```
<CFPOP ACTION="GETALL"
       NAME="qGetMail"
       MESSAGENUMBER="1"
       ATTACHMENTPATH="c:\mail\attach\"
       GENERATEUNIQUEFILENAMES="Yes"
       SERVER="mail.daemon.com.au"
       USERNAME="modius"
       PASSWORD="secret">
```

In this instance, two additional columns are returned:

- ATTACHMENTS—A tab-separated list of all the source attachment names
- ATTACHMENTFILES—A tab-separated list of the actual temporary filenames written to the server

In the event that there are no attachments, both of these columns are returned as empty strings. By setting the GENERATEDUNIQUEFILENAMES attribute of <CFPOP> to "Yes", you can avoid duplicate filenames when saving attachments to the ColdFusion server. You can then use <CFFILE> to move temporary files to a more permanent storage area on the server.

Attachments need to end up with their original names, but POP is an open and portable protocol available on many different operating systems. Unfortunately, not all operating systems that support POP (servers and clients) support the same filenames. For example, if you send a file named super green price list.xls from Windows 2000 to someone on a DOS box you'll have problems. DOS supports only 8.3 filenames. Perhaps you need to send two files with exactly the same names except for the letter casing from a Unix box to an NT box. To solve this problem, POP keeps two pieces of information for each file: the original source filename and the name of the actual attached file (which can be different). The physical attachments are named by their alternative names when they are retrieved from the POP server; those names are safe. <CFPOP> returns these filenames in two tab-separated lists, ATTACHMENTS and ATTACHMENTFILES, respectively.

➔ File manipulation on the ColdFusion server was covered in Chapter 27, "System Integration." Lists were discussed in Chapter 13, "Lists."

Deleting Mail

Deleting messages from a POP server is different from deleting records from a database. Each message on the POP server is uniquely identified by the MESSAGENUMBER. For example, from the oldest message, you have 1, 2, 3, and so on to the total number of messages in the mailbox. However, this unique assignment is only temporary.

Message numbers are reassigned at the end of every <CFPOP> delete action. If three messages are retrieved from a POP mail server, the message numbers returned are 1, 2, 3. If message 2 is deleted, message 1 remains 1 and message 3 is assigned message number 2. Therefore, unlike a typical database primary key, the MESSAGENUMBER key is reassigned depending on what is present in the message queue.

> **NOTE**
>
> Although Internet Message Access Protocol (IMAP)is a very popular mail protocol on the Internet, it is not directly supported by ColdFusion. However, several third-party extensions to the ColdFusion engine provide complete IMAP integration.

Troubleshooting ColdFusion Mail

To understand where to look when things go wrong with mail services, we need to inspect what ColdFusion does when it sends email.

The <CFMAIL> command generates a mail spool file containing information about the server to use, recipients, sender, and so on, and places it in the \cfusion\mail\spool directory. A special low-level thread sweeps the spool directory every 15 seconds, sending any spool files to the SMTP server specified in the mail headers.

> **NOTE**
>
> A mail spool file is a simple text file specifically formatted for an SMTP server. It starts with a series of mail headers and finishes with the body of the mail message.

If the specified SMTP server refuses to send the message or ColdFusion is unable to contact the SMTP server, an error is logged in `\cfusion\mail\log\errors.log` and the spool file is moved to the `\cfusion\mail\undelivr` directory. The name of the spool file is specified in the `errors.log`.

> **NOTE**
>
> UNIX versions of ColdFusion use the following default directory tree for mail services:
>
> ```
> /opt/coldfusion/mail/log/errors.log
> /opt/coldfusion/mail/spool/
> /opt/coldfusion/mail/undelivr/
> ```

You can set mail error logging options in the ColdFusion Administrator. Your SMTP server's log may be another place to look for enlightenment.

> **CAUTION**
>
> ColdFusion uses a low-level thread to process mail in the spool directory. If the ColdFusion server is very busy processing Web page requests, email waiting to be sent is delayed until such time as the server is less busy. ColdFusion has been designed this way so that large email spools do not slow down the server and that optimum performance is guaranteed for the delivery of Web pages to users. However, this may lead to significant delays in email delivery on high-traffic systems with large amounts of email to send.

> **CAUTION**
>
> SMTP servers have a multitude of configuration options. A common cause of undelivered mail is anti-relay measures on the SMTP server. This can prevent unauthorized senders from using the mail server at all. Depending on your environment, you might need to ensure that the ColdFusion server is authorized to use the SMTP server and that the sender field has a correctly formatted email address, among other things.
>
> The ColdFusion `errors.log` and your SMTP server's transaction log are good places to look when email inexplicably appears in the `undelivr` directory.

Undelivered mail can be reprocessed by simply moving the spool file from `/cfusion/mail/undelivr/` back to `/cfusion/mail/spool/`. This procedure can be done programmatically through ColdFusion or manually by an administrator. This can be automated by scheduling a process to scan the `undelivr` directory and move any files back to the `spool` directory. However, malformed spool files or files with incorrect header information (such as a bad email address) may be in the undelivr directory for a very good reason—that is, they are undeliverable!

➔ Scheduling periodic processes was covered in Chapter 28, "Scheduling and Event Execution."

> **CAUTION**
>
> The message numbers returned by <CFPOP> are relative to the position of the emails in the POP message queue. Message numbers should not be stored as unique identifiers because they change whenever email is deleted from the mail box queue. They should be used immediately because of the transient nature of POP mail storage.

Summary

ColdFusion offers comprehensive email integration with both SMTP and POP servers. Text and HTML mail messages can be sent. Query-driven mail can be generated and personalized to combine database content with the mail output. POP accounts can be queried for stored email and associated MIME file attachments. Overall, the depth of support provided enables you to generate sophisticated Web applications that seamlessly leverage the Internet's most ubiquitous information system—email.

Sample Questions

1. ColdFusion does not require any external services to send email.
   A. True
   B. False

2. ColdFusion supports which of the following mail services?
   A. SMTP
   B. POP
   C. IMAP
   D. MIME attachments

3. If the SMTP server has been incorrectly specified, how does ColdFusion respond?
   A. It generates a runtime error and halts processing.
   B. It logs an error in the ColdFusion `application.log`.
   C. It creates a spool file in the `/cfusion/mail/undelivr` directory.
   D. It creates a spool file in the `/cfusion/mail/spool` directory.

CHAPTER 30

LDAP

Understanding LDAP

LDAP (Lightweight Directory Access Protocol) was originally conceived as a simplified interface to X.500 directories. Today, LDAP is both an interface to all sorts of proprietary directory services including MS Exchange and Novell and a directory server protocol in its own right.

LDAP is a protocol that enables organizations to store and access directory style information. For example, developers can build central stores of contact lists, user authentication, and security policy stores. This central repository might form the basis of a single login for a myriad of different services, such as Novell's NDS, cc:Mail, NT domains, and more. Because LDAP is an Internet standard, client programs and applications can be built to common specifications to hook into the directory's information repository. `<CFLDAP>` is the tag in ColdFusion that enables developers to communicate with any LDAP interface.

A directory is similar to a database, but contains more descriptive, attribute-based information. The information in a directory is generally read much more often than it is written. As a result, directories don't normally implement the complicated transaction schemes that regular databases use for doing high-volume, complex updates. LDAP updates are typically simple all-or-nothing changes. Directories are tuned to give quick response to high-volume lookup and search operations.

→ LDAP version 3 is defined in detail within RFC 2251, "The Lightweight Directory Access Protocol" (`http://www.ietf.org/rfc/rfc2251.txt`).

The LDAP directory data model is based on collections of attributes called *entries*. The unique reference to an entry is called a *distinguished name (DN)*. Each of the entry's attributes has a type and one or more values. The types are typically mnemonic strings, such as `"cn"` for common name and `"mail"` for email address. The values depend on what type of attribute it is. For example, a mail attribute might contain the value `"paumier@realtennis.org"`.

LDAP directory entries are arranged in a tree-like structure. Entries representing countries appear at the top of the tree. Below them are entries representing organizations. Further down the branch, you might find entries representing people, organizational units, printers, documents, and just about anything else you can think of. Figure 30.1 shows a sample LDAP directory tree.

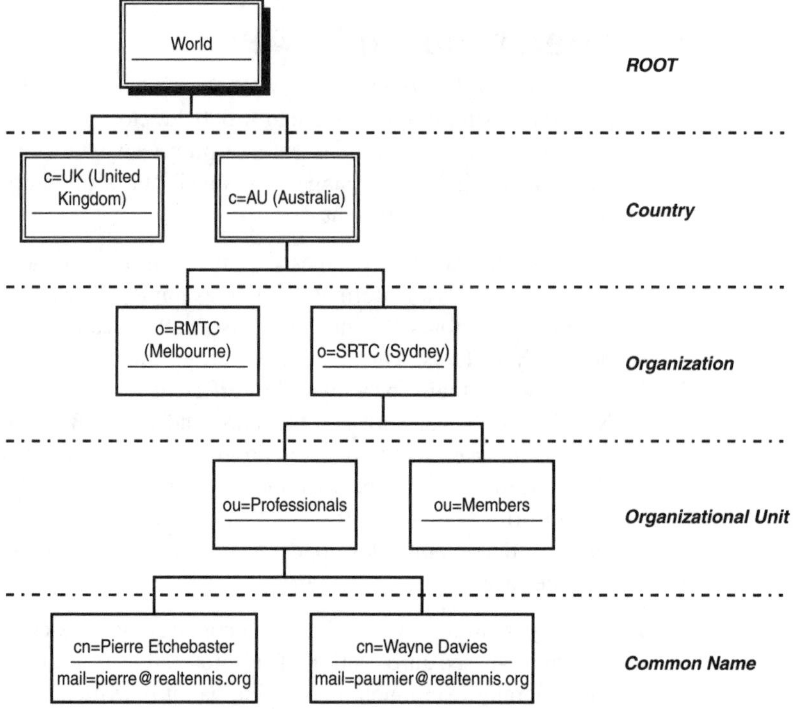

Figure 30.1

An LDAP directory tree.

You can control which attributes are required and allowed in an entry through the use of a special LDAP attribute called an `objectclass`. The values of the `objectclass` attribute determine the directory schema rules to which the entry must adhere.

An entry is referenced by its distinguished name, which is constructed by concatenating the name of the entry itself (called the *relative distinguished name*, or *RDN)* and the names of its ancestor entries. For example, the entry for Wayne Davies in Figure 30.1 has an RDN of "cn=Wayne Davies" and a DN of "cn=Wayne Davies, ou=Professionals, o=SRTC, c=AU".

➔ The full DN format is described in RFC 1779, "A String Representation of Distinguished Names" (http://www.ietf.org/rfc/rfc1779.txt).

➔ The University of Michigan originally developed the LDAP specification. However, its work has been taken up by The OpenLDAP Project (http://www.openldap.org/). The OpenLDAP slapd server is derived from University of Michigan LDAP 3.3 release.

Connecting to LDAP

LDAP defines directory operations for adding or deleting an entry, modifying an existing entry, and changing the name of an entry. However, LDAP is used primarily to search for information in the directory. The LDAP search operation allows a section of the directory to be searched for entries that match criteria specified by a search filter. From a programming perspective, LDAP is just another client/server data management system.

For example, if you had an LDAP directory of all the members of the Real Tennis Clubs of the world, you might search the index for all the players in Sydney, Australia and display them.

```
<CFLDAP ACTION="QUERY"
        NAME="qPlayers"
        ATTRIBUTES="cn,o,l,c,mail,telephonenumber"
        START="o=SRTC, c=AU"
               SORT="cn ASC"
        SERVER="ldap.realtennis.org">

<!--- Display qPlayers --->
<CFOUTPUT>
There were #qPlayers.RecordCount# players found.
</CFOUTPUT>
<TABLE>
   <TR>
        <TH>Player</TH>
        <TH>Club</TH>
        <TH>Location</TH>
        <TH>EMail</TH>
        <TH>Phone</TH>
   </TR>
  <CFOUTPUT QUERY="qPlayers">
   <TR>
     <TD>#qPlayers.cn#</TD>
     <TD>#qPlayers.o#</TD>
     <TD>#qPlayers.l#, #qPlayers.c#</TD>
     <TD><A HREF="mailto:#qPlayers.mail#">#qPlayers.mail#</A></TD>
     <TD>#qPlayers.telephonenumber#</TD>
   </TR>
```

```
  </CFOUTPUT>
</TABLE>
```

The ATTRIBUTES parameter dictates which entities—or in a database sense, columns—will be returned by the search. START nominates the branch in the directory hierarchy in which the search should start (organization, Sydney Real Tennis Club and Country, Australia). We are sorting by common name in ascending order. Matching information is returned as a query object specified by the NAME attribute. See Table 30.1 for more <CFLDAP> attributes.

→ Displaying query objects with <CFOUTPUT> is discussed in Chapter 7, "Using Databases."

Table 30.1 <CFLDAP> Attributes and Their Usage

Variable Names	Description
SERVER/PORT	Required to locate the LDAP server. SERVER can be a qualified domain name or an IP address. PORT defaults to 389.
USERNAME/PASSWORD	These attributes are needed for authenticated directory access. This is typically required to perform updates on the directory.
ACTION	Must be ADD, MODIFY, MODIFYDN, DELETE, or QUERY.
NAME	The name of the query object returned by <CFLDAP>.
TIMEOUT	Operational timeout. Defaults to 60 seconds.
MAXROWS	Maximum number of rows returned. May be superceded by a maxrows setting on the LDAP directory itself.
START	Specifies the DN of the entry branch from which to start the search.
SCOPE	The depth to which the search will run in the directory hierarchy. Defaults to ONELEVEL.
ATTRIBUTES	Comma-delimited list of attributes to be returned in the QUERY or updated on the directory.
FILTER	The FILTER attribute is more akin to the search criteria of a query rather than an actual filter per se. No filter returns all entries.
FILTERFILE	An absolute file path or filename in \cfusion\ldap that conforms to the LDAP filter file format as defined in RFC 1558 (http://www.ietf.org/rfc/rfc1558.txt).
SORT	An attribute listed in ATTRIBUTES. SORT can be either ascending (ASC) or descending (DESC). For example, "cn DESC".
SORTCONTROL	Enter NOCASE for case-insensitive sorting.
DN	Distinguished name (DN) is the directory key for the entity being updated.
STARTROW	Start row of a query; useful for building a Next/Previous style results page. Defaults to 1.
REBIND/REFERRAL	These attributes modify how <CFLDAP> treats referrals to other directories.
SECURE	Provides security options for encrypting the transmission of data to and from the LDAP server.

LDAP offers a collection of `FILTER` operators. These can be used to apply Boolean and wildcard searches on the directory entries. For example, restricting a search to an organization name of `"RMTC"` and a country of `"AU"` could be done using the following line:

```
FILTER=(&(o=RMTC)(c=AU))
```

➔ A partial list of `FILTER` operators can be found in the ColdFusion documentation in Chapter 16, “Scripting.”

> **TIP**
>
> Bigfoot (`http://www.bigfoot.com/`) runs a public LDAP server that you can practice queries against at `ldap.bigfoot.com`.

`<CFLDAP>` provides actions for updating LDAP directories. Typically a `USERNAME` and `PASSWORD` with appropriate permissions are required to perform additions or modifications to the directory. For modifications or deletes, you will need to know the distinguished name, which acts like a database primary key. Lastly, the `ATTRIBUTES` parameter is used to specify a list of LDAP attributes to be updated or added to the hierarchy.

```
<CFLDAP ACTION="ADD"
        DN="cn=Wayne Davies, ou=Professionals, o=realtennis.org"
        ATTRIBUTES="objectclass=top, person, organizationalPerson;
               mail=paumier@realtennis.org;
               telephonenumber=+61 2 5555 2244;
               ou=Professionals"
        MODIFYTYPE="REPLACE"
        SERVER="ldap.realtennis.org"
        USERNAME="cn=modius, ou=Members, o=realtennis.org"
        PASSWORD="champion">
```

In this example, a `DN` for an administrator, `"modius"`, is used as the `USERNAME`, the particular record being updated is specified in the `DN` attribute, and the `ATTRIBUTES` list the values for updating an entry for `"Wayne Davies"`.

> **NOTE**
>
> If a single attribute value contains a comma, you must escape it by adding an extra comma. For example, a value of
>
> `uid=wdavies,ou=professionals,o=realtennis.org`
>
> must be entered as
>
> `uid=wdavies,,ou=professionals,,o=realtennis.org`

Summary

LDAP is a directory protocol used as an interface to many disparate directory vendors. It allows a common coding interface for developers to access directory information. LDAP is similar to other data management systems, such as databases, and is read optimized for fast, high-volume lookup searches. ColdFusion uses the `<CFLDAP>` tag to provide both query and update actions on LDAP-compliant servers.

Sample Questions

1. What does LDAP use as a unique reference or primary key in the directory hierarchy?
   A. `UUID` (Universally Unique Identifier)
   B. `DN` (Distinguished Name)
   C. `RDN` (Relative Distinguished Name)
   D. `objectclass`

2. Which `<CFLDAP>` attribute is used to specify the distinguished name of the entry for a directory branch within which a search is performed?
   A. `START`
   B. `STARTROW`
   C. `DN`
   D. `SCOPE`

3. In LDAP, the distinguished name is (choose two)
   A. A unique reference to an attribute in the directory
   B. A concatenation of an `RDN` and its ancestor attributes
   C. The name of an entry in the directory
   D. The `objectclass` definition

CHAPTER 31

Other Internet Protocols

Using HTTP Agents

HTTP agents provide developers with the opportunity to leverage other Web servers as an information resource. ColdFusion uses `<CFHTTP>` to connect to and retrieve content from remote servers. The agent (your ColdFusion code) behaves just like a Web browser, retrieving the entire contents of the designated URL. Combined with other ColdFusion technologies, HTTP agents form the basic transport for content and application syndication services. HTTP agents fall into two camps: unilateral and cooperative.

Unilateral agents retrieve the contents of a Web page without any type of cooperation with the remote information resource. The developer has to determine flexible methodologies for coping with the returned data to accommodate potential changes in the structure of the information returned. For example, syndicating headlines from the home page of a news portal. The portal owner might change the layout of his Web site from time to time. Consequently, unilateral agents are generally more complex to code, can break easily, and are prone to copyright infringements.

Cooperative agents are those that work in concert with a back-end page or robot on the remote server. A back-end page is not designed to be seen by a user with a Web browser; rather, it is specifically coded to respond to an HTTP agent. As a result, cooperative agents are generally very easy to put together and do not break often. On the other hand, a back-end page can be fairly complex depending on the level of functionality being delivered to the incoming agent. For example, a news portal delivering an XML news feed to syndicate partners.

Creating HTTP Agents

The <CFHTTP> tag spawns an external agent that goes to a specified URL and retrieves the contents via HTTP. The agent is sophisticated and remarkably simple to implement.

```
<CFHTTP URL="http://www.allaire.com/"
        METHOD="GET"
        RESOLVEURL="true"
        USERAGENT="Mozilla/4.0 (compatible; MSIE 5.5; Windows NT 5.0"></CFHTTP>

<CFOUTPUT>
#CFHTTP.FileContent#
</CFOUTPUT>
```

In this example, <CFHTTP> is sending an agent to retrieve and then display the Allaire home page. The entire contents of the page are returned as the variable `CFHTTP.FileContent`. The `METHOD="GET"` attribute is used to get any text or binary file from the URL.

When a file is brought back from a remote server, any relative links to images, other Web pages, and so on will no longer be valid. `RESOLVEURL` determines whether to resolve URLs found in `CFHTTP.FileContent` to absolute addresses. Absolute links will then point to the correct remote address.

When a Web browser accesses a Web server, it indicates the type and version of browser it is. The `USERAGENT` attribute can be used to nominate the agent or browser of your choice. The default is `"ColdFusion"`.

TIP

Web sites often use routines to detect the type of browser the user is operating. This information is then used to deliver a different client-side experience depending on the browser detected. To ensure that your HTTP agent returns the Web page you expect, make sure that the `USERAGENT` attribute is set to an appropriate Web browser type.

Microsoft's Internet Explorer 5.5 uses

```
Mozilla/4.0 (compatible; MSIE 5.5; Windows NT 5.0)
```

You can determine a Web browser's user agent value by browsing a ColdFusion server with debugging turned on. Check the `CGI` variables for `HTTP_USER_AGENT`.

→ ColdFusion debugging is covered in Chapter 20, "Debugging."

The <CFHTTP> agent has the same issues as any other Web browser. If your server is located in a network that must use a proxy server to reach the Web, you will need to specify a proxy using the appropriate attributes for the <CFHTTP> agent as well.

TIP

<CFHTTP> is not clever enough to tell the proxy server to bypass the cache. Therefore, depending on how your proxy server has been configured, a <CFHTTP> agent might continue to retrieve the cached version of a Web page even though the actual page has long since been modified.

You can often trick the proxy server's cache by adding a different URL parameter onto the end of the remote address each time you request a page. A URL encoded time stamp works well.

```
<CFHTTP URL="http://www.allaire.com/index.cfm?#URLEncodedFormat(Now())#"
        METHOD="GET">
```

<CFHTTP> returns a number of useful variables in addition to CFHTTP.FileContent. These are listed in Table 31.1.

Table 31.1 <CFHTTP> Return Variables

Variable Names	Description
CFHTTP.FileContent	Returns the entire contents of the remote file for text and MIME files.
CFHTTP.MimeType	Returns the MIME type of the file; for example, "text/html".
CFHTTP.ResponseHeader	Returns the entire response header in a structure. If there are multiple instances of a header key, the values are placed in an array within the ResponseHeader structure. For example, multiple cookies.
CFHTTP.Header	Returns the entire response header in its raw text format as a simple variable.
CFHTTP.StatusCode	Returns the HTTP error code and associated error string; for example, "200 Success".

<CFHTTP> can send variables to a URL ahead of its retrieval of the Web page. This is as you would expect given that a standard Web browser can submit form variables, cookies, and URL parameters to the Web server. By submitting variables to the Web server directly, you can activate form action pages and other dynamic content, effectively bypassing the user interface that a normal Web user would navigate.

To submit variables, you must change to METHOD="POST" and specify the variables to send using a series of <CFHTTPPARAM> subtags nested within the <CFHTTP></CFHTTP>. For example, submitting variables to a contact form action page:

```
<CFHTTP URL="http://www.barrowdowns.com/contact.asp"
    METHOD="POST">
    <CFHTTPPARAM TYPE="FORMFIELD" NAME="ContactName" VALUE="Gandalf the Grey">
    <CFHTTPPARAM TYPE="FORMFIELD" NAME="Occupation" VALUE="Wizard">
    <CFHTTPPARAM TYPE="FORMFIELD" NAME="Message" VALUE="Where's that hobbit?!">
</CFHTTP>
```

<CFHTTPPARAM> can be used to specify any combination of the following variable types:

- FORM variables, including file uploads
- COOKIE variables
- URL parameters
- CGI variables

<CFHTTP> can also be used to retrieve a file and save it direct to disk. This is particularly useful if you are grabbing binary files such as images, but it works equally well with Web pages and other text files. You need to specify the PATH where the file is to be saved. If you don't specify a FILE attribute, the original filename will be used.

```
<CFHTTP URL="http://www.daemon.com.au/images2/daemonlogo_medium.gif"
        METHOD="GET"
        PATH="C:\x"
        FILE="logo.gif"
        RESOLVEURL="false"
        THROWONERROR="yes">
```

Remote Data File Queries

<CFHTTP> can be used to retrieve a remote data file and dynamically generate a query object. <CFHTTP> sends out an agent to retrieve the file and then parses the data according to the DELIMITER attribute. TEXTQUALIFIER indicates the character at the start and finish of a column. The COLUMNS attribute can be used to dictate column headings otherwise the very first record is used for column names.

```
<CFHTTP URL="http://www.stockbroker.com/closing_quotes.txt"
        METHOD="GET"
        NAME="qQuotes"
        COLUMNS="code,open,close,low,high,volume"
        TEXTQUALIFIER=""""""
        DELIMITER=","
        RESOLVEURL="false"></CFHTTP>
<CFOUTPUT QUERY="qQuotes">
#qQuotes.Code#: #qQuotes.Close#<BR>
</CFOUTPUT>
```

NOTE

To specify quotes as a TEXTQUALIFIER, you need to escape each quote with yet another quote!

```
TEXTQUALIFIER=""""""
```

There are six quotes in this example: two to define the value of the attribute and two for each quote in the value.

Troubleshooting HTTP Agents

<CFHTTP> spawns an additional process that sends out an HTTP agent. The calling application page waits until the agent has traveled onto the network and returned before it continues processing. The agent's activity on the Web is largely beyond the developer's control. Any number of issues, from network congestion to the remote host simply being unavailable, can cause the agent to fail.

If the agent fails or takes an inordinate amount of time to complete its mission, it might jeopardize the processing of the calling page. It is good idea to set a TIMEOUT attribute for the agent so that you can code appropriate error handling to deal with long-running agents. Set THROWONERROR="Yes" if you want to raise a standard exception if <CFHTTP> times out or alternatively check the CFHTTP.Status variable.

➔ Trapping errors is covered in Chapter 21, "Error Handling."

> **TIP**
>
> Where you have an agent that is notorious for taking a long time to complete its mission, be careful not to be timed out by the ColdFusion server. Place a RequestTimeOut parameter on the end of the URL to make sure that the agent has the time it needs.
>
> ```
> <CFHTTP URL="http://www.allaire.com/index.cfm?RequestTimeout=500"
>         METHOD="GET">
> ```

On occasion, the remote host might respond with an error. In other words, the remote host is available on the network but the Web service has failed for some reason. You can test the CFHTTP.Status variable to detect whether things have gone wrong and respond accordingly.

> **NOTE**
>
> A successful HTTP agent will return a STATUSCODE of "200 Success" or "200 OK". A complete list of HTTP status codes can be found at the W3C Web site: http://www.w3.org/Protocols/rfc2616/rfc2616-sec10.html

Page Scraping

A page scrape involves capturing an HTML page from another Web server and then processing the page for information. For instance, you might be interested in harvesting a list of contacts from an affiliates Web site and displaying them on your own. However, you might want to get rid of the header and footer displayed on the affiliate's site and substitute your own.

Excising a particular piece of content from a Web site is done using string parsing. Typically this is achieved by locating a region on the page above and below the desired content. A region is identified as a constant string (such as a heading or a comment) or, alternatively, a pattern that can be reliably matched using a regular expression. Using string functions, you then remove all the text above and below the content you want in the `CFHTTP.FileContent` variable.

```
<CFHTTP URL="http://www.daemon.com.au/news.cfm"
        METHOD="GET"
        RESOLVEURL="true"></CFHTTP>

<!--- find the beginning of the headlines less one char --->
<CFSET count = Find('<!-- START INDEX1 -->', CFHTTP.filecontent) - 1>

<!--- remove characters to this point in the string --->
<CFSET news = RemoveChars(CFHTTP.filecontent, 1, VARIABLES.count)>

<!--- find the end of headlines --->
<CFSET count = Find('<!-- END INDEX1 -->', VARIABLES.news) - 1>

<!--- remove characters for the rest of the page --->
<CFSET news = RemoveChars(VARIABLES.news, VARIABLES.count,
➥len(VARIABLES.news))>
```

This form of syndication can be useful when you are dealing with a partner who has a basic Internet site. As long as the structure of the page (that is, the regions you are matching) does not change, you can syndicate content from the Web page with the partner providing little or no input.

Back-End Pages and Robots

Back-end pages, or robots, are application pages specifically designed to respond to HTTP agents. To this end, they normally provide an agreed data format that can be retrieved to reduce the amount of work involved in processing the information at the agent's end. Normally we are talking about the exchange of text-based information, so an ideal structured format for the data is XML. In ColdFusion, the native XML format is WDDX, so this is often preferred by ColdFusion developers.

→ WDDX and XML in ColdFusion are discussed in Chapter 25, "WDDX."

An example of a cooperative agent might include a back-end page that queries a database and outputs a query object as a WDDX packet. The following code will also accommodate an optional `FORM` parameter to modify the sort behavior of the query.

```
<!--- Mordor Forces of Darkness, Troop Bot --->
<!---Suppress debug output --->
<CFSETTING SHOWDEBUGOUTPUT="No">

<CFQUERY NAME="qTroops" DATASOURCE="#application.dsn#">
   SELECT Orc_ID, CommonName, Breed, Regiment, PlaceOfSpawning
   FROM   Warrens
   <CFIF IsDefined("FORM.sort")>
   ORDER BY #FORM.sort#
```

```
    </CFIF>
</CFQUERY>

<CFWDDX ACTION="CFML2WDDX" INPUT="#qTroops#">
```

The cooperative agent is designed to contact the robot, using `<CFHTTP>` and pass a `FORM` parameter with a sort value. It returns with a WDDX packet, which it then converts into a native ColdFusion query variable. The query is used with `<CFOUTPUT>` to build a report table.

```
<CFINCLUDE TEMPLATE="header.cfm">
<CFPARAM NAME="FORM.SORT" DEFAULT="REGIMENT">

<H2>Hordes Of Mordor - Troop Locator</H2>

<CFHTTP URL="http://www.mtdoom.com/robots/troops_wddx.cfm"
        METHOD="POST"
        RESOLVEURL="false">

<CFHTTPPARAM TYPE="FORMFIELD"
             NAME="SORT"
             VALUE="#FORM.SORT#">

</CFHTTP>

<!---Deserialize the packet into a native result set qTroops --->
<CFWDDX ACTION="WDDX2CFML"
        INPUT="#CFHTTP.FileContent#"
        OUTPUT="qTroops">

<!---This form allows the passing of a sort parameter to the syndicated troop
➥locator --->
<CFOUTPUT>
    <FORM ACTION="#CGI.SCRIPT_NAME#" METHOD="post">Sort by:
        <SELECT NAME="SORT" SIZE="1">
            <OPTION VALUE="REGIMENT"> Orc Regiment
            <OPTION VALUE="BREED"> Orc Breed
        </SELECT>
        <INPUT TYPE="submit" VALUE="refresh">
    </FORM>
</CFOUTPUT>

<!---Print out the troop list --->
<TABLE>
    <TR>
        <TH>Name</TH>
        <TH>Breed</TH>
        <TH>Regiment</TH>
    </TR>
```

```
    <CFOUTPUT QUERY="qTroops">
        <TR VALIGN="top">
            <TD>#qTroops.CommonName#</TD>
            <TD>#qTroops.Breed#</TD>
            <TD>#qTroops.Regiment#</TD>
        </TR>
    </CFOUTPUT>
</TABLE>
<CFINCLUDE TEMPLATE="footer.cfm">
```

FTP Agents

<CFFTP> enables developers to implement File Transfer Protocol operations from the ColdFusion server to an FTP server. The <CFFTP> tag governs all the actions that you require to connect to and perform file actions on the FTP server.

> **NOTE**
>
> The <CFFTP> tag is specifically for transferring files between a ColdFusion server and an FTP server. <CFFTP> is unable to move files between a ColdFusion server and a browser (client). Use <CFFILE> with ACTION="UPLOAD" to copy files from the client to a ColdFusion server; use <CFCONTENT> to move/copy files from a ColdFusion server to the browser.

➔ <CFFILE> and <CFCONTENT> are covered in Chapter 27, "System Integration."

You need to first establish or "open" a connection with the FTP server. After a connection is made, the details (server, username, password, and so on) can be cached by <CFFTP>, so you need only refer to the name of the CONNECTION for subsequent actions on the server for that FTP session. If the FTP session times out or your connection is closed for whatever reason, you will need to reopen the connection.

```
<CFFTP ACTION="OPEN"
       SERVER="ftp.zipworld.com.au"
       USERNAME="anonymous"
       PASSWORD="modius"
       STOPONERROR="Yes"
       CONNECTION="zip">
```

After a connection has been made, the other ACTION attribute values can be used to perform operations on the FTP server. Generally the ACTION performs some task and returns a variable, CFFTP.ReturnValue. The value of this variable depends on the task being performed. For example, for an ACTION="ExistsFile" operation to test whether a file exists on the FTP server, CFFTP.ReturnValue will be either YES or NO. The exception to this is ACTION="ListDir", which instead generates a query object containing a directory listing of the specified directory.

```
<CFFTP ACTION="LISTDIR"
       STOPONERROR="Yes"
```

```
        NAME="qFiles"
        DIRECTORY="/"
        CONNECTION="zip">

<CFOUTPUT QUERY="qFiles">
#qFiles.Name#: #qFiles.URL#<BR>
</CFOUTPUT>
```

On the FTP server, you must navigate to the directory you want before performing a file operation. For example, you might log in to a home directory on the FTP server, but then need to change directory to `/pub/uploads` before being able to upload a file. You cannot just nominate the directory and file in one operation. FTP uses a slightly different vocabulary than you might be used to. `PUT` is used for uploading a file to the FTP site and `GET` is used for retrieving files.

```
<!--- check to see if the directory is there --->
<CFFTP ACTION="EXISTSDIR"
       STOPONERROR="No"
       DIRECTORY="/pub/uploads"
       CONNECTION="zip">
<CFIF CFFTP.returnvalue is "NO">
        <CFABORT SHOWERROR="Uploads directory does not exist!">
</CFIF>

<!--- change directory --->
<CFFTP ACTION="CHANGEDIR"
       STOPONERROR="No"
       DIRECTORY="/pub/uploads"
       CONNECTION="zip">

<!--- upload file to the current directory --->
<CFFTP ACTION="PUTFILE"
       STOPONERROR="No"
       LOCALFILE="c:\tolkien\frodo.gif"
       REMOTEFILE="frodo.gif"
       TRANSFERMODE="AUTO"
       CONNECTION="zip">
```

> **NOTE**
>
> When your application is finished with the FTP connection, it is polite to close the FTP session by using `ACTION="CLOSE"`. If you neglect to close the session, it will remain open until the connection times out. This would be considered particularly poor etiquette if a connection limit existed on the FTP server you were contacting.

CAUTION

Use of <CFFTP> on the ColdFusion server can be blocked using basic security under ColdFusion Administrator. There are obvious security issues when enabling developers to move any file off the server to any remote FTP server.

Summary

ColdFusion provides HTTP agent technology through the use of <CFHTTP>. <CFHTTP> can be used to retrieve Web pages and files from remote Web servers and build query objects from remote data files. Cooperative agent technology can provide very sophisticated content and application syndication services. Using HTTP agents and XML as a transport medium provides a powerful platform for utilizing the Web as an information resource for your applications.

FTP remains one of the primary Internet services for transferring files. <CFFTP> enables you, as a developer, to integrate FTP communication between servers from within your applications.

Sample Questions

1. <CFHTTP> with METHOD="GET" can send what type of parameters to the remote URL?
   A. FORM variables
   B. COOKIE variables
   C. URL parameters
   D. FILE variable

2. What tags would be needed to upload a file from a client's browser to the ColdFusion server and then syndicate the file to a remote FTP site?
   A. <CFFILE> and <CFCONTENT>
   B. <CFFILE> and <CFFTP>
   C. <CFCONTENT> and <CFFTP>
   D. <CFFILE> only

3. <CFHTTP> can be used to retrieve both Web page and its corresponding images in a single agent call.
   A. True
   B. False

PART 7

DATABASES

CHAPTER 32

Basic SQL

Database Basics

The term *database* is used in many different ways, but for our purposes (and indeed, from SQL's perspective), a database is a collection of data stored in some organized fashion.

Databases contain tables, and data itself is stored in *tables* (not in databases). A table is a structured container that can store data of a specific type. A table might contain a list customers, a product catalog, or any other list of information.

Tables are made up of *columns*. A column contains a particular piece of information within a table. Each column in a database has an associated *data type*. A data type defines what type of data the column can contain. For example, if the column is to contain a number (perhaps the number of items in an order), the data type would be a numeric data type. If the column were to contain dates, text, notes, currency amounts, and so on, the appropriate data type would be used to specify this fact.

Data in a table is stored in *rows*. Each record saved is stored in its own row. If you envision a table as a spreadsheet-style grid, the vertical columns in the grid are the table columns, and the horizontal rows are the table rows.

Every row in a table should have some column (or set of columns) that uniquely identifies it. A table containing customers might use a customer number column, a table containing orders might use the order ID, and an employee list table might use an employee ID or the employee Social Security number column. This column (or set of columns) that uniquely identifies each row in a table is called a *primary key*. You use the primary key to refer to a single row. Without a primary key, updating or deleting specific rows in a table becomes extremely difficult.

> **TIP**
>
> Although primary keys are not actually required, most database designers ensure that every table they create has a primary key so that future data manipulation is possible and manageable.

Any column in a table can be established as the primary key, as long as it meets the following conditions:

- No two rows can have the same primary key value.
- Every row must have a primary key value (a column cannot allow NULL values).
- The column containing primary key values can never be modified or updated.
- Primary key values can never be reused (if a row is deleted from the table, its primary key cannot be assigned to any new rows).

The SELECT Statement

SELECT is the most frequently used SQL statement. It retrieves data from one or more tables. At minimum, SELECT takes two clauses: the data to be retrieved and the location to retrieve it from.

> **NOTE**
>
> Technically, SELECT statements don't even need table names. It is perfectly valid (although uncommon) to do something like this:
>
> ```
> SELECT 100 AS id
> ```
>
> This statement returns a single row with a single column—data not retrieved from any table at all.

In practice, however, most basic SELECT statements are made up of four parts that must appear in this order:

- The data to retrieve
- The location to retrieve it from
- Filtering conditions (to restrict the data being retrieved)
- Sort order (to specify how returned data is sorted)

Specifying the Data to Retrieve

You specify the data to be retrieved by listing the required table column names as the first clause (right after the keyword SELECT). At least one column must be specified.

> **NOTE**
>
> The maximum number of columns (or width of a retrieved row) that may be retrieved varies from one DBMS (Database Management System) to the next. There is no standard size or limitation.

The following example retrieves a single column (named product_id) from a table (named products):

```
SELECT product_id
FROM products
```

To retrieve multiple columns, you must separate the column names with commas:

```
SELECT product_id, product_name
FROM products
```

NOTE

To retrieve unique values, use the DISTINCT keyword before the column name.

You also can retrieve all columns without listing them individually. You do so by using the wildcard character * as follows:

```
SELECT *
FROM products
```

TIP

For performance reasons, it is generally not a good idea to use SELECT * (unless you actually need every column). As a rule, retrieve just what you need and nothing more.

You can also rename columns when retrieving them by assigning aliases to them. You do so by using the AS keyword, which lets you specify an alternative name for a column, as follows:

```
SELECT product_id AS id, product_name AS name
FROM products
```

In this example, the returned columns are id and name even though the actual table names are product_id and product_name.

TIP

You most often use aliases when working with aggregate functions (covered in Chapter 34, "Aggregates"), but another important use allows you to rename illegally named columns. For example, some databases allow you to include spaces and special characters (such as the # sign or plus and minus) in column names, and these characters could render the column names unusable in other applications (such as ColdFusion). Using aliases, you can rename the columns, giving them safe (and legal) names when they are retrieved.

Specifying the Table

The table name is always specified using the `FROM` keyword, as follows:

```
SELECT product_id, product_name
FROM products
```

Data can be retrieved from multiple tables, in which case the table names must be separated by commas. You usually do so only in Join operations.

➔ Joins are covered in Chapter 33, "Joins."

> **NOTE**
>
> Some databases require that table names be fully qualified (with a prefix that indicates the table owner and database).

Filtering

Retrieved data is filtered using the `WHERE` clause, which must contain one or more filter conditions using supported operators. Table 32.1 lists the operators supported by most SQL implementations.

Table 32.1 `WHERE` Clause Operators

Operator	Description
`=`	Equality
`<>`	Nonequality
`<`	Less than
`<=`	Less than or equal to
`>`	Greater than
`>=`	Greater than or equal to
`IN`	One of a set of
`LIKE`	Wildcard match
`BETWEEN`	Between two specified values
`IS NULL`	Is a `NULL` value
`AND`	Combine clauses
`OR`	Or clauses
`NOT`	Negate clauses

The basic mathematical type operators are used as follows:

```
SELECT product_id, product_name
FROM products
WHERE product_id=1
```

You use the IN operator to specify multiple values, which must be separated by commas and enclosed within parentheses:

```
SELECT product_id, product_name
FROM products
WHERE product_id IN (1,3,7,18,45)
```

TIP

You can use lists and the list functions to pass values to the IN operator. See Chapter 13, "Lists," for more information.

You use the LIKE operator for wildcard searches. The SQL specification supports three wildcards, as shown in Table 32.2 (although some databases do not support them all).

Table 32.2 Wildcard Operators

Operator	Description
%	Match zero or more characters
_	Match a single character
[]	Match one of a set of characters

You use wildcard searches to search for patterns within column text. The following example finds all products beginning with the letter s:

```
SELECT product_id, product_name
FROM products
WHERE product_name LIKE 's%'
```

Wildcards can be used anywhere within a string, not just at the beginning. The following example finds all products that contain the text widget:

```
SELECT product_id, product_name
FROM products
WHERE product_name LIKE '%widget%'
```

TIP

Wildcard matches are generally the slowest form of filter. This is particularly true of wildcards used in the middle or end of a search pattern. And as such, they should not be overused unnecessarily.

You can combine searches by using the AND and OR operators. The following example finds all products with the text widget in the name and a cost of $5 or more:

```
SELECT product_id, product_name
FROM products
WHERE product_name LIKE '%widget%' AND product_price >= 5
```

> **CAUTION**
>
> When using multiple search conditions (using AND and OR), you should use parentheses to group clauses appropriately. They prevent ambiguity and prevent clauses from being evaluated in an unexpected order.

To negate a condition, you use the NOT operator before the condition as follows:

```
SELECT product_id, product_name
FROM products
WHERE NOT product_id IN (1,3,7,18,45)
```

Sorting

Retrieved data can be sorted using the ORDER BY clause. Data can be sorted in one or more columns (if more than one column is specified, data is sorted by the first column and then by the second if multiple rows have the same first column value and so on).

The following example retrieves all products and sorts them by name:

```
SELECT product_id, product_name
FROM products
ORDER BY product_name
```

Data is sorted in ascending or descending order, which you specify by using the ASC or DESC keywords, respectively. If neither keyword is provided, ASC is assumed by default.

The INSERT Statement

The INSERT statement inserts one or more rows into a table. INSERT always takes the name of the table into which data is to be inserted, as well as the appropriate columns and values. The columns are listed comma delimited in parentheses after the table name, and the values for each column are listed comma delimited in parentheses after the VALUES keyword.

> **NOTE**
>
> Data cannot be inserted into more than one table in a single operation. The same is true for UPDATE and DELETE operations.

The following example inserts a new row into a products table:

```
INSERT INTO products(product_name, product_price)
VALUES('Super deluxe widget', 299)
```

> **CAUTION**
>
> Unlike ColdFusion, SQL is not *typeless*. Strings must be enclosed within quotation marks, and numbers must not be.

You cannot use INSERT to insert multiple rows unless the data is the result of a SELECT operation (known as an INSERT SELECT). The following example inserts all the data from one table into another:

```
INSERT INTO products(product_name, product_price)
SELECT product_name, product_price
FROM new_prods
```

> **TIP**
>
> ColdFusion developers often use INSERT SELECT as a way to insert multiple user selections. They do so by passing the user selections (usually from form fields) to an IN clause in the SELECT statement so that it selects only the user-selected data.

The UPDATE Statement

The UPDATE statement updates data in one or more rows. UPDATE takes the name of the table to be updated, as well as the rows to be affected, and the new values.

The following example updates a single row in a table:

```
UPDATE products
SET product_price=49.99
WHERE product_id=235
```

The WHERE clause restricts the rows being updated, and without it, *all* rows are updated. The following example increases the price of all products by 10:

```
UPDATE products
SET product_price=price+10
```

To update multiple columns, you must separate each column=value pair with a comma.

> **CAUTION**
>
> Care must be taken to ensure that a WHERE clause is specified where needed (usually it will be). If you want to update a single row, the WHERE clause should always filter by the primary key.

The DELETE Statement

The DELETE statement deletes one or more rows from a table. DELETE takes the name of the table to be processed, as well as the rows to be affected.

The following example deletes a single row from a table:

```
DELETE FROM products
WHERE product_id=235
```

The WHERE clause restricts the rows being deleted, and without it, *all* rows are deleted.

CAUTION

Care must be taken to ensure that a WHERE clause is specified where needed (usually it will be). If you want to delete a single row, the WHERE clause should always filter by the primary key.

Summary

The basic SQL statements are SELECT, INSERT, UPDATE, and DELETE. These four statements, combined with features and functions to be reviewed in the next few chapters, account for the majority of SQL written by ColdFusion developers.

Sample Questions

1. Which of these keywords are used in SELECT statements?
   A. SET
   B. ORDER BY
   C. RETRIEVE
   D. WHERE
2. Which of the following wildcard searches are valid for use in WHERE clauses?
   A. LIKE 'widget'
   B. LIKE NOT '%widget%'
   C. LIKE 100%
   D. LIKE '%a%b%c%d%e%'
3. To delete data from specific columns in a row, which statement should you use?
   A. DELETE
   B. UPDATE
   C. NULL

4 Primary keys are required.
   A. True
   B. False

CHAPTER 33

Joins

Understanding Relational Database Design

You use SQL joins to perform operations and extract data from relational databases. As such, an understanding of relational database design is a prerequisite to successfully using joins.

Relational databases are sets of tables that each store parts of a complete data set, parts that relate to each other (and thus the term *relational*). The underlying principle here is that data should be organized so that it never has to be repeated (stored more than once), while at the same time keeping data in small manageable sets.

> **NOTE**
>
> Databases that are not relational are often referred to as being *flat*.

Some examples will help you understand this concept:

- A list of employees could be stored in a flat table—one big (and wide) table with employee and department information in each row. But employees are members of departments, and many employees share the same department information. Relational database design would then dictate that the data be broken into three tables—an employee table, a department table, and a third table that connects the two by storing the primary keys of employees and departments to relate them to each other.

- An orders database is another classic example of data that should be stored relationally. Customer information is not tied to a specific order (a customer may have many orders), order items are not tied to a specific order (an order may have multiple order items), and products are not tied to specific orders (a single product could be part of many orders). Relational design might require a table for products, a table for customers, a table for orders (which relates to the customers table), and a table for order items (which relates to both the orders and products tables).

When you're planning relational databases, there is no real right or wrong design, and there is always more than one way to lay out the tables. The following are some of the issues that you need to consider when planning relational table design:

- Data access—The less relational the data is, the harder it will be to extract required data filtered or ordered as needed.
- Maintainability—Relational databases can be maintained far more easily, but special attention has to be paid to the links between tables so as not to break them.
- Storage—A well-designed relational database can use disk space far more efficiently.
- Performance—Relational databases can perform far quicker than flat databases, if the design is well thought out and implemented.

> **NOTE**
>
> Primary keys, which were introduced in Chapter 32, "Basic SQL," are columns within tables that uniquely identify every row within those tables. Primary keys are an important part of relational database design because they are the values that connect tables to each other.
>
> Another important type of key used in relational databases is the *foreign key*. It is a column within a table whose value is that of another table's primary key. For example, an orders table might use the order number as a primary key, in which case the order number stored in the related order items table is a foreign key. Unlike primary keys, foreign keys need not be unique, and they can be updated as needed. Like primary keys, they always have values (and should not be `NULL`).

> **NOTE**
>
> A full discussion of relational database design is beyond the scope of this chapter and book. For an explanation of relational databases from a ColdFusion perspective, see *ColdFusion Web Application Construction Kit* (ISBN: 0-7897-1809-X).

Understanding Joins

Data broken up across relational databases has all the advantages listed previously. It also has a disadvantage in that retrieving the data is more complex. To retrieve a list of customers with matching orders information, you might have to retrieve data from two tables. And to retrieve a list of employees with the department data, you might have to retrieve the information from three tables.

If you want to retrieve data from multiple tables (within a single operation, a single `SELECT` statement), the tables must be *joined* (and thus the term *joins*).

> **NOTE**
>
> Joins are logical entities; that is, data is not actually stored in any joined format, and joins do not exist or persist. Data is joined as needed—while a SQL statement is being executed.

Basic Join Syntax

You join tables by using the SQL `SELECT` statement to specify all the tables to be joined. For example, the following code snippet retrieves every customer and order joined into a single resultset:

```
SELECT customers.customer_name, customers.customer_id,
       orders.order_id, orders.order_date
FROM customers, orders
```

In this example, `customers` and `orders` are both tables, and both are listed in the `FROM` clause. The database processes this SQL statement and returns data from both tables.

> **TIP**
>
> When retrieving columns from multiple tables, you need to provide the fully qualified table column name in the format `table.column` if any column appears in more than one table. Many developers find that using this fully qualified format prevents ambiguity, so they always use it for all SQL statements.

But how does the database engine know which rows in the `orders` table to relate to rows in the `customers` table? The answer is that it does not; the join condition must be specified, or *all* rows will be joined to each other. So, if you had 100 customers and 200 orders, the preceding SQL statement would return 20,000 rows (100 times 200) instead of 200. This kind of output is known as a *Cartesian product* or a *cross join*, and is seldom the desired output.

> **NOTE**
>
> Although join syntax is, for the most part, consistent across database implementations, some subtle differences can have an impact on your `SELECT` statements. Refer to your database's documentation for more information.

To properly join tables, you must explicitly provide the join condition. You can choose from two primary forms of syntax for doing so:

- Most databases allow you to join data in the `WHERE` clause, specifying the columns in each table that must be matched.
- ANSI SQL syntax requires that you specify joins in the `FORM` clause using the `JOIN` keyword.

The following example retrieves customers and orders (the same SQL statement used previously) joined using a `WHERE` clause:

```
SELECT customers.customer_name, customers.customer_id,
       orders.order_id, orders.order_date
FROM customers, orders
WHERE customers.customer_id=orders.customer_id
```

The condition provided in the `WHERE` clause instructs the database to join the tables by a common column—in this case, `customer_id`, which is the primary key of table `customers` and a foreign key in table `orders`.

> **TIP**
>
> You can join tables by using any comparison operators (not just =), and you can use multiple comparison operators (using AND, for example), too.

The following is the ANSI SQL version of this same statement:

```
SELECT customers.customer_name, customers.customer_id,
       orders.order_id, orders.order_date
FROM customers JOIN orders
     ON (customers.customer_id=orders.customer_id)
```

Using ANSI SQL syntax, you specify the join condition itself by using the `ON` keyword immediately after the names of the tables being joined.

> **NOTE**
>
> The number of tables that you can join in a single SELECT statement varies from one database to the next. SQL Server, for example, allows you to join 256 tables, whereas Oracle has no limit. Consult your database documentation for more information.

Inner Joins

The most commonly used join is the *inner join* (the type of join used in the previous sections). Inner joins use a join condition (including a comparison operator) to match rows from both tables using values in common columns. In other words, the join condition must match rows in both tables, and values that appear in one table, but not in the other, are not retrieved.

Using ANSI SQL, you can specify the join type in front of the `JOIN` keyword as follows:

```
SELECT customers.customer_name, customers.customer_id,
       orders.order_id, orders.order_date
FROM customers INNER JOIN orders
     ON (customers.customer_id=orders.customer_id)
```

> **TIP**
> If no join type is specified, INNER is assumed by default.

> **NOTE**
> There are actually two forms of INNER JOIN. The syntax shown here (testing for equality between two tables) is known as an *equi-join*. Another (lesser used) form of INNER JOIN is the *natural join* in which repeated values are eliminated from the resultset.

> **NOTE**
> Although ANSI SQL requires that you specify joins in the FROM clause, an exception is made for inner joins. It is the only form of join that ANSI SQL allows you to specify in the WHERE clause.

Outer Joins

Outer joins join tables while including rows that do not have corresponding (related) rows in the other tables. For example, to retrieve all customers (including those with no orders), you could use an outer join. The outer join assigns NULL values to all columns that are empty (because they have no matching row).

Three forms of outer joins are supported:

- LEFT OUTER JOIN (or LEFT JOIN) retrieves all rows from the left table (the left of the JOIN clause) and only related rows from the right table.
- RIGHT OUTER JOIN (or RIGHT JOIN) retrieves all rows from the right table (the right of the JOIN clause) and only related rows from the left table.
- FULL OUTER JOIN (or FULL JOIN) retrieves all rows from both tables and assigns NULL values to the columns for all rows that do not have a match in the other table.

The following example uses the ANSI SQL syntax to retrieve all customers (including those who don't have orders):

```
SELECT customers.customer_name, customers.customer_id,
       orders.order_id, orders.order_date
FROM customers LEFT OUTER JOIN orders
     ON (customers.customer_id=orders.customer_id)
```

In this example, the columns order_id and order_date contain NULL for all customers with no orders.

The following SELECT statement uses a WHERE clause join:

```
SELECT customers.customer_name, customers.customer_id,
       orders.order_id, orders.order_date
FROM customers, orders
WHERE customers.customer_id*=orders.customer_id
```

Here, `*=` creates the join. Because the `*` is on the left of the equal sign, all rows from the left table are retrieved (just like the `LEFT OUTER JOIN`). To retrieve all rows from the right table, you could use `=*` instead.

> **TIP**
>
> The only difference between `LEFT OUTER JOIN` and `RIGHT OUTER JOIN` is the order of the tables (which table is on which side of the `JOIN` keyword). You can change join types by simply switching the positions of the table names within the `SELECT` statement.

> **TIP**
>
> Regardless of the join type you're using, you can filter the data being retrieved by using additional conditions (known as *predicates*) in the `ON` clause.

Self-Joins

Tables can be joined to themselves to perform filtering based on data derived from the same table. This is known as a *self-join*. Self-joins do not require a special join syntax, so you can use all the standard join types and syntax. What makes a join a self-join is that the same table name is used twice, and this use obviously presents a syntax difficulty because SQL does not allow names to be duplicated within a `SELECT` statement.

To create self-joins, you must assign *aliases* to tables, temporary names used in the SQL statement in lieu of the real names. You specify table aliases after the table names as follows:

```
SELECT customers.customer_name
FROM customers c1 INNER JOIN customers c2
     ON (c1.customer_city=c2.customer_city)
WHERE c1.customer_state='CA'
```

In this example, the `customers` table is self-joined, so each occurrence of the table is given a unique alias (here, `c1` and `c2`) in the `FROM` clause. Once assigned, aliases are used like any other table names.

Summary

Relational database design is an important part of application design in general, and one that has a significant impact on everything from application performance to data manageability to resource usage to SQL complexity. Relational data is joined for retrieval, and several join types are supported (the most common being the `INNER JOIN`). Tables are usually joined by their primary and foreign keys.

Sample Questions

1. Every table must have a primary key in order to be joined to another table.
   A. True
   B. False

2. What kind of join is being used in this statement?

```
SELECT customers.customer_name, customers.customer_id,
       orders.order_id, orders.order_date
FROM customers, orders
WHERE customers.customer_id=*orders.customer_id
```

   A. Inner
   B. Equi
   C. Right outer
   D. Full outer

3. Which of these keywords are used in `JOIN` statements?
   A. `INNER`
   B. `SELF`
   C. `LEFT`
   D. `FULL`

CHAPTER 34

Aggregates

Understanding Aggregate Functions

Although you usually access a database to retrieve stored data, you often need to access calculations performed against data (and not the data itself). The SQL aggregate functions are a set of special functions that perform mathematical calculations against data, returning the results of those calculations to the calling application.

The SQL aggregate functions are both powerful and flexible, and can be used in conjunction with tables, joins, and any other database features.

> **TIP**
>
> Many database developers find using the aggregate functions troublesome and even complex at a times. So, instead of using them, they retrieve large amounts of data and then programmatically perform the calculations themselves. This practice should be avoided at all costs. First, the database engine can process these calculations far quicker than any client application could. And second, sending unneeded data across a connection from a database server to a client host can have a significant effect on network traffic and performance.

Using Aggregate Functions

The following five primary aggregate functions are supported by most major databases:

- `AVG` calculates the average value of a numeric column.
- `COUNT` obtains the number of rows that match a specific condition.

- MAX obtains the greatest value in a numeric column.
- MIN obtains the smallest value in a numeric column.
- SUM obtains the total of all values in a numeric column.

You can use these functions in two locations within SELECT statements:

- The SELECT list (the list of columns being selected)
- The HAVING clause (discussed later in this chapter)

The following example retrieves the cost of the most expensive product in a products table:

```
SELECT MAX(product_price) AS expensive
FROM products
```

Here, the MAX function is assigned to an alias using AS so that it can use the value.

➔ The use of aliases within SELECT statements was discussed previously in Chapter 32, "Basic SQL."

Multiple aggregate functions can be used within a single SELECT statement. This next example retrieves both the most and least expensive items in a products table:

```
SELECT MAX(product_price) AS expensive, MIN(product_price) AS cheap
FROM products
```

> **NOTE**
>
> Some databases extend the standard set of aggregate functions with additional proprietary functions. Examples are SQL Server's STDEV (statistical standard deviation) and VAR (statistical variance of all values) functions. If your database supports these functions, you can use them in the same way you use the standard functions. The only downside is that the SQL code is not portable to other databases.

Handling NULL Values

With the exception of COUNT, aggregate functions ignore NULL values. So returning the MIN of a column returns the actual value (and not NULL). COUNT obtains the number of rows that match a condition and as such can (optionally) include rows with NULL values. You determine whether or not to include NULL values by specifying (or not specifying) a column to count.

This first example counts the number of rows in a products table:

```
SELECT COUNT(*) AS num_products
FROM products
```

This next example counts only the rows that have a product description (not NULL in the prod_desc column):

```
SELECT COUNT(prod_desc) AS num_products
FROM products
```

As you can see, if * is used, all rows are counted. If a column name is specified, only rows that do not have a NULL value in that column are counted.

Another important distinction between COUNT and the other aggregate functions is the returned value. With the exception of COUNT, the aggregate functions return NULL if no rows are processed (for example, the SUM of no rows). COUNT, however, returns 0 if no rows are processed (or match selection criteria).

Processing Distinct Values

By default, the aggregate functions perform calculations on all rows. To calculate only unique values, you can use the DISTINCT keyword. This example counts the number of unique products in a table:

```
SELECT COUNT(DISTINCT prod_name) AS num_prods
FROM products
```

> **TIP**
>
> The opposite of DISTINCT is ALL, which you can use when all rows are to be processed. But because that is the default behavior, if neither ALL nor DISTINCT is specified, most developers ignore that keyword.

> **NOTE**
>
> You can use DISTINCT with AVG, COUNT, and SUM, but not with MAX and MIN. Obviously, if you want to know the greatest or smallest values in a column, DISTINCT would have no relevance.

Grouping Results

Thus far, we have reviewed the basic use of aggregate functions, applying them to entire tables. Aggregate functions can also be used to perform analysis on groups of data. For example, instead of counting all the employees in a company, a function can count them by department. Or instead of returning the highest priced item in a table, a function can return the highest priced item in each category. This type of calculation involves grouping (specifying how data is to be grouped), and when grouped, the aggregate functions return multiple rows—one per group.

You accomplish grouping by using the GROUP BY keyword. GROUP BY takes one or more columns to be grouped on (comma delimited if more than one is specified)—columns that must be specified in the SELECT list.

The following example returns a list of department IDs and the number of employees in each department:

```
SELECT department_id, COUNT(*) AS num_employees
FROM employees
GROUP BY department_id
```

Joined tables can be grouped in the same way. This next example joins two tables (using a WHERE clause) to return a list of department names and the number of employees in each department:

```
SELECT department_name, COUNT(*) AS num_employees
FROM employees, departments
WHERE employees.department_id=departments.department_id
GROUP BY department_name
```

➔ Joins and join clauses were covered in Chapter 33, "Joins."

NOTE

If a SELECT statement includes a WHERE clause, you must use GROUP BY after it. Similarly, if you use an ORDER BY clause, you must use GROUP BY before it.

GROUP BY does not sort data, and although grouped columns may be sorted in ascending order, this order must never be assumed. The only guaranteed safe way to sort grouped data is to use the ORDER BY clause.

Filtering Results

Aggregated data can be filtered in two ways to allow you complete flexibility within SELECT statements:

- You can use the WHERE clause to filter rows before they are grouped. Rows excluded by the WHERE condition are not included in aggregate calculations and processing. WHERE conditions can be used regardless of whether grouping is used and can reference any valid expression.
- You can use the HAVING clause to filter entire groups. This condition is applied after groups have been processed to eliminate aggregate values that do not match a specific condition. HAVING can be used only in conjunction with grouping and can reference any items in the select list.

➔ The WHERE clause was reviewed in Chapter 32, "Basic SQL."

The following example returns the number of employees in each department, including only employees residing in the specified country:

```
SELECT department_name, COUNT(*) AS num_employees
FROM employees, departments
WHERE employees.department_id=departments.department_id
      AND employees.country='USA'
GROUP BY department_name
ORDER BY department_name
```

This next example returns the number of employees in each department that has 100 or more employees:

```
SELECT department_name, COUNT(*) AS num_employees
FROM employees, departments
```

```
WHERE employees.department_id=departments.department_id
GROUP BY department_name
HAVING COUNT(*) >= 100
ORDER BY department_name
```

> **NOTE**
> You can use both `WHERE` and `HAVING` in the same `SELECT` statement if necessary. `WHERE` must always be the first clause after the tables (specified in the `FROM` clause).

Summary

The SQL aggregate functions perform calculations on data, returning the calculation results instead of the data itself. The standard aggregate functions are `AVG`, `COUNT`, `MAX`, `MIN`, and `SUM`. Aggregate calculations can filter data as needed using combinations of `WHERE` and `HAVING`, and data can be grouped using `GROUP BY`.

Sample Questions

1. Aggregate functions should not be overused because they tax the database server.
   A. True
   B. False

2. What is wrong with the following SQL statement?
   ```
   SELECT product_name, COUNT(*)
   FROM products
   GROUP BY product_name
   HAVING MAX(prod_price) > 10
   ```
   A. It doesn't have a `WHERE` clause.
   B. The `ORDER BY` clause is missing.
   C. The alias is missing.
   D. The `HAVING` clause does not match the `SELECT` list.

3. Which of the following are valid aggregate functions?
   A. `AVERAGE`
   B. `COUNT`
   C. `TOTAL`
   D. `MIN`

CHAPTER 35

Advanced Database Features

Constraints

Relational databases require that information be broken into multiple tables, each storing related data. Keys are used to create references from one table to the other (and thus the term *referential integrity*) so as to be able to join tables.

➔ Relational databases and joins were discussed in Chapter 33, "Joins."

For relational database designs to work properly, you need a way to ensure that only valid data is inserted into tables. For example, if an `Orders` table stored order information and `OrderItems` stored order details, you'd want to ensure that any order IDs referenced in `OrderItems` exist in `Orders`. Similarly, any customers referred to in `Orders` would have to be present in the `Customers` table.

Although you could perform checks yourself before inserting new rows (do a `SELECT` on another table to make sure that the values are valid and present), that is generally a practice to avoid because:

- If database integrity rules are enforced at the client level, every client will have to enforce those rules—and inevitably some clients won't.
- You'd also have to enforce the rules on `UPDATE` and `DELETE` operations.
- Performing client-side checks is a time-consuming process; having the DBMS do the checks for you is far more efficient.

DBMSes enforce referential integrity by imposing constraints on database tables. Most constraints are defined in table definitions by using a `CREATE TABLE` or `ALTER TABLE` statement.

> **TIP**
>
> Constraints force databases to throw errors (rejecting SQL statements) when they are violated. Within ColdFusion these errors can be trapped using `<CFTRY>` and `<CFCATCH>` (covered in Chapter 21, "Error Handling").

> **CAUTION**
>
> There are several different types of constraints, and each DBMS provides its own level of support for them. Refer to your DBMS's documentation before proceeding.

Unique Constraints

Unique constraints are used to ensure that all data in a column (or set of columns) is unique. This is similar to primary keys, but there are some important distinctions:

- A table may contain multiple unique constraints, but only one primary key is allowed per table.
- Unique constraint columns may contain `NULL` values.
- Unique constraint columns may be modified or updated.
- Unique constraint column values may never be reused.
- Unlike primary keys, unique constraints may not be used to define foreign keys.

→ Primary keys were discussed Chapter 32, "Basic SQL."

An example of using unique constraints might be an employees table. Every employee has a unique Social Security number, but you would not want to use that for the primary key because it is too long (and you might not want that information easily available). So, every employee would have a unique employee ID (a primary key) in addition to his Social Security number.

Because the employee ID is a primary key, you can be sure that it'll be unique. But you also might want the DBMS to ensure that Social Security numbers are unique, too (to make sure that someone does not make a typo and reuse someone else's number). You could do this by defining a `UNIQUE` constraint on the Social Security number column.

The syntax for unique constraints is similar to that for other constraints: either the `UNIQUE` keyword is defined in the table definition or a separate `CONSTRAINT` is used.

Check Constraints

Check constraints are used to ensure that data in a column (or set of columns) meets a set of criteria that you specify. Common uses of this are

- Checking minimum or maximum values—for example, preventing an order of `0` items (even though `0` is a valid number).
- Specifying ranges—for example, making sure that a ship date is greater than or equal to today's date and but not greater than a year from now.
- Allowing only specific values—for example, allowing only `M` or `F` in a gender field.

In other words, a datatype restricts the type of data that may be stored in a column. Check constraints place further restrictions within that datatype.

The following example creates a table named `OrderItems` and applies a check constraint to it to ensure that all items have a quantity of greater than `0`:

```
CREATE TABLE OrderItems
(
    order_num    INTEGER       NOT NULL,
    order_item    INTEGER       NOT NULL,
    prod_id    CHAR(10)    NOT NULL,
    quantity    INTEGER       NOT NULL    CHECK (quantity > 0),
    item_price    MONEY       NOT NULL
);
```

To check that a column named `gender` contained only `M` or `F`, you could do the following:

```
CONSTRAINT CHECK (gender LIKE '[MF]')
```

> **TIP**
>
> Some DBMSes enable you to define your own datatypes. These are essentially simple datatypes with check constraints (or other constraints) defined. So, for example, you could define your own datatype called `gender` that would be a single-character text datatype with a check constraint that restricted its value to `M` or `F` (and perhaps `NULL` is unknown). The advantage of custom datatypes is that the constraints are applied only once (in the datatype definition) and they are automatically applied each time the datatype is used. Check your DBMS's documentation to determine whether user-defined datatypes are supported.

Understanding Indexes

The best way to understand indexes is to envision the index at the back of a book (this book, for example).

Suppose that you wanted to find all occurrences of the word "datatype" in this book. The simple way to do this would be to turn to page 1 and scan every line of every page looking for matches. Although that would work, it is obviously not a workable solution. Scanning a few pages of text might be doable, but scanning an entire book is not. As the amount of text to be searched increases, so does the time it takes to pinpoint the desired data.

And so books have indexes. An index is an alphabetical list of words with references to their locations in the book. To search for "datatype," you would find that word in the index to determine what pages it appears on. You could then turn to those specific pages to find your matches.

So, what is it that makes an index work? Simply, the fact that it is sorted correctly. The difficulty in finding words in a book is not the amount of content that needs to be searched; rather, it is the fact that the content is not sorted by word. If the content were sorted like a dictionary, an index would not be needed (which is why dictionaries don't have indexes).

Database indexes work in much the same way. Primary key data is always sorted—that's just something the DBMS does for you. So, retrieving specific rows by primary key is always a fast and efficient operation.

But searching for values in other columns is usually not as efficient. For example, what if you wanted to retrieve all customers who lived in a specific state? Because the table is not sorted by state, the DBMS would have to read every row in the table (starting at the very first row) looking for matches—just as you would have to do if you were trying to find words in a book without using an index.

The solution is to use an index. You may define an index on one or more columns so that the DBMS keeps a sorted list of the contents for its own use. After an index is defined, the DBMS uses it in much the same way that you would use a book index. It searches the sorted index to find the location of any matches, and then retrieves those specific rows.

But before you rush off to create dozens of indexes, bear in the mind the following:

- Indexes improve performance of retrieval operations, but they degrade the performance of data insertion, modification, and deletion. This is because when those operations are executed, the DBMS has to dynamically update the index.
- Index data can take up lots of storage space.
- Not all data is suitable for indexing. Data that is not sufficiently unique (a state, for example) will not benefit as much from indexing as data that has more possible values (first name or last name, for example).
- Indexes are used for data filtering and for data sorting, so if you frequently sort data in a specific order, that order might be a candidate for indexing.
- Multiple columns may be defined in an index (for example, State plus City), in which case that index will be of use only when data is sorted in that order. If you wanted to sort by City, that index would not be of any use.

There is no hard and fast rule as to what should be indexed and when. Most DBMSes provide utilities that you can use to determine the effectiveness of indexes, and you should use these regularly.

Indexes are created with the `CREATE INDEX` statement (the syntax of which varies dramatically from one DBMS to another). The following statement creates a simple index on a `Products` table's product name column:

```
CREATE INDEX prod_name_ind
ON PRODUCTS (prod_name)
```

Every index must be uniquely named. Here the name `prod_name_ind` is defined after the keywords `CREATE INDEX`. `ON` is used to specify the table being indexed, and the columns to include in the index (just one in this example) are specified in parentheses after the table name.

TIP

Index effectiveness changes as table data is added or changed. Many database administrators find that what was once an ideal set of indexes might not be so ideal after several months of data manipulation. As such, it is a good idea to revisit indexes on a regular basis to fine-tune them as needed.

NOTE

Index use is essentially transparent to ColdFusion development.

Stored Procedures

Stored procedures are SQL statements that are stored on the DBMS server itself. Instead of entering SQL directly, you can call the stored procedure by name to execute the stored SQL.

Stored procedures are invaluable for several reasons:

- Stored procedures execute more quickly than straight SQL statements because the code saved on the server is already parsed and ready for use.
- Stored procedures may contain multiple SQL operations, which enables you to call a single command and execute a set of statements (without having to specify them individually).
- Depending on the DBMS being used, stored procedures might be able to return multiple result sets as well as output parameters.
- Stored procedures can be used to hide complex data structures, so users can call the procedures and pass them values as needed, and the procedures can internally manipulate tables as required.
- Stored procedures can be used to secure underlying data. Users might not be given access to underlying tables (to prevent abuse or misuse); instead, they communicate with a stored procedure that in turn interacts with the underlying tables.

There are lots of reasons to use stored procedures, which are created using the SQL `CREATE PROCEDURE` statement (which varies dramatically from one database to the next).

➔ For information about invoking stored procedures from within your ColdFusion code, see Chapter 18, "Stored Procedures."

Triggers

Triggers are special stored procedures that are executed automatically when specific database activity occurs. Triggers may be associated with `INSERT`, `UPDATE`, and `DELETE` operations on specific tables (or any combination thereof).

Unlike stored procedures (which are simply stored SQL statements), triggers are tied to individual tables. A trigger associated with `INSERT` operations on an `Orders` table will be executed only when a row is inserted into that `Orders` table. Similarly, a trigger on `INSERT` and `UPDATE` operations on that `Customers` table will be executed only when those specific operations occur on that table.

Within triggers, your code has access to the following:

- All new data in `INSERT` operations
- All new data and old data in `UPDATE` operations
- Deleted data in `DELETE` operations

Depending on the DBMS being used, triggers may be executed before or after the specified operation is performed.

Triggers have three primary uses:

- Ensuring data consistence—for example, converting all states to uppercase during `INSERT` and `UPDATE` operations
- Performing actions on other tables based on changes to a table—for example, writing an audit trail record to a log table each time a row is updated or deleted
- Performing additional validation and rolling back data if needed—for example, making sure that a customer's available credit has not been exceeded and blocking the insertion if it has

Trigger creation syntax varies from one database to another. The following example creates a trigger that converts the `cust_state` field to uppercase on all `INSERT` and `UPDATE` operations on a `Customers` table. This is the SQL Server version:

```
CREATE TRIGGER customer_state
ON Customers
FOR INSERT UPDATE
AS
UPDATE Customers
SET cust_state = Upper(cust_state)
WHERE Customers.cust_id = inserted.cust_id
```

This is the Oracle version:

```
CREATE TRIGGER customer_state
AFTER INSERT UPDATE
FOR EACH ROW
BEGIN
       UPDATE Customers
       SET cust_state = Upper(cust_state)
       WHERE Customers.cust_id = :OLD.cust_id
END;
```

> **TIP**
>
> As a rule, constraints are processed quicker than triggers, so whenever possible use constraints instead.

Bind Parameters

Most databases provide a mechanism to bind SQL parameters to specific datatypes. Doing so prevents the database (and database drivers) from having to perform implicit type conversions. The major benefits of parameter binding are

- Improved performance
- Support for large columns
- From a ColdFusion perspective, preventing hacking via URL parameter manipulation

Parameter binding requires that a parameter be specified along with a datatype with which it is to be bound. The following are the names of the ColdFusion-supported types:

- CF_SQL_BIGINT
- CF_SQL_BIT
- CF_SQL_CHAR
- CF_SQL_DATE
- CF_SQL_DECIMAL
- CF_SQL_DOUBLE
- CF_SQL_FLOAT
- CF_SQL_IDSTAMP
- CF_SQL_INTEGER
- CF_SQL_LONGVARCHAR
- CF_SQL_MONEY
- CF_SQL_MONEY4
- CF_SQL_NUMERIC
- CF_SQL_REAL
- CF_SQL_REFCURSOR
- CF_SQL_SMALLINT
- CF_SQL_TIME

- CF_SQL_TIMESTAMP
- CF_SQL_TINYINT
- CF_SQL_VARCHAR

ColdFusion parameter binding is implemented via the <CFQUERYPARAM> tag, which must be used in between <CFQUERY> and </CFQUERY> tags. The following query uses <CFQUERYPARAM> to bind a URL parameter to a specific datatype (an integer):

```
<CFQUERY DATASOURCE="DSN" NAME="Product">
SELECT product_id, produce_name
FROM products
WHERE <CFQUERYPARAM VALUE="#URL.product_id#" CFSQLTYPE="CF_SQL_INTEGER">
</CFQUERY>
```

The <CFQUERYPARAM> CFSQLTYPE attribute defaults to CF_SQL_CHAR if not specified. Additional attributes may be used optionally to specify value lengths and ranges.

> **CAUTION**
> SQL query parameter binding is not supported by all database and database drivers. Refer to the ColdFusion documentation to determine whether your database is supported.

> **NOTE**
> The exact syntax used by the database for query parameter binding varies dramatically from one database to the next. Fortunately, this is handled internally by the <CFQUERYPARAM> tag so that you need not worry about it.

Summary

Databases support a wide range of advanced features, and some support more features than others do. These features can, and should, be used to improve performance, to ensure data integrity, and to help protect data.

Sample Questions

1. Which of the following technologies could you use to ensure data consistency?
   A. Stored procedure
   B. Trigger
   C. Index
   D. Bind parameter

2. Which of the following statements are true?
   A. Stored procedures execute quicker than regular SQL statements.
   B. Stored procedures are supported by all databases.
   C. Stored procedures cannot be called from within ColdFusion code.
   D. Stored procedures can help secure your data.

3. Which of the following statements support triggers?
   A. `INSERT`
   B. `UPDATE`
   C. `DELETE`
   D. `SELECT`
4. Which of the following technologies could be used to prevent database hacking via URL tampering?
   A. Stored procedure
   B. Trigger
   C. Index
   D. Bind parameter

CHAPTER 36

Improving Performance

Eliminating Unnecessary Database Access

Database access (and waiting for databases) is the single biggest bottleneck in ColdFusion applications. As such, ColdFusion developers invest (or should invest) a significant amount of time into improving database access time (and even eliminating it when possible). There are lots of things that can negatively impact database performance:

- Poor database and table design
- Non-relational tables
- Incorrect data types used
- Poorly written SQL
- Lack of indexes
- Not using stored procedures
- … and much more

➔ Stored procedures, relational databases, and SQL are covered in the previous four chapters (Chapters 32–35).

Even if all these issues were to be addressed properly, they'd still be a potential database bottleneck in that most Web-based applications have to make frequent databases requests—often for the same data over and over. This being the case, an important part of optimizing database performance is preventing unnecessary database access by saving query results for later use.

ColdFusion provides two very different ways to accomplish this, each designed for very different situations:

- Variable-based query caching
- Query result caching

Variable-Based Query Caching

Some database queries change infrequently (or never), and are thus perfect candidates for caching. Examples of these types of queries are

- Countries
- U.S. states and Canadian provinces
- Company information (such as addresses and phone numbers)
- Product catalogs
- Employee extensions and email addresses

Variable-based query caching takes advantage of ColdFusion's support for persistent data by using the scopes designed for just that purpose. Three scopes are supported:

- Data that needs to persist for a single user can be stored in the `SESSION` scope.
- Data that needs to be available application wide can be stored in the `APPLICATION` scope.
- Data that needs to be available across all applications on a server can be stored in the `SERVER` scope.

➔ For an explanation of how to use these persistent scopes see Chapter 10, "`APPLICATION` and `SERVER` Variables," and Chapter 11, "Session State Management."

> **CAUTION**
>
> As a rule, use of the `SERVER` scope should be avoided. Most variable-based query caching belongs in the `APPLICATION` scope unless it is user specific (in which case it belongs in the `SESSION` scope). The `SERVER` scope is shared by all applications and is therefore far more susceptible to the introduction of bugs or corruption by other developers or applications.

Storing a variable in the `APPLICATION` scope (for example) is as simple as prefixing the variable name with the scope specifier, as follows:

```
<CFSET APPLICATION.dsn="my_data_source">
```

Caching queries into the `APPLICATION` scope is just as simple. The following example reads the list of U.S. states into a query within the `APPLICATION` scope (using the previously assigned `APPLICATION` variable as the datasource):

```
<CFQUERY DATASOURCE="#APPLICATION.dsn#" NAME="APPLICATION.states">
 SELECT state_name, state_abbrev
 FROM states
 ORDER BY state_name
</CFQUERY>
```

This query now resides within the `APPLICATION` scope and will persist for as long `APPLICATION` variables are configured to persist. The query can be used like any other query, and must be referred to be the fully qualified name (scope plus name). The following example populates a drop-down list box with the list of states:

```
<SELECT NAME="state">
 <CFOUTPUT QUERY="APPLICATION.states">
  <OPTION ID="#state_abbrev#">#state_name#
 </CFOUTPUT>
</SELECT>
```

Of course, if the query is in the `APPLICATION` scope then the majority of times it is used it will not need to be retrieved from the database. As such, the code that creates the query should always first check whether the query exists. The following code snippet demonstrates this process:

```
<CFIF NOT IsDefined("APPLICATION.states")>
 <CFQUERY DATASOURCE="#APPLICATION.dsn#" NAME="APPLICATION.states">
  SELECT state_name, state_abbrev
  FROM states
  ORDER BY state_name
 </CFQUERY>
</CFIF>
```

Using this code, the list of U.S. states can be read from the database just once (or as often as needed) and then used and reused without ever having to access the database again. This can dramatically reduce redundant database access, which in turn can dramatically improve application performance.

> **TIP**
>
> The `Application.cfm` is the perfect place for initializing `APPLICATION` scope data. See Chapter 6, "The Application Framework," for more information.

Of course, the other scopes can be used just as easily; just specify the appropriate prefix and ColdFusion does the rest.

> **NOTE**
>
> Persistent query initialization and access code must be locked to prevent memory corruption. See Chapter 12, "Locking," for details.

Variable-based query caching is not suited for queries that need to persist for short periods. Nor is it well suited for dynamic queries (for example, queries that are driven by form field).

Query Result Caching

Variable-based query caching is ideal for queries that change infrequently, are not highly dynamic, and are of use across users or parts of applications. For all other queries, ColdFusion features another form of caching: query result caching.

This form of query caching is ideally suited for

- Search results
- 'Next N'–style interfaces
- User-specific queries

Query result caching is specified within the <CFQUERY> tag by using one of two optional (and mutually exclusive) attributes:

- CACHEDWITHIN is used to cache data for a specified interval (relative time) specified as a time span (using the CreateTimeSpan() function).
- CACHEDAFTER is used to cache data after a specific date is reached (absolute time) specified as a valid ColdFusion date.

The following example attempts to cache the results of a dynamic, form-driven SELECT statement:

```
<CFQUERY DATASOURCE="dsn" NAME="product_search"
 CACHEDWITHIN="#CreateTimeSpan(0,0,10,0)#">
 SELECT prod_id, prod_name, prod_desc
 FROM products
 WHERE prod_name LIKE '%#Trim(FORM.prod_name)#%'
 ORDER BY prod_name
</CFQUERY>
```

Here the CACHEDWITHIN attribute specifies a time span of 10 minutes (0 days, 0 hours, 10 minutes, and 0 seconds). If the query is cached, any further queries for the same data within that interval will use the cached data automatically.

> **TIP**
>
> Most developers find that CACHEDWITHIN is the more useful of the two cache attributes. CACHEDAFTER is of use only when data is being retrieved from databases that are updated at known regular times.

But it is important to understand that CACHEDWITHIN (and CACHEDAFTER) are not instructions to cache data, they are *requests*. Data will be cached only if the administrator so allows, and if there is sufficient space in the cache. If the data can be cached, it will; if not, it won't. In fact, there is no way for developers even to know whether or not the query was cached. This is deliberate and by design, as this form of caching is designed to be as hands-off and transparent as possible.

> **NOTE**
>
> The number of queries that may be cached server-wide is specified in the ColdFusion Administrator.

Using cached queries is no different from using any queries—just refer to the query name. If a cached query can be used, it will; if not, it will not be used. The cached query will not be used if neither of the cache attributes is specified. But, if either of them is specified, and a cached query exists, ColdFusion will use it automatically.

NOTE

What makes a cached query unique is *not* the query name. In fact, a query can use a cached query even if the name is different as long as it is the same query. So, what is it that makes a query unique? The combination of

- Datasource name
- Datasource type (if specified)
- SQL text (post and dynamic and programmatic processing)
- Login information (if specified)

TIP

If debugging output is enabled, ColdFusion will let you know that a cached query was used (in lieu of the standard execution time output).

Reducing Data Transfer Time

Database clients (like database drivers used with ColdFusion) typically retrieve rows of data from the database one row at a time. If a query returns multiple rows, the client makes multiple requests, one per row. The number of rows retrieved at once is referred to as the *block factor*, and the default block factor is always `1` (a single row).

Retrieving data piecemeal in this fashion affects performance in two ways (if multiple rows are being retrieved). First, the database must work harder because it has more requests to respond to. Second, sending lots of smaller results forces lots of extra traffic over the network between the client (the ColdFusion server) and the server (the database server).

ColdFusion enables developers to specify the block factor to be used for a query in an attribute appropriately named `BLOCKFACTOR`. The number specified in this attribute is the number of rows to be retrieved in a single operation.

The following example retrieves the list of U.S. states and sets the `BLOCKFACTOR` to `50` (the number of rows to be retrieved):

```
<CFQUERY DATASOURCE="dsn" NAME="states" BLOCKFACTOR="50">
 SELECT state_name, state_abbrev
 FROM states
 ORDER BY state_name
</CFQUERY>
```

Specifying a `BLOCKFACTOR` can improve performance, but there is a risk here, too. Specifying too high a `BLOCKFACTOR` can hurt performance because the database and drivers have to allocate and free larger blocks of memory to handle the anticipated data.

Ideally, specifying a BLOCKFACTOR requires knowing the number of rows that will be retrieved. In practice this does not occur frequently, and so developers must resort to using educated guesses to determine the optimum BLOCKFACTOR (and most decide to ignore it altogether).

> **TIP**
>
> The best option is to not use BLOCKFACTOR at all for searches that will likely return a single row (for example, primary key searches). For searches that are expected to return large blocks of data, pick an average result size, but err on the side of caution.

> **CAUTION**
>
> Don't use BLOCKFACTOR unless you know that the database and driver support it. If use is not supported, no error will be thrown, but database retrieval will be even slower than not having used the attribute at all.

Summary

Database response and access times play a pivotal role in the performance of ColdFusion applications. Most performance issues are caused by bad SQL, poor database design, and other fundamental database related concerns. But in addition to those, eliminating unnecessary database and network load can help application performance, and ColdFusion provides the mechanisms to accomplish this.

Sample Questions

1. Database queries can be cached into which of the following scopes?
   A. VARIABLE
   B. CLIENT
   C. COOKIE
   D. APPLICATION
   E. SERVER

2. Which of the following statements are true?
   A. Query-based caching can be disabled.
   B. Variable-based caching can be disabled.
   C. Query-based caching requires the use of locks.
   D. Variable-based caching requires the use of locks.

3. Which <CFQUERY> attribute is used to reduce the number of roundtrips to the database server during data retrieval?
   A. CACHEDWITHIN
   B. CACHEDAFTER
   C. BLOCKFACTOR
   D. PACKETSIZE

PART 8

TUNING AND OPTIMIZATION

Application Performance Tuning and Optimization

Server Performance Tuning

CHAPTER 37

Application Performance Tuning and Optimization

Employing Effective ColdFusion Coding

You can employ many strategies to improve performance of a Web application. The first place to start is writing code that runs efficiently. Tuning the server and caching are also effective but do not act as cure-alls for poorly written code. What follows is a list of techniques that can increase the performance of your ColdFusion application. Remember that ColdFusion is like any other language. You can write code that is efficient and performs well. However, you also can write ColdFusion code in a way that is sloppy, and it will perform poorly because of that.

Different Variable Scopes and Performance

Variable scopes that are stored in memory should be locked. When a lock is applied to a read or write, performance can suffer. Using the `REQUEST` scope, which does not have to be locked, to store these variables is a good strategy for performance improvement.

→ For a discussion on locking variables, see Chapter 12, "Locking."

Don't Nest <CFIF>, <CFCASE> and <CFLOOP> Unless Absolutely Necessary

Although sometimes nesting is critical in implementing an algorithm, nested `<CFIF>`, `<CFCASE>`, and `<CFLOOP>` tags are processing expensive.

<CFCASE> Versus Multiple <CFELSEIF> Tags

Rather than use a number of `<CFELSEIF>` tags in a conditional statement, use the `<CFSWITCH>`/`<CFCASE>` tag set.

➔ For exact syntax and more information on conditional statements, see Chapter 3, "Conditional Processing."

Optimize Conditional Expressions in <CFIF>

Often in ColdFusion, logical operators used in `<CFIF>` statements are not necessary. For instance, you might use the `ListFind()` function to see whether an element appears in a list. If it does not, the function returns a `0`; otherwise, it returns the index position of the element. The conditional expression can check whether the returned value is `0` as follows:

```
<CFIF ListFind(TheList,"Testing") IS NOT 0>
```

You don't actually need to use `IS NOT 0` because the value returned by the function is inherently true or false. If any number other than `0` is returned by the function, it is true, and the comparison using the operator is not necessary.

Since version 4.0.1, ColdFusion uses shortcut Boolean evaluation. You should take advantage of this type of evaluation when writing conditional expressions. For example, if you're checking for the existence of a variable and then for a certain value, use the `IsDefined()` function and then use a logical `AND` with the next check. If the existence test is false, when ColdFusion sees the logical `AND`, it knows that the result will be false no matter what, and it will stop evaluation of the expression.

Unnecessary Dynamic Expression Evaluation

The `Evaluate()`, `DE()`, and `IIF()` functions permit you to write highly flexible and dynamic code, but they are processing intensive and should not be overly used.

➔ You can find more information about dynamic expression evaluation in Chapter 17, "Dynamic Functions."

Code Reuse: <CFINCLUDE> Versus Custom Tags

Reusing code with `<CFINCLUDE>` costs almost no extra processing time. Custom tags, although tremendously powerful and flexible, are more resource intensive because they must set up their own environment when used.

➔ The `<CFINCLUDE>` tag was discussed fully in Chapter 5, "Redirects and Reuse," and custom tags in Chapter 22, "Custom Tags."

Type Your Variables When Performance Counts

ColdFusion is considered a typeless language, which can have a small impact on performance. For instance, if the code permits, you could use the `<CFPARAM>` tag's `TYPE` attribute when assigning values to help performance. If this condition exists

```
<CFIF TheVar IS 10>
```

it would be evaluated marginally faster if TheVar were assigned a value using

```
<CFPARAM NAME="TheVar" DEFAULT="10" TYPE="Numeric">
```

rather than

```
<CFSET TheVar=10>
```

> **NOTE**
> As mentioned above, the impact on performance is minimal. The real benefit of using <CFPARAM> with the TYPE attribute is error checking.

Use Variable Prefixes

If you do not use variable prefixes, ColdFusion must scan a list of variable scopes in a predetermined order to find the variable specified. When you use a prefix, the variable's value can be retrieved directly.

➔ See Chapter 2, "Working with Variables and Expressions," for a full discussion of variable prefixes.

Don't Do the Database's Job with ColdFusion

Databases are built and optimized to manipulate data. For instance, SQL's aggregate functions are faster at finding an average or sum of a set of numbers than reading the set of numbers and then looping over them with a <CFOUTPUT QUERY=""> tag and doing the arithmetic in ColdFusion. So, you should use your database to enforce referential integrity, apply constraints, and use triggers when one database activity needs to cause another to be performed.

Enforcing Strict Attribute Validation

In the ColdFusion Administrator, you can find the Enforce Strict Attribute Validation check box under Settings. When this option is checked, ColdFusion makes sure that no extraneous attributes are used with CFML tags during p-code creation rather than at execution time. Checking this option saves time because, during execution, ColdFusion does not have to see whether the attribute is valid and then ignore it if it is not.

Using <CFCACHE>

Many ColdFusion templates do not change with every request. Often in an application, these pages are built dynamically every time one of the pages is requested. An example of this scenario would be a home page that has no personalization on it. Why should the page be built dynamically from the ColdFusion template when it rarely changes? This is a good question, and the <CFCACHE> tag can help resolve this issue.

When the <CFCACHE> tag is used on a page, it takes the HTML that is generated by the page and saves it as a separate file. When the page is requested again, instead of dynamically building the page, it sends the Web server the generated HTML that was saved earlier. This means that complete pages that do not change often can be cached, thus saving processing and improving performance.

Not all pages are good candidates for <CFCACHE>. When a page is cached, it is considered unique by URL. For instance, `Product.cfm`, `Product.cfm?Prod_ID=6`, and `Product.cfm?Prod_ID=11` would all be considered unique pages and cached as different pages. All these pages would be considered good candidates for <CFCACHE>. Conversely, an action page from a form that varies depending on user input in form controls is a terrible candidate in most cases for <CFCACHE>. The first user to fill in the form would generate output from the action page, and that output would be cached. All users following, no matter how they filled in the form, would see the cached page until it timed out or was deleted.

The attributes used with <CFCACHE> are shown in Table 37.1. They are all optional.

Table 37.1 <CFCACHE> Tag Attributes

Attribute	Description
ACTION	Specifies the action the tag should perform. The options are `Cache` (the default), `Flush`, `ClientCache`, and `Optimal`.
CACHEDIRECTORY	Specifies a directory where the generated HTML files should be stored, as well as the MAP file that records information about the caching process.
TIMEOUT	Specifies the oldest date that the cached page is acceptable. By default, ColdFusion uses the cached pages unless a timeout is specified.
DIRECTORY	Used with `ACTION="Flush"` to specify from which directory cached files should be flushed.
EXPIREURL	Used with `ACTION="Flush"` to specify the generated HTML files of which original files should be deleted; for instance, `EXPIREURL="Product.cfm?*"`.
PROTOCOL	Specifies which protocol will be used when communication between the tag and server takes place. The choices are either `HTTP://` (the default) or `HTTPS://`.
PORT	Specifies which port will be used when communication between the tag and server takes place. The default is 80.

You can create a template as follows:

```
<CFCACHE>
<HTML>
<HEAD>
    <TITLE>Untitled</TITLE>
</HEAD>
<BODY>
<CFSET THEVAR="Pass the test!">
<CFOUTPUT>#VARIABLES.TheVar#</CFOUTPUT>
</BODY>
</HTML>
```

A file is created and saved with a name generated by ColdFusion. The saved file looks like this:

```
<HTML>
<HEAD>
    <TITLE>Untitled</TITLE>
</HEAD>
<BODY>
Pass the test!
</BODY>
</HTML>
```

After the ColdFusion tags are processed, the HTML is generated and then saved as a separate file. The next time this page is browsed, ColdFusion sees the `<CFCACHE>` tag and checks to see whether the generated code already exists. This check uses a file named `cfcache.map` that was created or modified at the same time the generated HTML was saved.

The `cfcache.map` file is structured with references to the following:

- The name of the original ColdFusion template cached, in square brackets
- The full path to the place where the generated HTML file is stored
- A time stamp of the original ColdFusion template

Here's an example:

```
[test.cfm]
Mapping=C:\Inetpub\wwwroot\CFC23.tmp
SourceTimeStamp=12/04/2000 06:47:19 AM
[C:\Inetpub\wwwroot\dupfilename\test.cfm]
Mapping=c:\inetpub\wwwroot\benbook\chap38\CFC24.tmp
SourceTimeStamp=12/04/2000 06:59:56 AM
```

NOTE

By default, the map file and generated HTML file are saved in the same directory as the ColdFusion template. Using the `CACHEDIRECTORY` attribute, you can set the location of the `<CFCACHE>` files. The sample `cfcache.map` file shows what happens if you try to cache two ColdFusion templates of the same name in the same directory. The first, `[test.cfm]`, is the entry made when the same directory default is made; the `CACHEDIRECTORY` attribute from another file named `test.cfm` points to that same directory. Notice that the second entry shows the full path to the second `test.cfm` file.

Now the generated HTML is cached, and the `cfcache.map` file is in place (see Figure 37.1).

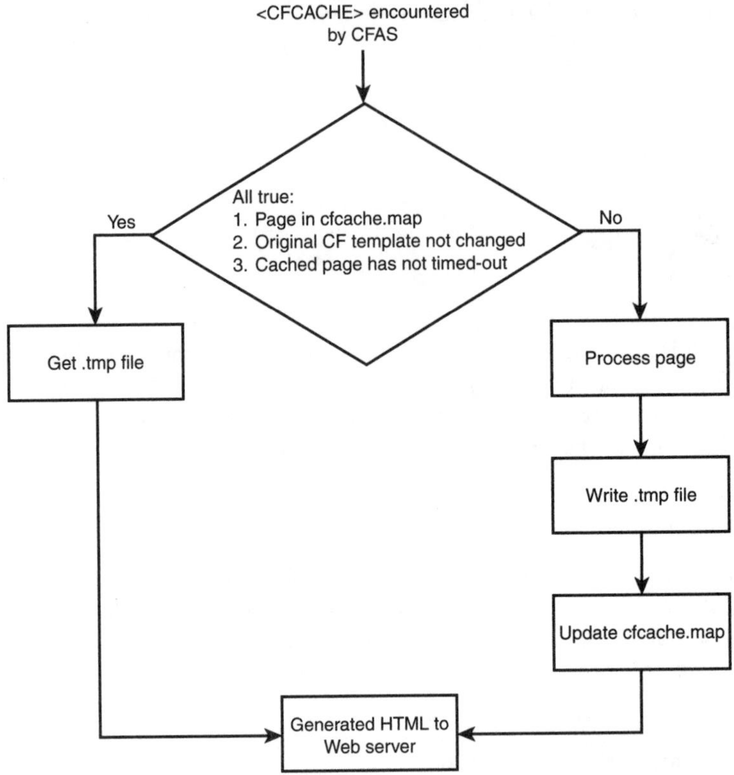

Figure 37.1

<CFCACHE> *logic.*

The cached page can be timed out in a number of ways. One possible way is to use the TIMEOUT attribute with the <CFCACHE> tag. The following example would time out the cache in five hours:

```
<CFCACHE ACTION="Cache" TIMEOUT="#DateAdd("h","-5",Now() )#">
```

You also can schedule a page to run at certain intervals, or dynamically, by using the Flush value for the ACTION attribute as follows:

```
<CFCACHE ACTION="Flush" EXPIREURL="*">
```

> **CAUTION**
>
> The ColdFusion documentation is contradictory about using attributes when ACTION="Flush". In some places, it implies that no attributes are needed, and in others, it indicates that both EXPIREURL and DIRECTORY are required. In practice, at least the EXPIREURL must be used.

Measuring Performance

In this chapter, we've suggested a number of techniques to improve performance, and you will hear and read of others while learning about ColdFusion. How can you tell whether they are helping in your application? A number of ColdFusion tools are available to help with this task.

Execution Time

In the ColdFusion Administrator, you can select the Show Processing Time check box under Debugging. It displays the total time of page processing and execution after the page. So you could run a page and record the total time of execution. You then could make changes to improve performance and run the page again to see whether the new technique helped.

Exploded Benchmarking

Knowing execution time is helpful, but the total time for a page may not be enough, or it may even be misleading. In the ColdFusion Administrator, the Detail View check box under Debugging is related to the Show Processing Time check box described in the preceding section. When you select this box, more than just the total time of page execution is shown. After the total, a time breakdown reports how long each component that made up the page took to execute. For instance, the time to run `Application.cfm` and any included templates and custom tags is reported. Exploded Benchmarking is when both the total execution time and the execution time for every component are displayed. This is a much better tool to use to try to find bottlenecks. After you find them, you can use some technique to improve them.

Using `GetTickCount()`

If you know a number of different ways to perform some programming task, using the `GetTickCount()` function is an ideal way to see which of the approaches is most efficient. This function retrieves a measurement in milliseconds. So, to time a block of code, you could use the following:

```
<CFSET Start=GetTickCount()>
      Code to time
<CFSET TotalTime=GetTickCount()-Start>
<CFOUTPUT>The time to process is: #VARIABLES.TotalTime#</CFOUTPUT>
```

Finding Bottlenecks

Now that we've covered techniques to improve and measure performance, it would be helpful to learn a simple process to find bottlenecks, which you can then address with tools discussed in this chapter.

The first step in the process is finding long-running pages. High-end load testing tools are built for this process, but in a worst-case scenario, you can simply identify these pages through use, or you can open the ColdFusion Administrator and choose Logging, Settings, Log Slow Pages to log pages based on a time you set.

Next, you can view that page, under load if possible, and look at the exploded benchmarking to see what template or templates involved in fulfilling the request are taking the most time.

Finally, you can go to that page, break it into some logical sections, and use `GetTickCount()` to identify the slowest running section. If the tag that is causing the bottleneck is still not clear, use `GetTickCount()` again to break the offending sections into smaller sections. You can continue this process until you identify the tag that is causing the bottleneck.

Summary

ColdFusion code can execute very efficiently or run very poorly, depending upon how you write the code. You can use a number of techniques to write code that will perform optimally. These techniques can be roughly broken into the following categories: identify effective ColdFusion coding techniques; don't have ColdFusion do the database's job; enforce strict attribute validation; use `<CFCACHE>` when logical.

To be sure that the particular technique employed has actually increased performance, you can use a number of ColdFusion tools, such as the `GetTickCount()` function, to show processing time in both normal and exploded fashion.

Sample Questions

1. For best performance, a set of numbers should be read from the database and then summed by using a loop in ColdFusion.
   A. True
   B. False

2. When many conditions will be tested, what tag is best to use?
   A. `<CFIF>/<CFELSEIF>`
   B. `<CFTESTCASE>`
   C. `<CFSWITCH>/<CFCASE>`
   D. `<CFLOOP>`

3. Which of the following reuses code most efficiently?
   A. `<CFINCLUDE>`
   B. `<CF_CustomTag>`
   C. `<CFPARAM>`
   D. `<CFMODULE>`

4. What does the `SourceTimeStamp` file used in the `cfcache.map` file refer to?
   A. The time stamp of the generated HTML file
   B. The time the cached file should time out
   C. The time the cached file should be reached
   D. The time stamp of the original ColdFusion template

5. When you use exploded benchmarking, it includes timings for which of the following?
   A. "Housekeeping chores" in getting the template started, parsed, and shut down
   B. Included templates
   C. Breakouts of database access times
   D. Custom tags used

CHAPTER 38

Server Performance Tuning

OS

An operating system is the underlying software that issues commands to the computer's hardware, such as

- Allocating storage space
- Scheduling tasks
- Acting as an interface to the user's computer when an application is running

Web sites are putting ever more demands on the operating system of the server. It is important that an operating system be selected that is flexible, can protect itself from multiple server processes competing for system resources, and can support essential server-side processes such as application servers and search engines. All the while, the OS must continue to perform well.

Certainly performance is a critical factor in operating system selection, but other factors should also be considered. In determining which operating system best meets your needs, you should take the following criteria into consideration:

- Scalability/flexibility—Can it scale to a platform capable of handling large traffic loads? Is it flexible enough to handle a variety of Internet services? How many CPUs can it handle?
- Network management—Can it support common IP network management applications? Does it integrate with your existing network environments and directory services?

- Application availability—Can it run the applications you run today? Are new applications being developed for it? How much do the applications that you need cost?
- Management—Does it provide flexible, accessible management utilities?
- Cost—What are the costs for related hardware, the operating system itself, and a required Internet server? Is the operating system so complex that it will require additional costs for specialized personnel to install and maintain the system?
- Performance—How many users can you support with a single system? Does the OS support symmetric multiprocessing (SMP)? Does it let you balance loads across multiple systems?
- Application development—Are the development tools you use available for this platform? Are there standard OS services and industry-standard interfaces to support development?
- Reliability—Does it support RAID or clustering? Can you hot-swap components?

NOTE

You can find tuning tips for running ColdFusion on specific operating systems at Allaire's Web site. See KnowledgeBase article number 11772, "Platform-Specific Performance Settings." Another KnowledgeBase article with a wide range of performance-related links is number 11773, "Performance-Related Resources."

Web Server

The decision of which Web server to use is a difficult one complicated by many factors. The most important considerations are which operating system you intend to use and which Web server software has the feature set and performance potential to handle the expectations and traffic load of your Web site. Following is a list of factors that might be important in considering the selection of a Web server:

- Operating system
- Familiarity with operating system
- Price
- Access to support and other resources
- Ability to host multiple Web sites on a single Web server
- Log reporting
- Server side includes
- User access security
- Transaction security
- Server programming and database support
- Current equipment (hardware, network, NOS)
- Scalability
- Applications server support
- Management tools

There are many factors that can affect the performance of a Web server including:

- Server's processor
- Type and quantity of RAM
- Type of bus used for the network adapter card and the disk controller
- Disk drive's operating characteristics
- LAN utilization
- WAN bandwidth
- Type of content included on Web pages (multimedia versus text)

When an Internet or intranet Web site gets very busy, performance will suffer. The first option to improve the situation is to add memory so that more requests can be serviced from cache. It is possible, though, that this might not help, especially if the server is busy because of background or communication tasks. At this point, two options are available:

- Purchase a new, more powerful server and no longer use the older one
- Add individual servers and a load balancer

Load balancers distribute the incoming requests among a group of Web servers. Load balancing provides the opportunity to utilize your existing resources and then add servers as needed. It also adds fault tolerance. If one server goes down, the others can keep providing service. This fault tolerance feature also provides uninterrupted service during routine maintenance in which servers need to be offline. A load balancer functions by sitting between the Internet and the Web servers, connected on one side to the Internet router, and a hub or switch on the other. The load balancer uses a virtual IP address to communicate with the router. This address is what is advertised to the Internet for all Web servers. This masks the actual IP address of the Web server, which aids security. The hub or switch connected to one side of the load balancer is the point of connectivity for all Web servers.

Application Server

An application server provides the services that connect applications and databases, and should also have development tools that work with it. It should provide a framework to link the Web site to existing applications and data. The application server should provide these services at the fastest speed possible.

Many criteria should be used when selecting an application server. A few of these are

- Language used, and its learning curve
- Database connectivity options, and throughput
- Load balancing and fail-over options
- Supported operating systems and Web servers
- Development tool availability
- Ability to work with various industry standards
- Security options

> **NOTE**
>
> ColdFusion does all these things, which is part of the reason you are using it and becoming certified in it.
>
> Many KnowledgeBase articles concerning ColdFusion's load balancing and fail-over options are available from Allaire's Web site. To find all the articles, search Allaire's KnowledgeBase for "clustering."
>
> A White Paper on load balancing and fail-over, called "Achieving High Availability and Scalability in Allaire Multiserver Environments," is also available on Allaire's Web site.

Separate Servers for Separate Tasks

Even after careful selection of the OS and Web server, expecting one computer to do all the tasks associated with a Web site will most likely be too much. A single piece of hardware to act as the host for all services will shortly overwhelm its resources. To correct this problem, run separate servers for ColdFusion, the Web server, the database, email, and so on.

> **NOTE**
>
> Running the ColdFusion application server on a different machine than the Web server is discussed in the "Administering the ColdFusion Server" book of the ColdFusion documentation.

Specific Tuning Techniques (CF Admin Settings)

After decisions have been made about the OS and Web server, attention can turn to tuning the ColdFusion application server. There are a number of "knobs to turn" to optimize the performance of the ColdFusion server.

> **NOTE**
>
> You can find other ColdFusion performance tuning tips in KnowledgeBase article 922, "ColdFusion Performance Tuning," article 2497, "ColdFusion Performance Tuning (Part 2)," and article 8627, "ColdFusion Performance Debugging."

Template Cache/P-Code Caching

When a ColdFusion template is requested, it first needs to be parsed and turned into p-code. The p-code is then executed and the HTML generated from this execution is returned to the Web server, which sends it to the requesting browser. To optimize performance, the parsing of the page should be done once, and then the p-code held in cache unless the underlying ColdFusion template changes. Figure 38.1 further explains the process.

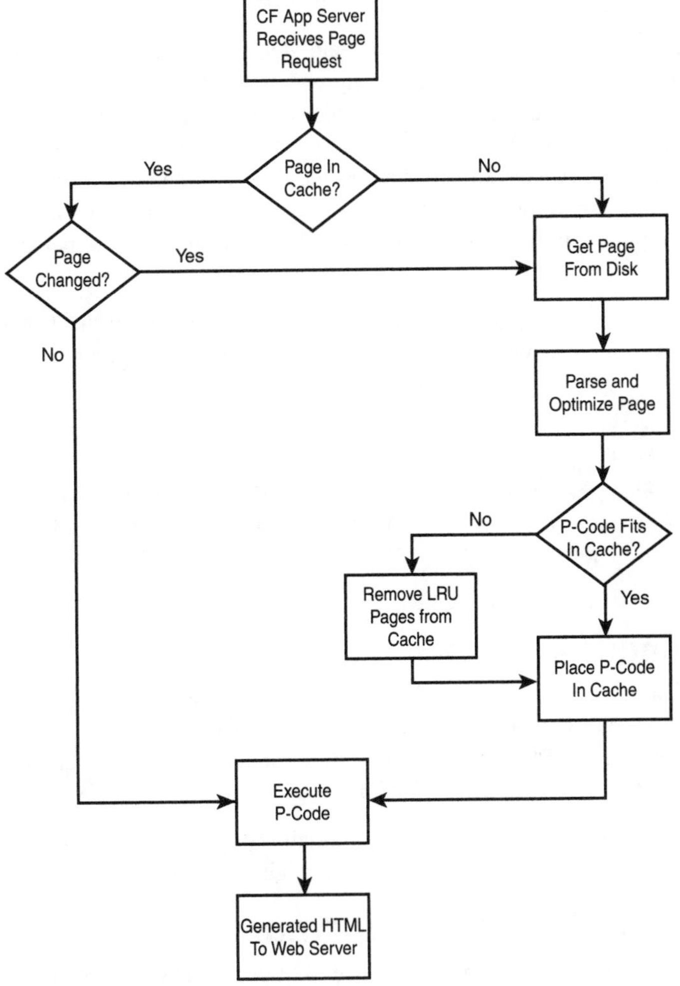

Figure 38.1

ColdFusion page caching logic.

The first decision in the flowchart is whether the page is in cache. If there is not enough memory, pages will constantly have to be pulled from disk, parsed, and swapped in and out of cache, causing excess disk access. Disk access is one of the worst events that can occur for performance.

In the ColdFusion Administrator Caching option there is a Template Cache Size setting. This setting controls how much of the server's memory is set aside to hold parsed templates. For optimal performance, the amount of memory allocated for this setting should be from three to five times the total size of all your ColdFusion templates.

Trusted Cache

In the flowchart for the previous section, one step of the template p-code caching process was checking whether the underlying CFML of the cached page had changed. If a site has been launched and few, if any, changes to the site are occurring, checking whether the underlying CFML has changed is not a necessary step. The decision to check for changes every time a page is requested can be turned off. In the ColdFusion Administrator Caching option is a Trusted Cache check box. If this box is checked, the ColdFusion Application Server trusts that the CFML of the template being requested has not changed.

If changes are made to templates, the changes will be ignored until the Trusted Cache box is unchecked and the particular templates are browsed. After that, Trusted Cache can be turned on again.

> **TIP**
>
> If Trusted Cache is being used and a substantial number of templates are changed, every template has to be browsed before Trusted Cache could be turned on again. In that case, it might be easier to cycle the ColdFusion services to clear all cached pages.

Simultaneous Requests

In the ColdFusion Administrator, Settings option is the Limit Simultaneous Request to *x* tunable. This setting determines the number of listener threads set up by the ColdFusion Application Server to receive requests made by the Web server. When all the threads are busy, new requests will be queued.

There is no rule of thumb that will set this optimally for your application. Only testing under load can determine the ideal setting for any given configuration.

Monitoring Server Performance

In this chapter, several suggestions were made to improve the ColdFusion Application Server's performance. There are tools available to watch and see the affect of the changes. Using a good load-testing tool with a well-planned load testing script is the best way to see the effects of the changes when the server is under load. It is also possible to gain a look into how the ColdFusion server is behaving using Performance Monitor or `CFSTAT`.

Performance Monitor

Performance Monitor is built into Windows NT and Windows 2000. It looks at resource use for specific components and program processes. In the ColdFusion Administrator, Debugging option is an Enable Performance Monitoring check box. Checking this box and applying the changes will expose ColdFusion counters to Performance Monitor.

> **CAUTION**
> Unlike some of the other settings in debugging, the ColdFusion Application Server service must be restarted for Performance Monitor to be able to see the ColdFusion object's counters.

The counters available are shown in table 38.1.

Table 38.1 ColdFusion Counters Available in Performance Monitor

Counter	Description
`Average DB Time (msec)`	This is a running average of the amount of time in milliseconds that an individual database operation, launched by CF, took to complete.
`Average Queue Time (msec)`	This is a running average of the amount of time in milliseconds that requests spent waiting in the CF input queue before CF began to process that request.
`Average Request Time (msec)`	This is a running average of the total amount of time in milliseconds that it took CF to process a request. In addition to general page processing time, this value includes both queue time and database processing time.
`Bytes In/Sec`	This is the number of bytes received by the ColdFusion Server per second.
`Bytes Out/Sec`	This is the number of bytes returned by the ColdFusion Server per second.
`Cache Pops/Sec`	This is the number of times (per second) that a cached template had to be ejected from the template cache to make room for a new template.
`DB Hits/Sec`	The number of database operations performed per second by the ColdFusion Server.
`Page Hits/Sec`	The number of Web pages processed per second by the ColdFusion Server.
`Queued Requests`	The number of Web pages processed per second by the ColdFusion Server.
`Running Requests`	This is the number of requests currently being actively processed by the ColdFusion Server.
`Timed Out Requests`	This is the total number of requests that timed out waiting to be processed by the ColdFusion Server. These requests never got to run.

To help you better understand the first three time counters listed in Table 38.1, they are diagrammed in Figure 38.2.

The average request time is shown at the top. Remember that this is the average of how long it took ColdFusion to process a request. In the middle, you see that the average request time is broken into two pieces: how long the request was waiting to be serviced (that is, the average queue time) and how long ColdFusion actually spent processing the request (that is, the execution time). Finally, at the bottom of the figure you see that the execution time is separated into how long ColdFusion worked on the request and how long the database worked on the request. Not all the times shown in Figure 38.2 are counters, only the ones marked with an asterisk (*). For instance, the execution time is not reported directly by a counter, but you can calculate it from available counters by taking the average request time minus the average queue time.

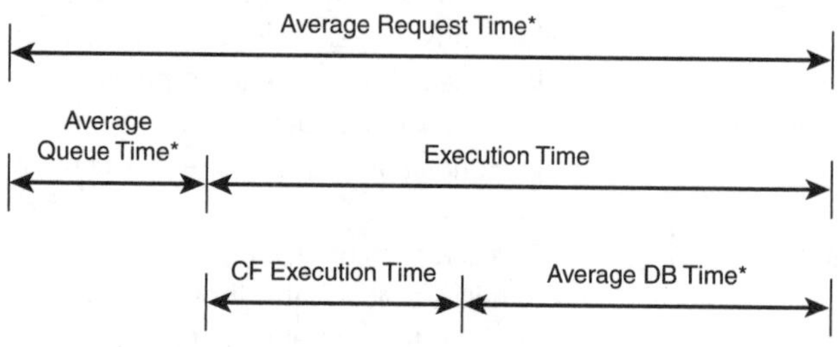

Figure 38.2

The relationship between the average request time, average queue time, and average DB time counters.

The server tuning options mentioned in this chapter have, either directly or indirectly, affected some of these counters. For example, `Cache Pops/Sec` reports the number of times a template was removed from cache to make room for a newly parsed template. If this number is not at or near zero, it indicates that the Template Cache Size setting in the ColdFusion Administrator needs to be increased, and possibly more memory added in the server.

The `Running Requests` counter will never be more than the Limit Simultaneous Requests To setting in the ColdFusion Administrator.

Performance Monitor has a GUI interface that enables you to graph any of the counters and also to log the counters and then look at the log graphically.

CFSTAT

Performance Monitor is not available in non-Windows operating systems. Also, you might want a command-line interface in Windows to see the ColdFusion Application Server's counters. `CFSTAT` is a command-line utility that is available for all platforms on which ColdFusion runs.

> **TIP**
>
> The counters can be used in a ColdFusion template by using the `GetMetricData("monitor_name")` function. In Windows, the *`monitor_name`* is `PerfMonitor`; on Unix/Linux, it is `CFStat`.

`CFSTAT` has two optional switches to modify its behavior. They are listed in table 38.2 below.

Table 38.2 *CFSTAT Switches*

Switch	Description
`-n`	This instructs `CFSTAT` not to display column headers. This is helpful if you are redirecting output to a file and do not want the column headers.
x	*x* is a number, in seconds, specifying how often the counters should be polled and displayed.

> **NOTE**
>
> As with Performance Monitor, the Enable Performance Monitoring option must be checked and the ColdFusion Application Server service must be restarted for `CFSTAT` to function.

Summary

Critical to the Web server's performance is the underlying operating system and Web server software selected. After the ColdFusion Application Server is installed and running on the system, a number of tuning options are available, including template cache size, trusted cache, and the number of simultaneous requests. Use Performance Monitor and `CFSTAT` to determine whether the tuning did in fact aid performance.

Sample Questions

1. Which of the following are counters for the ColdFusion object in Performance Monitor?
   A. `Average ColdFusion Execution Time`
   B. `Average Request Time`
   C. `Average DB Time`
   D. `Average Queue Time`

2. It is possible to have ColdFusion NOT check whether templates that are currently cached have changed.
   A. True
   B. False

3. Which counter is an indicator of sufficient memory for template cache?
   A. `Bytes In/Sec`
   B. `DB Hits/Sec`
   C. `Queued Requests`
   D. `Cache Pops/Sec`

PART 9

APPENDIX

Answers

APPENDIX A

Answers

Chapter 1

1. A, B, and D. CGI variables are usually sent when a URL is requested, but they are not part of the URL itself.
2. B. ColdFusion runs on the server, not on the client, and therefore can access only server resources.
3. A and C. XML has nothing to do with CFML, and JavaScript is a client technology.

Chapter 2

1. A and C. `MOD` is an operator, and `LCase()` is a function.
2. B. Order of evaluation dictates that URL appears before the others.
3. D. Although all are legal, the best use of # signs, or in this case lack of # signs, is shown in D.
4. B. When you're using constant string manipulation, you must know the exact string.

Chapter 3

1. C. The normal operator symbols cannot be used.
2. A, C, and D. Remember that any number except zero evaluates to true.
3. True. Either the actual string could match the expression, or a `DELIMITERS` attribute is used to specify the semicolon as the delimiter.

Chapter 4

1. C. Index loops can iterate only over numeric values.
2. D. Because the counter "i" is incremented and then displayed, the first value displayed is 2. The number 4 is shown because the loop does not terminate immediately when the condition is false, but finishes the loop.
3. A. The variable specified in the ITEM attribute takes on the keys of the structure in the loop.
4. A. Yes they are logically equivalent, but the <CFLOOP> will perform better.
5. B and D. The Conditional loop has only one attribute, CONDITION, and the Collection loop uses ITEM.

Chapter 5

1. C. Cookies are not sent on to the redirection page; ADDTOKEN at least sends on CFID and CFTOKEN.
2. B and C. <CFHEADER> is used on the server side to alter response headers. The response header is sent to the browser and can tell it not to cache a page.
3. B. The first character after the quotation mark is a forward slash (/), so a ColdFusion mapping is used.
   D. RESET="Yes" clears any display before the tag, so ABC is not shown.

Chapter 6

1. B. False. ColdFusion will search all the way to the hard drive root if it has to.
2. A. True. Each OnRequestEnd.cfm is paired with an Application.cfm file. OnRequestEnd.cfm will run only if it is located in the same directory as the Application.cfm file that was executed.
3. C. The Application.cfm file is reserved for business logic only and should never be used to render HTML or other client-side scripting.
4. B. False. Although an Application.cfm cannot be called from a URL, it can be included in another application page.

Chapter 7

1. A, B, and C. MaxRow is an attribute of the <CFQUERY> tag used to restrict the maximum number of records returned.
2. B. Although the <CFOUTPUT> GROUP attribute can be used in conjunction with SQL GROUP BY operations, they are not related.
3. A, B, C, and D. Any SQL statement can be passed to the database by using <CFQUERY> providing the designated driver can handle it.

Chapter 8

1. B. Val() checks whether a string can be converted to a number. Trim() removes whitespace around a string. URLEncodedFormat() converts URL-unfriendly characters (such as a space) into its ASCII equivalent. StripSpaces() is not a valid ColdFusion function.

2. A. A URL variable exists only on the page to which the link points—target page. Multiple URL variables can be passed on a link, each variable separated from the other by an ampersand (&). Everything after the question mark (?) in a link is referred to as the *query string*. While URL variables can be created using <CFSET>, they are normally created as part of the HTML <A> tag.
3. C. Answer A does not specify a name for the URL variable. URLVar in answer B is not a valid prefix for URL variables—the proper prefix is URL. In answer D, the <A> tag's NAME attribute is used to name the target location for a link on a page, not create the link.

Chapter 9

1. D. FORM and ACTION.
2. C. A select control that allows multiple options but has none selected essentially acts like a set of check boxes. However, this question lists a drop-down select control. Drop-downs, by default, always pass a value.
3. A. FavCountry=CAN,FRA. Because both form controls have the same name, their values are concatenated.

Chapter 10

1. D. Answer A uses a fictitious function. Although APPLICATION variables are, indeed, structures, the StructIsEmpty() function merely checks to see whether the variable contains data, not whether it exists. The <CFSWITCH> statement merely evaluates the value of the variable and does not check for its existence.
2. A. The other options are false.
3. C. The other options are false.

Chapter 11

1. D. Session and browser are not valid settings for the EXPIRES attribute. now would expire the cookie immediately. By not setting an EXPIRES attribute at all, you create a browser session cookie.
2. D. The other options are valid.
3. C. CFID and CFTOKEN are set to maintain session and client variables. CFDOMAIN is fictional.

Chapter 12

1. The answer is D. A is incorrect because CFLOCK requires either the SCOPE or the NAME attribute. B is incorrect because NAME and SCOPE are mutually exclusive attributes. C is incorrect because the SCOPE attribute must be a valid scope name such as APPLICATION or SESSION.
2. Both A and C are correct.
3. Both A and B are correct. C and D are incorrect because missing read locks would cause errors only when read checking is set.
4. Both A and B are correct. C is incorrect because deadlocks only occur when locks are nested. D is incorrect because the CLIENT scope is not a variable type that requires locking.

Chapter 13

1. A and D. Strings can always be accessed as lists. Dates can be treated as strings and therefore are lists (usually a list delimited by slashes or hyphens). Arrays and structures, however, can never be accessed as lists.
2. A, C, and D. B is not valid because it is an empty string (ColdFusion will not throw an error, but the list will always contain one element).
3. A, B, C, and D. By default (comma-delimited list), the list has one element. If a space is used as a delimiter, the list has two elements. If two characters are used as delimiters (for example, `"er"` or `"no"`), the list has three elements. If the delimiter contains all the characters `"Ben Forta"`, the list has no elements at all (just delimiters).

Chapter 14

1. A and B are both valid ways of creating an array. C is incorrect as there is no function named `ArrayCopy`. Therefore D is the correct answer.
2. B is the correct answer. When an array is declared in a given index, it does not automatically create arrays in other indexes. In the example, there is only an array in `aThat[1]` but not in `aThat[2]`. Therefore, a second index cannot be added to `aThat[2]`.
3. A is incorrect as of ColdFusion 4.5 because no equal sign is required in a CFSET. B is also incorrect as an Array can be resized to any size. C and D are both correct. As the loop iterates, the size of the array will decrease because of the deleted indexes.
4. A is false because an associative array not officially an array in ColdFusion (it is a structure). B is true as is D. C is the other false choice because arrays can have more than three dimensions through the repetitive use of ArrayNew(). Therefore A and C are the correct answers (both false).

Chapter 15

1. B. Remember that structures are pointers. Both of the structures (a and b) are the same structure and each equals 2 after being set a second time.
2. B. The attributes that are used with a `CFLOOP` and a structure are `ITEM` and `COLLECTION`. `#` signs must be used around the structure within the `COLLECTION` attribute.
3. A, B and D. C is incorrect because dot notation must follow ColdFusion variable naming conventions. D is perfectly valid even though it is not an array.
4. B, C, and D. A is false because structure keys have no reliable order.
5. C. `StructDelete` will only clear a certain key from the `APPLICATION` structure and never takes the value "all" unless that was a key itself.

Chapter 16

1. C. The only answer are valid `CFSCRIPT` features except for C (HTTP requests). The `CFHTTP` tag has been exposed through a tag based interface only.

Remember none of ColdFusion's services (query, HTTP, FTP, and so on) are available in a CFSCRIPT block.

2. D. A is false because the same operators are used in CFML as in CFSCRIPT blocks. B is false because CFML is capable of doing things that CFSCRIPT blocks are not (such as a database query). C is false because SWITCH/CASE statements are available in both syntaxes.
3. D. When a SWITCH block runs, each case will run *once* in sequential order provided that their conditions are all true. Because the first CASE statement changes X to 2 the second CASE statement will run.

Chapter 17

1. B and C. One of the purposes of DE() is to stop ColdFusion from evaluating an expression. This can be used in an IIf() to return a literal rather than a value. Answer A is incorrect because DE() is rarely used for output. Answer B is incorrect because DE() stands for "delay evaluation."
2. C. The condition ("1 is 1") is true and will return the first of the two arguments. The first argument has three expressions within it ("1;2;3" are three separate expressions). Because ColdFusion always returns the last expression, the rightmost is returned ("3").
3. B. The Evaluate() function can create expressions by concatenating strings and literals. The complete expression evaluates to "p=ArrayNew(1)", which creates a new array.
4. A. It might appear that the answer is B ("y"). Because x is not equal to y (x = "y" and y = "x"), the second of the two expressions will run. The second expression is simply "x." If the expression had quotes around it, then x would be evaluated as the value "y." But because x has no quotes around it, it is actually evaluated twice. First, it is evaluated to see what it equals (y), and then that value is evaluated as an expression in itself, which equals "x." It is doubtful that anything this difficult would be on the exam, but it is sure good practice!

Chapter 18

1. A and B. Stored procedures are much faster than passing SQL or calling a view because they are precompiled in the database server. Therefore, A is one of the correct answers. B is also correct because stored procedures can hide certain columns and introduce layers of abstraction. The other two answers (C and D) are not valid reasons to use stored procedures as they can be difficult to create and are not standard across database platforms.
2. C. The TYPE attribute of <CFPROCPARAM> is "INOUT" when a stored procedure names a variable the same as the parameter it returns. An example would be a stored procedure that takes a product's price (itemPrice) and returns the price (as itemPrice again) with all discounts applied.
3. B. <CFPROCPARAM> can return arrays but <CFPROCRESULT> always returns queries.

Chapter 19

1. A, B, and C. The <CFTRANSACTION> tag has an ISOLATION attribute. Whether the database respects this ISOLATION is beyond your control. Isolation levels can affect performance with SERIALIZABLE as the worst performing and READ COMMITTED as the best. Isolation levels also affect the way records are locked. D is the only answer that is false because the database has full control over what is locked.
2. C. A is incorrect because <CFTRANSACTION> supports rollbacks as well as commits. B is incorrect because a dirty read is possible depending on the isolation level. D is also incorrect because <CFLOCK> has nothing to do with a database transaction, per se.
3. B. If the <CFTRANSACTION> tag used XML syntax, the code would work.
4. A. A SERIALIZABLE read is the worst performing.

Chapter 20

1. C. To expose SESSION variables, you must use manual debugging or the ColdFusion Studio debugger.
2. A. To make sense of GetTickCount, it must return more than one count. This count equals elapsed time when an earlier count is subtracted from a later one.
3. B, C, and D. Error codes are not shown in the ColdFusion Studio debug window.

Chapter 21

1. B. When the type is Validation, <CFERROR> checks server-side form validation.
2. B and D. Any catches any exception; and Application is used specifically for this purpose.
3. A. All the others redirect processing and then terminate processing when the template is finished.

Chapter 22

1. B. By prefixing a variable with Caller. inside of a custom tag, you tell ColdFusion to make it available to the calling page.
2. D. This merely states the name of the tag, not where you can find it. <CF_MyCustomTag> will look for the file in the same directory or in the C:\Cfusion\Bin directory. <CFMODULE TEMPLATE="/files/mycustomtag.cfm"> will look for the custom tag file in a directory called FILES mapped in the ColdFusion Administrator. Modifying the registry key with a new path will force ColdFusion to always search that directory for custom tags.
3. A. B simply creates a variable, not a default value. C creates a hidden form variable, which has no direct effect on the custom tag. D explicitly passes a custom tag attribute and value, but does not set a default.

Chapter 23

1. D. ThisTag.GeneratedContent gives you direct access to text created between the start and end tags. ThisTag.StartOrEnd is a fictitious variable. ThisTag.HasEndTag is a variable that lets you know whether the current tag has an end tag. ThisTag.ExecutionMode lets you know if you're in start, end, or inactive mode.
2. B. Although any of the answers would work, the question asked for the best method. GetBaseTagData() is simply called from within the child tag to reach out and grab the base tag's, or parent tag's, data.
3. C. The other answers are incorrect.

Chapter 24

1. A and B. CFX custom tags can only be written in either C++ or Java.
2. The answer is false. Although JSP allows you to more easily implement Java servlets using a scripting interface, in order to perform some tasks, such as the querying of a database, you will have to use Java. However, JRun can help you because it provides a tag library for many of the more common tasks.
3. A. The *D* in DCOM stands for Distributed.

Chapter 25

1. A. The other three are valid.
2. C. The others are not true.
3. A. By not declaring an OUTPUT attribute, you are telling ColdFusion to write the results of the WDDX packet to the page.

Chapter 26

1. A, B, and D. The NEAR operator is available only in explicit search expressions.
2. A and B. <CFCOLLECTION> with the ACTION="OPTIMIZE" attribute is the preferred method for optimization. However, <CFINDEX> with the ACTION= "OPTIMIZE" attribute is the old, deprecated method and is still backwardly compatible.
3. A, B, and C. Searching requires only a READONLY lock.

Chapter 27

1. A, B, C, and D. Access to <CFFILE>, <CFCONTENT>, <CFDIRECTORY>, and <CFREGISTRY> can all be restricted through the ColdFusion Administrator in Basic Server Security.
2. D. <CFLOG> does not exist, <CFCONTENT> cannot write files to the server, and <CFSCHEDULE> is used to schedule events. <CFFILE> is used for writing and appending logs.
3. B. The HTML <INPUT> tag with TYPE="File" specified is also required.

Chapter 28

1. A. Scheduled events are executed using a <CFHTTP> agent.
2. B. The Registry stores persistent task information. cfexec.ini does not exist.
3. A, B, and C. <CFEVENTEDIT> is not a ColdFusion tag.

Chapter 29

1. B. False. ColdFusion needs access to an SMTP-compliant mail server to send email.
2. A, B, and D. ColdFusion supports IMAP only through third-party extensions.
3. C and D. ColdFusion creates a spool file in the /cfusion/mail/spool directory with the incorrect SMTP server information in the mail header. When it attempts to send the message, it fails, logs an error to /cfusion/mail/log/errors.log, and then moves the spool file to the /cfusion/mail/undelivr directory.

Chapter 30

1. B. The distinguished name is used as the unique reference in LDAP hierarchies.
2. A. START nominates the directory branch for searching.
3. A and B. The distinguished name is a unique reference to a specific attribute. The distinguished name is made up of the relative distinguished name and all the attributes up to the root of the LDAP hierarchy.

Chapter 31

1. C. Ordinarily you must specify METHOD="POST" with a relevant <CFHTTPPARAM> tag to send variables. However, URL parameters can be sent on the URL attribute itself.
2. B. <CFFILE> is required to receive an uploaded file from a client browser. <CFFTP> is used to manage a remote FTP connection and file transfer.
3. False. <CFHTTP> can retrieve both text and binary files, but not at the same time.

Chapter 32

1. B and D. A is used in UPDATE operations. B is not a valid keyword.
2. A and D. A is valid. Wildcard characters are actually not required when you use LIKE; the search will effectively be an equality test. B is invalid; NOT must precede LIKE. C is invalid; wildcards can be used with strings, not numbers. D is valid; there is no limit to the number of wildcard characters that you can use in a search.
3. B. You use UPDATE when columns are affected (as opposed to rows). A, DELETE, deletes entire rows. C, NULL, is not a statement; it represents no value and can be used with UPDATE to set a column to no value.
4. B. Primary keys are not required but should always be created and used anyway.

Chapter 33

1. B. Primary keys are never actually required, but joining tables without one is exceedingly error-prone and should be avoided at all costs.
2. C. Using =* is equivalent to using the ANSI `RIGHT OUTER JOIN`.
3. A, C, and D. No keyword is required for self-joins.

Chapter 34

1. B. Yes, aggregate functions make the database work harder, but that's what databases are designed for. Client applications usually cannot perform these calculations as quickly as the database server.
2. D. `WHERE` and `ORDER BY` are not required, and neither is an alias (although one should ideally be used). The `HAVING` clause, however, must contain entries from the `SELECT` list.
3. B and D. The average function is `AVG`, and the function used to total values is `SUM`.

Chapter 35

1. A and B. Indexes are of significance only to data retrieval, and bind parameters perform no data conversion.
2. A and D. Many databases (especially non-client/server databases) do not support the use of stored procedures, and stored procedures are fully supported in ColdFusion.
3. A, B, and C. `SELECT` does not change data and therefore does not support the use of triggers.
4. A and D. Bind parameters do this automatically, but so can stored procedures because they prevent users from passing explicit SQL to be executed.

Chapter 36

1. A, D, and E. This is a trick question. Queries cannot be cached in `CLIENT` or `COOKIE` variables. They can, however, be stored in `VARIABLE` variables (in fact, that is what most queries are).
2. A and D. Query-based caching can be disabled in the ColdFusion Administrator, but there is no way to prevent users from caching queries to variables. Locking is an issue only with variable-based caching.
3. C. `CACHEDWITHIN` and `CACHEDAFTER` are used in query caching. Option D does not exist.

Chapter 37

1. B. Whenever possible, let the database do the job—in this case, using the aggregate function `SUM`.
2. C. The `<CFSWITCH>/<CFCASE>` tag is best used with many conditions.
3. A. Includes perform better than custom tag calls.

4. D. This value is used to decide whether the page must be recached because the original file was changed.
5. A, B, and D. Exploded benchmarking reports individual template times, not what has happened in the template.

Chapter 38

1. B, C, and D. The average ColdFusion execution time must be calculated from the other counters.
2. A. Enabling the Trusted Cache option can do this.
3. D. `Cache Pops/Sec` will tell you how many pages are taken out of cache to make room for more.

INDEX

SYMBOLS

A

B

C

D

G

H

I

M

P

S

W

X

Other Related Titles

JavaServer Pages Application Development
Ben Forta, et al
ISBN: 0-672-31939-X
$49.99 US/$74.95 CAN

WAP Development with WML and WMLScript
Ben Forta, et al
ISBN: 0-672-31946-2
$54.99 US/$81.95 CAN

Sams Teach Yourself Homesite 4 in 24 Hours
Ben Forta, et al
ISBN: 0-672-31560-2
$24.99 US/$37.95 CAN

Sams Teach Yourself ColdFusion Express in 24 Hours
Ben Forta and Sue Hove
ISBN: 0-672-31662-5
$29.99 US/$42.95 CAN

SQL Unleashed
Youness, Boutquin, et al
ISBN: 0-672-31709-5
$49.99 US/$74.95 CAN

JavaScript Unleashed
Richard Wagner and R. Allen Wyke
ISBN: 0-672-31763-X
$49.99 US/$74.95 CAN

Sams Teach Yourself SQL Server 2000 in 21 Days
Richard Waymire and Rick Sawtell
ISBN: 0-672-31969-1
$39.99 US/$59.95 CAN

Sams Teach Yourself Dreamweaver UltraDev 4 in 21 Days
John Ray
ISBN: 0-672-31901-2
$39.99 US/$59.95 CAN

Flash for the Real World: e-Commerce Case Studies
Steve Street
ISBN: 0-672-32079-7
$49.99 US/$74.95 CAN

XML Unleashed
Michael Morrison et al
ISBN: 0-672-31514-9
$49.99 US/$74.95 CAN

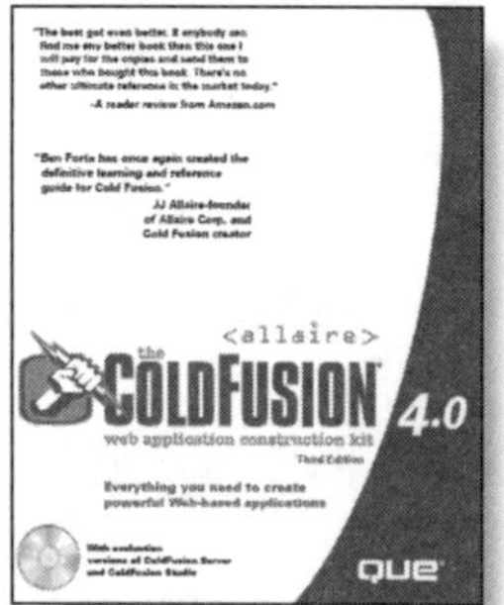

The ColdFusion 5.0 Web Application Construction Kit, 4th Edition
Ben Forta, et al
ISBN: 0-7897-2584-3
$49.99 US/$74.95 CAN

Advanced ColdFusion 5.0 Application Development, 2nd Edition
Ben Forta, et al
ISBN: 0-7897-2585-1
$49.99 US/$74.95 CAN

Sams Teach Yourself SQL in 10 Minutes, Second Edition
Ben Forta
ISBN: 0-672-32128-9
$14.99 US/$22.95 CAN

www.quepublishing.com

All prices are subject to change.